What Others Are Saying...

"Wine tasting should be fun. That's why the wineries have clubs – to introduce their members to limited releases, pre-releases and other rare wines as well as provide exciting club events for their enjoyment. Mike's book will introduce even more guests to taste our incredible wines and join our club."

—Claire Silver, Co-owner, Tobin James Cellars

"So many wineries, so little time. With this book, wine enthusiasts will discover wineries they would have missed and taste wines that lots of people never get to enjoy."

—Mandy Taylor-Gratzer, Tasting Room and Wine Club Manager, Beckmen Vineyards

"It's a great reference tool for the wine novice to the connoisseur. We will recommend this book to all of our customers."

—Jennifer Salisbury Rucks, Owner, Salisbury Vineyards

"With this book and a AAA road map, wine lovers will be all set. We can't wait until they discover our "secret" winery."

—Marc Goldberg, Owner/Winemaker, Windward Vineyard

"Finally, a book with all the tasting rooms along the Central Coast! What a great idea!"

—Alicia Summers, Sales & Marketing Manager, Casa Cassara Winery

THE
Wine Tasting Guide
to California's Central Coast

230 Wineries –From Paso to Malibu–
You Won't Want to Miss!

Mike O'Beirne

Old Vine Publishing Company
Pine Mountain Club, CA

THE Wine Tasting Guide to California's Central Coast

230 Wineries – from Paso to Malibu – You Won't Want to Miss!

Old Vine Publishing Company
PO Box 6774
Pine Mountain Club, CA 93222-6774 U.S.A.

First Edition 2007
ISBN 978-0-9794291-3-2

Book design by www.KareenRoss.com
Library of Congress Control number: 2007902128

O'Beirne, Mike.
    The wine tasting guide to California's central coast
: 230 wineries--from Paso to Malibu--you won't want to
miss! / Mike O'Beirne.
    p. cm.
    LCCN 2007902128
    ISBN-13: 978-0-97942913-2
    ISBN-10: 0-9794291-3-7

    1. Wine and wine making--California--Pacific Coast--
Guidebooks. 2. Wineries--California--Pacific Coast--
Guidebooks. 3. Pacific Coast (Calif.)--Guidebooks.
I. Title.

TP547.O27 2007   641.2'209794
                        QBI07-600098

Dedication

This work could only be dedicated to one person, and by all rights, her name should appear as co-author.

My wife joined with me in planning the contents, visiting the wineries, taking photographs and spending hours reading and improving my writing. Without her help, this guide might never have made it to your hands.

So I dedicate this book to my wife, partner and best friend, Jo-Ann O'Beirne for her love, patience and continued understanding.

Acknowledgements

I can honestly say that the beginnings for this guide occurred in the early 1980's when my wife and I discovered Central Coast wineries. We've been returning ever since, often many times each year. The commitment of the winery tasting hosts and their interest in imparting their knowledge to us, started us on a trip that continues to this day.

I must express my gratitude to the many people in the Central Coast wine industry who learned of my plans for this guide and urged me to bring it to fruition. Their encouragement and positive reaction to the need for this guide made the long hours of research worthwhile. It would be impractical to name them all, but the support given me by John Niven of Baileyana Winery/Tangent Winery was evident from our first phone visit, to our meeting at the winery to the many emails he sent offering advice and support. My thanks are heartfelt.

To all the winery owners, their tasting room managers, the tasting room hosts and marketing managers, I send a deep thank you for the many hours you devoted to making the pages of this book informative and interesting. Your ideas to improve the contents were thoughtful and added greatly to the value of the guide for the readers. Special thanks go to Claire Silver of Tobin James Cellars, Meryl Capone of Gainey Vineyards and Brandon Lyons of Cass Winery for the time and effort they devoted to review.

And a special thanks to my good friend Carolyn Honsberger who applied her years of proofreading and editing experience to clean up my punctuation and incomplete sentences.

Finally, I offer sincere thanks to my "mentor" Dr. Douglas Markham, author of "Total Health Beyond the Zone" and "Beyond Atkins". When I first dreamed of this book, he was the one who guided me to dozens of the best resources available to authors and publishers. His experiences were both interesting and educational, and this book is the better for his sharing them with me.

Table of Contents

6.
Clubs 41

Most wineries have a club. Some good reasons to join, one reason to leave

7.
The Wineries 43

1.

Why This Book...
Why These Wineries?

If you've ever gone wine tasting, you probably have developed a tried and true routine. You drive to a winery, get your first taste and ask for the most recent map of that tasting area. And you plot your trip from there.

Nothing wrong with that...we've all done it and discovered some great wines. But have you ever wondered about the wineries you missed? Are there some wineries not shown on the map? You're darn right there are.

Because that map is published by a wine grower's association, or a vintner's group or some other group of wine producers who have banded together to promote themselves. Nothing wrong with that, either. Those wineries are practicing good marketing. But there are lots of wineries that don't belong to the group – they're too small, or they're brand new, or they're independent cusses who just don't believe in belonging or they're just too far out in the country to benefit from the group promotion.

For example, one vintner's group map lists 15 wineries. We know of at least 23 wineries in the area. And three that aren't listed are among our favorites. So you can see what we'd be missing if we just followed the map.

Let me tell you a story. Many years ago, my wife Jo-Ann and I took a trip up to the Mendocino area in Northern California. Our B&B had copies of the local wine association map and we decided to visit a few. We visited Handley Cellars and Husch Vineyards and ended up at Scharffenberger Cellars. Since Jo-Ann is a real sparkling wine lover, I thought we'd probably make that our last tasting. But the young lady serving us must have felt our love of wines. She asked: "Do you mind going to really neat wineries that nobody goes to." And she proceeded to tell us about this little winery that she'd discovered that she thought we'd really enjoy.

Let's go! So she called Lazy Creek Vineyards, got their okay for us to visit and we experienced our first trip "off the map." Almost off the road. We drove down a gravel drive with very low hanging trees, crossed a creek without a bridge and drove into what looked like a farmer's backyard.

And we were invited by the owner/winemaker himself to sit down at his picnic table while he got some wine for tasting. Into an old barn he went and returned with three or four bottles and a couple of glasses and he discussed each of his excellent wines as we tasted it. To top off the afternoon, we tasted his latest Pinot Noir directly from the barrel.

He was a Hungarian gentleman who left Hungary to escape persecution after the 1956 Revolution, traveled the United States and finally settled in the Anderson Valley and made wine. He didn't even have a sign at the entry to his drive. But thanks to the lady at Scharffenberger, we had an unusual and memorable experience. Off the map.

That's one reason for this book and these wineries. We want to help you find **all** the wineries; we want you to discover new favorites that none of your friends know about.

Another reason for this book relates to the lady at Scharffenberger. We want you to visit wineries that we've personally visited and experienced. Not just those with a short write-up on a map, or those you've learned about on the internet. We've been to these wineries – we've talked to these people - we'll tell you about them.

And not just about the wines. There are some wineries that deserve your visit just because of the view of the vineyards from their tasting room. Awesome! Inspiring!

There are some wineries that almost beg you to bring a picnic and enjoy their lawns with a bottle of their wine. Restful! Refreshing!

And there are some wineries that are just so much fun. Where the conversations just seem to constantly flow. Where the servers become instant friends and you hate to leave.

Or where the gift shop beckons and can't be ignored. Full of treasures you've been searching for – or never knew existed.

Or where you learn so much. Where the winemaker or owner (and in many of our small wineries, that's the same person) enjoys sharing, in language you understand, the daily struggles they endure to bring you that sip you just experienced. Where you leave saying "I never knew winemaking was that intense."

Memorable wineries and memories we want to share. So when you walk in the door of that winery, hopefully, you'll feel like you've been there before.

And the final reason. We want you to have a guide that you'll carry in your car. This isn't intended to be a "library" book designed to sit on a shelf. Carry it in your glove compartment and when you're driving through the Central Coast, pull it out and see what wineries are nearby. Use the book…wear it out. Write your impressions in the margins and the pages we've supplied through the book. And as you find new wineries that didn't exist when we went to print, add their vital information on the note pages provided.

Just one reminder. You've all heard the expression: One man's junk is another man's treasure." That was never more true than with antiques, or art, or food, …or wine!

I don't happen to like sweet wines. Or at least not many. But I know friends of mine that really appreciate sweet wines. They look forward to the end of dinner or a relaxing evening when they can sit back and enjoy a glass of their favorite late harvest Merlot.

So in this book, we're not going to tell you to avoid XYZ Winery. It may not be our favorite, but its doors are open and people keep carrying cases out. So there must be lots of people that find the wine enjoyable. Give it a try.

So let's talk about tasting the wine……

2.

How To Taste

(Isn't that what this is all about?)

Let's cover what happens when you enter a tasting room. Head for the tasting bar; the server there will be your guide during your visit, and the first thing he or she will probably do is offer you a taste of their driest white wines. So you sip or swig and say "That's nice. What's number two?"

I was hoping you wouldn't do that.

First, take a good look at the wine, is the color what you expect? Obviously, you expect a Chardonnay to be clear, maybe with a soft straw color. You expect Cabernet Sauvignon to be a clear red and not cloudy or dull. You might keep in mind that cool climate wines tend to be less richly colored, hence a Washington State Chardonnay will be paler than a Central Coast California version. Certain grapes have an almost characteristic hue, such as the green tinge of a Riesling. Usually a Pinot Grigio will be less golden than a Chardonnay.

Now swirl the wine in your glass to throw the wine up onto the side of the glass, increasing the surface area of wine in contact with the air. As wine meets air, aromas are released and increasing the surface area helps to make the aromas more apparent. Be gentle, however in agitating the wine, in order to bring the wine up on the side of the glass without spilling it. If you find you are spilling, place the base of the glass on the counter and use a few good circular motions on the table top to get the aromas going.

Before you sniff the aroma, let the wine run back into the bowl and check the "legs." This tasting term refers to the long droplets of wine that run down the inside of the glass after the wine has been swirled. Many believe that slowly forming, thicker legs, reflecting either high alcohol content or the presence of sugars, are an indication of quality. Less exciting, weaker wines would quickly form more watery legs. This is true to some extent, but you may want to wait to judge these qualities on the palate rather than with the eye, because lower alcohol wines may be more to your liking – high alcohol wines tend to bigger, heavier tasting.

If you're tasting sparkling wine, take a look at the "beads." The bead describes the size and quantity of the bubbles generated by the wine. Fine Champagne is said to generate a very fine bead (smaller bubbles) than lesser Champagnes or other sparkling wines, and I believe that's probably true.

Perhaps you've seen the cartoon of the wealthy gentleman in black tie who has his nose stuck way down inside a wine glass and he exclaims "I will drink no wine before it's time." As the IRS agents enter, the gentleman declares "It's time."

Well, at least as far as tasting is concerned, it's time for the nose. Let me explain.

Understand, your nose will lead you to more fine wines than your taste buds ever will. Before your tongue ever experiences the "taste," your nose will say "you're going to like this."

Stick your nose in the glass and take a good sniff, and think about what aromas are coming up from the wine as you do so. Young wines will have "primary" aromas, relating to the grape variety. Such smells are often fruit related, and hence wines are described as smelling of black currants, grapefruit, raspberries, and so on, or maybe simply as fruity.

As wines age, more aromas develop, which may be more earthy. The aromas developed by a glass of fine wine can be many, intertwined in a most intimate and complex manner.

Now it's time to take a sip of the wine. Sometimes the flavor is exactly what you expected from the aromas you detected earlier. You smelled grapefruit when you sniffed the Sauvignon Blanc, and you get a hint of grapefruit as you taste it. Often, some flavors will come as a surprise. On the "palate" (the characteristics of the wine detected in the mouth), you'll find flavors you weren't expecting when you studied the aromas. Judging the presence of these "flavors" tells you whether this is a wine you like. This enables you to select "good" (in your judgment) wines, and discard lesser ones, as you analyze the wines and understand what it is that you don't like about them.

Pay attention to the way the wine changes as you hold it in the mouth. The finish describes the sensations derived from swallowing the wine. It will often be different from how the wine came across on the palate, so take note. The way flavors linger for a while on the palate after the wine has been swallowed is referred to as the length. The more length a wine has, the more time you have to enjoy it, and it's probably true to say that such wines are generally of better quality.

Now you've experienced a full "taste." Wasn't that a lot more enjoyable than just tasting the way you used to?

Oh, a word about that receptacle that you see at the end of the counter. It's usually a vase or a pitcher. It's called a spit bucket and it's meant to hold any wine you want to get rid of. Some winetasters actually spit the wine out of their mouth before swallowing, and that's quite acceptable. Others, a bit less assured or wanting to enjoy every bit of the small amount of wine they receive, finish the entire taste then flush any residue into the spit bucket with water (usually also on the counter) in preparation for tasting the next wine.

Don't worry that your wine server will be offended if you discard some of your wine into the pitcher. They know that you're tasting a number of wines and can't be expected to like every one that's poured. Also, they're as concerned as you are about over-doing, so they won't be upset if you keep your tastes to a minimum.

Before you jump in the car, let's explore some tips that might make your trip more enjoyable.

3.

A Day on the Tasting Trail

Let's talk about your tasting day. The things you can do (or not do) that will make the day more memorable and enjoyable.

If you can afford the time, try to visit during the week when the tasting room is less hectic than on weekends. Spring is the best time of year. The kids are still in school, so there are mostly adults in the tasting rooms. Wineries are releasing their spring bottlings. The employees are less busy, so you'll find that tours of the winery are offered more frenquently.

And now for some random thoughts for your tasting day.

Groups

This might be a good place to discuss traveling with a group to visit wineries. Remember, many wineries are small – often just one server to pour tastings, gather your purchases and handle the cash register. So make a rule; anytime you're visiting with more than six people, call the wineries in advance to let them know. (In fact, some wineries demand that groups call ahead for tasting.) A simple "We'd like to visit with eight people on Friday afternoon – will that work for you?" will suffice. They can be prepared; they may even have special accommodations for groups, like special pricing, a private tasting room or private tours.

Another story. A few years ago, I formed a small group of five couples from a service club I belong to. On a Saturday – prearranged – we visited Sanford, Gainey and Brander. At one, we received a guided tour and tasted one wine straight from the barrel. At the other two, we were able to taste wines that were not being offered for tasting that day. Well worth three phone calls, wouldn't you say?

And if you're part of a group, you should probably consider having a designated driver – or use a bus or limo service. Wine tasting should be a fun day – don't let it be spoiled by a member driving after too many wines.

Here are a few of the services available to drive you and/or your group through the Central Coast:

AITS – Santa Barbara – 888-334-5466

Alexis Limousine – San Luis Obispo, Paso Robles, Santa

Ynez – 805-550-0112

Breakaway Tours – Paso Robles, San Luis Obispo, Santa Barbara - 800-799-7657

Central Coast Trolley – Paso Robles, San Luis Obispo - 800-992-9633

Classic Limousine – San Luis Obispo – 805-773-2211

Cloud Climbers (backcountry wineries by jeep) – Santa Barbara, Santa Ynez – 805-965-6654

Grapeline Shuttle – Paso Robles, San Luis Obispo - 805-239-4747

Roadrunner Shuttle and Limousine – Central Coast – 800-247-7919

The Wine Wrangler – Paso Robles - 866-238-6400

Wine Edventures – Santa Barbara, Santa Ynez – 805-965-9463

Speaking of groups, if I'm touring in a private car and there are tour buses in the winery parking lot, I make it a point to go on to my next winery and come back later. Tour busses mean there are lots of people in the tasting room, and you don't want to fight the crowd to get your pour. That bus will be gone in a half hour and you'll have saved a lot of aggravation.

Food and water

Be sure to have breakfast or lunch before you go, and take a snack for on the road. Food helps to absorb the alcohol, and alcohol, no matter how little, on an empty stomach is never a good idea. Maybe pack a picnic cooler – many wineries provide cool, comfortable areas for picnicking. But if you have a picnic or lunch at a winery, don't drink wine from a different winery with your picnic. And carry plenty of water - one effect of even just tasting alcohol is that you get dehydrated. Pack several bottles of water in the car, and take a swig often.

Fatigue

Choose a reasonable number of wineries to visit in the course of the day. Three or four is usually plenty. Your taste buds will begin to rebel after a while. Fatigue can set in, and it is better to have a good day visiting three wineries than a bad one trying to visit seven.

Holidays

Some wineries are open on holidays, some aren't. Some which are never open on weekdays, open for holidays that fall on Monday. Some which are open every weekend, close every weekend that includes a holiday. Again, be safe. If you're hoping to taste on a holiday, call ahead. You'll find many open; you'll avoid unnecessary trips to wineries that are closed.

Purchasing

Should you purchase wine at the tasting room? Prices may be higher at the winery, but the great advantage over the supermarket or wine shop is that you can taste before you buy, you know the wine has been stored and handled properly, and taking home a bottle will remind you to look for it in your favorite wine store in the future. Another advantage of the tasting-room experience is that many wineries feature special, limited-release bottlings available only at the winery. If your home is a distance away, ask the winery if they'll ship your purchase to you.

Perfume, aftershave, cigarettes and cigars

In other words, anything with a strong fragrance. You and your fellow tasters will make use of aroma a lot when you taste wine. Have mercy and try to take the day off from your personal aromas.

Talk

Unless they're swamped with visitors, most tasting room personnel love to chat about their wines and the region. Take the opportunity to strike up a conversation with those around you. This is often a good way to ask about other wineries that they have been to and recommend. Hosts will also have a good knowledge of the neighboring wineries and their wines.

Tasting notes

Most wineries will have a sheet of tasting notes. Read the tasting notes as you taste and see if you notice any of the aromas or flavors listed in the notes. And some wineries set up the sheet so you can make notations to take with you. Be sure to do so, you'll be reminded of wines you liked and those you didn't.

Tasting charge

Many tasting rooms will require that you pay a fee to taste the wine – usually in the $3-$10 range. Some wineries apply this fee to a purchase. Others might include a souvenir glass with the fee. When a fee is charged, it is usually okay for two people to share one glass and pay only one tasting fee.

What you'll taste

Usually tastings include between 3 and 6 wines starting with lighter white wines through reds and finally desert wines. You don't have to taste them all – you can ask to taste only the reds, for example. And if you are really interested in a wine that is not on the tasting menu, ask politely and you may be able to taste that as well. Ask quietly – your host may see you as a knowledgeable wine lover, but see the guests next to you as something less.

Tasting by appointment

In this book, you'll find a number of wineries that say they're open by appointment only. It's not that they don't look forward to your visit, it's just that they don't have tasting room personnel – often the owner is it, or hosts are part-timers who are employed only on the weekend.

Please follow that request - if an appointment is required, you should call well in advance - 1-3 weeks is usually sufficient. (Harvest time can present a different set of problems, as the smaller wineries often pull tasting room staff to work the crush.)

But please, don't drive through the gate and ask if they're available for tasting. Winery owners are some of the finest people you'll meet – be polite and you'll likely enjoy a great experience.

Tasting Room or Not?

I don't know whether they're unique to the Central Coast, but there are a number of wine stores/tasting bars in Los Olivos and Solvang that serve as tasting rooms for some of the smaller wineries. Some of those wineries do as few as 100 cases of commercial wine a year – many as few as 30 cases.

But they're not tasting rooms the way I think of tasting rooms. When I enter the Gainey tasting room, I know I'm going to taste a number of Gainey wines, but I won't be able to taste Sunstone wines – their tasting room is down the road. But when I enter "Wine Country", for example, wanting to taste Benjamin Silver's wines, I'll find a couple of Silver wines available for tasting. And 7-9 wines from other wineries.

"Wine Country" has made an agreement with Silver to serve as Silver's exclusive tasting room. And they've made agreements with a number of other wineries to serve as their tasting room – to the same or lesser degree. So, in addition to Silver, you'll always find a J Wilkes bottle or two open, you'll usually find a bottle of Core open, you'll sometimes find a bottle of Qupe or Waltzing Bear open. And sometimes a Cimarone, Verdad or Flying Goat.

So on the winery pages in this book, I indicate wineries that are tasted at these tasting bars. Be aware that their wines may not be poured on the day you arrive, unless they're a winery that has an exclusive arrangement with the tasting bar. A polite request to taste a bottle not open often brings results. Or you may want to call ahead to check.

The wine bars that represent wineries include:

Ballard Inn Tasting Room, 2436 Baseline Ave., Ballard. 800-638-2466 Tasting for Arcadian, Ken Brown, Lane Tanner, Kenneth-Crawford, Palmina, Ojai and Calzada Ridge. Open Fri-Sun 12-4

Cabana Cellars, 1539 Mission Dr. 'C', Solvang 805-686-9126 "Represents" a number of wineries including Blair Fox, Norm Yost, Ken Brown, East Valley Vineyards, Falcone Vineyard, Kenneth-Crawford Open Wed-Mon 11-6 (until 8 in the summer)

Los Olivos Café & Wine Merchant, 2879 Grand Ave, Los Olivos. 805-688-7265 ext 203. Exclusive tasting for their own two Bernat Wines, plus tastes an additional three wines that change every Wednesday. Tasting 11-5 Daily

<u>Los Olivos Tasting Room,</u> 2905 Grand Ave. Los Olivos 805-688-7406   Tastes DiBruno, Happy Canyon, J Kerr, Jaffurs, Stephen Ross, Lane Tanner, Ken Brown and others. Tasting Daily 11-5:30

<u>Olde Mission Wine Co.,</u> 1539 Mission Dr 'B', Solvang 805-686-9323 Tastes Michael Grace, William James Cellars, Huber Cellars, Carr Winery and Labyrinth Open Daily 9:30-5:30

<u>Tastes of the Valley,</u> 1672 Mission Dr., Solvang 877-622-9463 Exclusive tasting of Au Bon Climat and Lane Tanner and offers around 12 other wineries on a partial basis including Verdad and Qupe. A bit different approach than the others, Tastes of the Valley offers flights of 6-7 wines each with a bit larger pour than most tastings. Open Daily 11-8 (or later)

<u>Wine Attic,</u> 1305 Park St Alley off 13th St, Paso Robles. 805-227-4107 Exclusive tasting for James Judd Wine. Tastes others on a weekly changing basis. Open Daily 11:30-8

<u>Wine Country</u> (used as the example above) 2445 Alamo Pintado Ave, Los Olivos. 805-686-9699 Exclusive tasting for Benjamin Silver, also tastes J Wilkes, Corr, Waltzing Bear, Qupe, Flying Goat and others. Open Daily 11-5

4.

Glossary

It seems to me there must be a bunch of wine nerds sitting around the barrel trying to come up with new words to use in describing wine. You'll hear words in the wine tasting room that you'll never hear anywhere else. Don't worry, this glossary will contain only the words you really need to know and be able to use. And many of the words not listed will just make sense, like "dry."

If you want to become a wine expert yourself, and want to learn all the terms, I suggest you "google" wine terminology and study away.

Acidity

The tart taste in wine. Too much acidity makes a wine unpleasant to drink – too little makes it flabby and dull. So look for balance.

Aftertaste

The flavor impression that's left after the wine is swallowed.

Alcoholic fermentation

The action of yeast on sugar results in alcohol. Fermentation often starts naturally with yeast on the grapes, but cultured yeasts may be added.

Aging

Aging of wines, and we're mainly referring here to red wines, either in the barrel at the winery or in the bottle at home, can add to the flavor and taste of wine. Your wine server can tell you how the winemaker "designed" the wine – for a few years aging or for immediate enjoyment.

Appellation

The French term that defines the vineyard location where the grapes were grown for the wine you're discussing. The idea is that the soil, climate, sun, water quality, and contour of a region combine to produce a style of wine that simply can't be duplicated elsewhere. In the U.S., appellations are known as AVAs (American Viticultural Areas), with slightly different rules than the French appellation of origin.

AVA

See Appellation

Balance

Wines that are balanced have a harmonious combination of acid, tannin, texture and flavor.

Blanc

White

Blind Tasting

Used when you don't know what you're tasting. Often used in social tasting with friends where the labels are covered and you must judge the wines on merit alone.

Bordeaux

The area in France that produces mostly Cabernet Sauvignon and Merlot in reds, Sauvignon Blanc and Semillon in whites.

Body

A tasting term that describes a wine that has plenty of flavor and is well balanced. Can be light-bodied or full-bodied.

Bouquet

The set of aromas that develop with aging. Young wines have aroma, not bouquet.

Brut

Very dry Champagne or other sparkling wine.

Burgundy

The area in France that produces mainly Pinot Noir in reds and Chardonnay in whites.

Champagne

Technically, sparking wine produced in the Champagne region of France. Legally, in France and many other countries, any other sparkling wine may not be called Champagne. The US has never adopted that law.

Chewy

Unusual thickness of texture or tannins that makes you almost "chew" the wine as you swallow. Old vine zinfandels are often chewy.

Clone

The offspring of grape vines that contains the genetic material of the parent. Clones further determine flavor, ripening, disease resistance, cluster size, etc.

Crisp

Brisk flavor, often from high acidity. Usually associated with dry white and rosé wines.

Club

It seems that every winery has a club by now. Membership is normally free and you receive 3-6 wines every 2-6 months (terms vary by winery) by UPS. You'll receive a discount on the shipped wine as well as any other purchases you make from the winery and you (and often your guests) can taste at the winery for free.

Corked

Describes a wine having the off-putting, musty, moldy-newspaper flavor and aroma and dry aftertaste caused by a tainted cork

Estate Bottled

Term used, always on the label and sometimes in the wine name, to signify that the wine was produced and bottled at the winery with grapes grown in vineyards owned by the winery.

Extra dry

Found on sparkling wine labels to signify not as dry as brut.

Late Harvest

A term applied to wines made from grapes that were left on the vine longer than usual. The grapes often look similar to raisins, but have naturally dehydrated while on the vine. Late harvest is usually indicative of a sweet desert wine, such a late harvest Zinfandel or late harvest Riesling.

Library wines

Refers to a winery's older wines that they're aging in the backroom and offering to the public for sale. Sometimes only available to "club" members. Almost always available at the winery. Very seldom available for tasting.

Malolactic fermentation

A bacterial process which converts the sharp tasting malic acid in the wine to a softer lactic acid. The winemaker decides whether to allow malolactic fermentation depending on the style of wine desired.

Mature

Developed, ready to drink. Some wines, usually reds, just require aging to reach full maturity.

Meritage

A blend of wines, often red, to make a winery specialty. The subtle blending of varietals allows the winemaker to experiment and find exciting new flavors.

Nose

Another tasting term. Describes how the wine smells. And as we've said, the nose is probably the most important sense in appreciating wine.

Oak

The number one wood choice for wine barrels. Some wines, such as Chardonnay, assume much of their flavor depending on length of time aged in the barrels.

Reserve

Originally used to designate the winemakers best effort using the best grapes from the best vineyards. But the term has become overworked by some wineries.

Rhone

A major river flowing from Switzerland to the Mediterranean. Wines from grapes grown along the river are referred to as Rhone wines – typically hearty red wines based on Syrah, Grenache and others. In the U.S., and especially along the California Central Coast, Rhone grapes have become important varietals and their wines a growing commercial success.

Screwcaps

The newest alternative to cork seals for wine. Cork, being a biological material, cannot be sterilized, and the fungal infections it contains can result in tainted wine aromas. Figures vary, but "corked" wine may occur in as many as 5% of all wines produced. Studies seem to show that the use of screwcaps does not affect the wine in any way.

Sulfites

A natural bi-product of fermentation, sulfites are naturally found in wine. Sulfites (in small quantities) may be added to wine to guard against spoilage.

Tasting fee

Probably started in Napa/Sonoma and now common on the Central Coast. The winery charges a fee for tasting – often a few dollars to taste 4-6 wines – sometimes a winery logo glass is your gift. Sometimes a few dollars more to taste their reserve or library wines. Often the fee is waved if purchases are made.

Tannin

Tannins are harsh, bitter compounds that can make a wine difficult to enjoy – creating a dry, puckering sensation in young red wines. But some tannin can't be avoided because it occurs, to different degrees, in all grape skins, pips and stalks. Especially found in red wines, tannic wine mellows with aging.

Terroir

A popular term to describe the external influence on the ripening grape. Like the soils, bedrock, gravel, exposure to wind and sun, depth of water and so on. Terroir plays a huge part in the flavors the grapes impart to the wines. See Appellation in this section and the short AVA discussion at the beginning of each winery region.

Texture

How the wine feels in the mouth.

Varietal Wine

Any wine that takes its name from the predominant grape variety. This naming is very common in the US, where the wine must contain a minimum 75% of the named grape.

Vintage

This term refers both to the actual grape harvest as well as the year of the harvest. Vintage wine is wine which is produced from grapes with at least 95% harvested in the year stated. Wines that are a blend of years are considered non-vintage wines (or N.V.).

Winemaker

The person engaged in the occupation of making wine. They are generally employed by wineries or wine companies, where their work includes; cooperating with viticulturists, monitoring the maturity of grapes to ensure their quality and to determine the correct time for harvest, crushing and pressing grapes, monitoring the settling of juice and the fermentation of grape material, filtering the wine to remove remaining solids, testing the quality of wine by tasting, placing filtered wine in casks or tanks for storage and maturation, preparing plans for bottling wine once it has matured and making sure that quality is maintained when the wine is bottled. In many of our Central Coast wineries, the owner is the winemaker.

Okay, now you have a good idea of the meaning of some of the terms you'll hear on the wine trail. But one thing is missing – how to pronounce the names of some of the wines you'll be introduced to. The next chapter will give you some of the most common – if you encounter others, just ask your server.

5.

How Did You Pronounce That?

Most of us are pretty secure when it comes to pronouncing Burgundy. We know it's a region in France and we may remember the days when most American red wines were called, simply, "Burgundy." But now we have varietals and regions and the wine names become more complicated.

So this chapter is designed to help you pronounce Viognier. And tell you just a bit about it. It's a wine you'll run into quite often along the Central Coast, and one that most winery visitors have a problem with.

Here we go, with words you'll run into along the Central Coast...

Barbera (bar-BEAR-ah)

A hearty red wine, as produced in northwestern Italy)

Bordeaux (bore-DOUGH)

A major wine region in southwestern France, known for red wine grapes Cabernet Sauvignon, Merlot, Cabernet Franc, Petit Verdot, and Malbec. Also known for producing excellent Sauternes.

Cabernet Franc (cab-air-nay frahN)

French red wine grape, often used in blends, as well as a varietal. Watch for blueberry aromas.

Cabernet Sauvignon (cab-air-nay so-veen-yawN)

One of the noblest red wines. Often produced for aging as opposed to immediate consumption.

Chardonnay (shar-doe-nay)

The most famous of the white wine grapes, Chardonnay was first recognized in Burgundy. There are two distinct styles of Chardonnay: rich fruit with substantial oak, and a more austere style

Chenin Blanc (shen-iN blaN)

French white grape, with pleasant honeydew and cantaloupe melon flavors and a light muskiness.

Cuvée (koo-vay)

The blend of different grapes that makes up a specific wine. Often used in the wine's name, as in "Cuvée Ten".

Fumé Blanc (foo-may blahN)

A California name for Sauvignon Blanc.

Gewürtztraminer (geh-VERTZ-tra-mee-nur)

White wine grape from Alsace, Germany. Highly aromatic, makes wines (from off-dry to sweet) with much concentration and a spicy (?) taste.

Grenache (gray-NAHSH)

Red-wine grape commonplace in the Rhone. In California, often used in blending. Typically makes hearty, peppery wines.

Melbec (mahl-bek)

Red-wine grape used as a nominal element of the Bordeaux blend, where its intense color and extract add to the wine's body.

Merlot (mare-low)

A red wine grape used heavily in Bordeaux/Meritage blends and bottled alone. It has become extremely popular because of its early drinking style of smooth tannins and bright fruit. Black-cherry and herbal flavors are typical.

Mourvédre (moor-VED'rr)

Red grape rich in color and extract, it often imparts earthy aromas to the wine.

Muscat (moos-caht)

Aromatic, ancient grape makes wines, often sweet and always fruity, with a characteristic grapefruity and musky aroma.

Nebbiolo (nay-BYOH-low)

From northwestern Italy, this red grape is frequently described as violet in aroma and intense black fruit in taste.

Petite Sirah (peh-teet see-rah)

California red grape makes an inky-dark red wine that can last forever, with warm, plummy notes.

Petit Verdot (peh-tee vehr-doe)

Red wine grape, fine quality, used in Bordeaux blends.

Pinot Blanc (pee-noe blahN)

White wine grape, making a dry, full white wine typically medium in body and sometimes showing melon scents.

Pinot Grigio (pee-noe gree-jzhee-o)

Typically makes a dry and very crisp and acidic white wine, often with a light musky aroma.

Pinot Gris (pee-noe gree)

Same as Pinot Grigio.

Pinot Noir (pee-noe nwahr)

Classic Burgundian red grape, widely accepted as one of the world's best. It has proven difficult to grow and vinify well elsewhere, but California and Oregon increasingly hit the mark. At its peak, it makes wines of incredible complexity, difficult to describe (although cherries and "earthy" qualities are typical), known as much for its "velvety" texture as its flavor.

Rhone (rone)

Great French wine region along the river of the same name. Best known for hearty red wines based on Syrah, Grenache and others, with a wine history certainly going back to the 14th Century, and at least by local legend, to the Romans.

Riesling (REESE-ling)

The classic German grape of the Rhine and Mosel, certainly ranks among the most noble white wine grapes. Germany's great Rieslings are usually made slightly sweet, with strong, steely acidity for balance. California Rieslings are often sweet without sufficient acidity for balance, although some compelling "Alsace-style" Rieslings are now found on the Central Coast. Another wine so complex that it defies easy description, but you'll often find fresh apples, with sometimes pleasantly resinous notes like pine.

Rosé (roe-zay)

Pink wine, traditionally made by using red grapes and removing the skins from the fermenter before they have had time to impart much color. Sometimes called Vin Gris, a good, dry, crisp rosé or Vin Gris can be a refreshing treat on a hot summer day.

Roussanne (roo-sahn)

White Rhone grape, often used in blends.

Sangiovese (sahn-joe-VAY-zeh)

The predominant red-wine grape of Tuscany in Central Italy, primary player in the Chianti blend; also sometimes used as a varietal there and in California. Makes a hearty, dry red with flavors of black cherries, often with a characteristic orange glint in the color.

Sauvignon Blanc (so-veen-yawn blahN)

Noble white grape, The wine comes in many styles, depending largely on canopy management or leaf pruning (shaded grapes make a "green," "grassy" style while grapes exposed to sunlight make a citric style) and whether the wine maker chooses to age the wine in oak.

Syrah (see-RAH)

Red Rhone grape, makes ageworthy wines easily identified by a very characteristic floral black-pepper fragrance.

Tempranillo (temp-rah-NEE-yo)

Spanish red-wine grape. Black fruit is the usual descriptor, although most Tempranillo-based wines show spicy oak as an integral component, and are also characterized by the hearty, robust and acidic structure that the grape imparts.

Viognier (vee-ohn-yay)

This white grape is gaining considerable attention as a varietal in California. It makes a light, lean wine with a very characteristic floral scent, not meant for aging but best consumed early.

Vin Gris (vaN gree)

Same as Rosé.

Zinfandel (zin-fahn-dell)

This tough and hearty grape shows its greatness in California. Red Zin is big and bold, with jammy raspberry and blackberry scents and a lasting finish.

You're almost ready to get in the car. But before you do, let me introduce you to a term you're sure to hear at 98% of the wineries you visit.......

6.

Clubs

(Some good reasons to join,
one reason to leave)

I'll be honest, I like wine clubs. I've belonged to a number of them over the years, and still do. Usually two to four at a time. And I'll tell you why.

I'm like a lot of wine drinkers; I sometimes pick up wine at the grocery to serve with tonight's dinner. And that's not the best way to buy good wines. Grocery store wines are pretty much mass produced wines, and hopefully, this book will convince you to get out on the back wine roads and taste some wines that are a whole lot tastier than mass produced.

Back in the Glossary, we told you about clubs. We said that *"membership is normally free and you receive 3-6 wines every 2-6 months (terms vary by winery) by UPS. You'll receive a discount on the shipped wine as well as any other purchases you make from the winery and you (and often your guests) can taste at the winery for free."*

So every couple of months, one of my wine club shipments arrives, and I'm reminded of the difference in wines. And I'm reminded that I like Penman Springs Syrah much more than the YellowTail I bought last week.

So next time Jo-Ann plans a nice meal, I'll be reminded to run down to Wade's Wines and pick up a better bottle. Gradually, I've upgraded the wines we drink because of the club memberships.

Clubs also introduce me to wines I would never have tasted because many wineries actually produce special wines just for club members. They produce just enough to meet club needs. So the club allows a winemaker to try his hand at a grape he's not worked with before and get instant feedback on his success. And if the wine's well received, the winery can add it to their regular offering.

And as a matter of fact, there are a lot of small wineries today that do not sell their wines through stores or restaurants – everything they make is sold to club members or visitors to the winery. So if you find a wine you particularly like that comes from one of those small wineries, you had better join the club to assure yourself a supply.

Another reason I like clubs is the special events they have just for club members. Special dinners, harvest parties, grape-stomping afternoons, concerts – all are used to keep you a loyal club member. And all are fun and offered at little or deeply discounted costs.

Finally, I like clubs because they give us a home when we're out tasting. It's nice to walk into a winery where we are members and be greeted like friends. To tell your server "I'm a member" and be served in a special glass or a larger than normal serving.

But I do drop my memberships. Usually after a year or a year and a half. I feel by that time I've been exposed to most of the wines that winery produces. And frankly, I always find other wineries that I want to explore in depth. So I drop A to join B.

And I've never had a winery become upset when I notified them, especially when I explain why. In fact, I dropped my memberships in Gainey and Brander a number of years ago, and I'm still greeted warmly every time I visit.

Winery tasting rooms are friendly places. Even more so when there's a club connection.

Let's go visit some wineries……..

7.

The Wineries

Paso Robles East

The Paso Robles AVA

The wines grown in the eastern portion (east of Highway 101) of the AVA, where it's warmer and more arid, are usually full bodied, rich in fruit and display soft tannins and lower acidity than those from the western portion. As a result, wines from the eastside tend to be more drinkable while young.

Cabernet Sauvignon, Chardonnay, Merlot and Zinfandel represent just under 80% of the planted acreage and some thirty-seven other varieties, lead by Syrah making up the remainder.

Sorry We Missed A Few

We believe the following wineries do offer tasting, but for some reason they chose not to respond to our requests for information. If you visit them, we hope you'll let them know what they missed.

Garretson, River Star, Turley

August Ridge Vineyards

8790 Hwy 41 East

Creston

805-239-2455

Tasting Sat-Sun 11:30-5

And By Appt

August Ridge was established in the spring of 2001 with the purchase of 40 acres of rolling hills in the Creston area of the Paso Robles AVA by John and Jill Backer. From the beginning their goal was to produce wines that combine the robust styling of the best California wines with the restrained elegance of the classic wines from northern and central Italy. Their passion for the project comes from a love of cooking, eating and sharing meals with friends which leads directly to August Ridge wine style.

August Ridge will release their first vintage in the spring of 2007. The release may include Sangiovese, Cabernet Sauvignon, Merlot and Arneis. The specific wines released will be determined by John, based on his sense of whether they have matured as necessary or will need further time in the barrel. In future years the August Ridge selection will expand to include Nebbiolo, Barbera and Pinot Grigio. Two reserve blends based on Sangiovese and Nebbiolo are planned with a first release in 2009. The work in the winery to date indicates these blends are sure to be something special!

The winery itself is a small, unassuming building that sits adjacent to the family home. Inside, the tasting area is just a small bar tucked away in one corner of the working winery and affords the visitor a clear perspective of the winemaking in progress. The farm and winery are such a natural extension of the family that daughter Isabella and cats Micky and Jerry are as likely to greet guests as are John and Jill.

August Ridge is located at 8790 Highway 41 East less than 15 minutes from downtown Paso Robles. They will open for tasting in the summer of 2007. Please phone to confirm details.

B & E Vineyards

10,000 Creston Road

Paso Robles

805-238-4815

Tasting Fri-Sun 11-5

And By Appt

B & E is a small, family-owned vineyard and winery featuring estate wines of Merlot, Cabernet Sauvignon and some red blends. The wines are carefully hand-crafted for 20 months in French oak barrels.

Jerry and Patricia Bello were typical farmers in Paso Robles, and as with many farmers in the area, the wine business came about because of outside forces. One hundred acres of hilly terrain was traditionally planted in alfalfa and the cost of irrigation of those acres became prohibitive in the 1980's. Vineyard plantings began in 1989, and today 58 of those acres are in grapes. In 1994, they began selling the grapes to other wineries. In 2002, they introduced their own label and began sales to the public.

That year, they started with 1000 cases and have been increasing production each year. B & E currently produces 4000 cases of Estate Merlot, Estate Cabernet Sauvignon, Reserve Merlot, Reserve Cabernet Sauvignon, Syrah and a blended red table wine they call *Red Rhythm*. Prices fall between $20 and $30.

The tasting room is a small western saloon located on the top of the hill, overlooking a small lake and the rolling countryside - the beautiful "back roads" of Paso Robles. And in case you're in a hurry to taste B & E wines, you can call ahead to arrange to visit by helicopter; they're one of only a few wineries with a maintained helicopter pad.

From Atascadero and Hwy 101, exit at Rte. 41 and travel east to Creston Rd. Turn left on Creston Rd. Winery on the right. Or from Paso Robles, take Rte. 46 east to Geneseo Rd. and turn right or south on Geneseo to Creston Rd. Turn left onto Creston, winery on your left.

Bella Luna Winery

1850 Templeton Rd

Templeton

805-434-5477

Tasting Sat-Sun 10-5

And By appt.

Some would say Bella Luna started some 30 or so years ago in the hearts and minds of its founders, Kevin Healey and Sherman Smoot. Kevin had just returned from honorably serving his country in Vietnam and Sherm was training as a Navy fighter pilot preparing to go to Vietnam. Having grown up together as best friends in the, now, Paso Robles AVA, both developed a real passion for wine.

The Bella Luna Estate is located on 5 acres in Templeton. Their boutique winery specializes in small lot productions of ultra-premium red wine. The estate's vineyard is planted with the noble Sangiovese and Cabernet Sauvignon varietals and is one of the only dry farmed, head trained, Sangiovese vineyards in California. They've recently added Tempranillo to round out their selection of fine red wines. Wines that sell in the $30-$40 price range.

Probably in keeping with their backgrounds, each year they produce a red wine blend named *Fighter Pilot Red,* named in honor of those courageous aviators who have put themselves in harm's way. And they always offer a 10% discount to all active duty military men and women.

The vineyard is farmed organically and the only water the vines get comes from "mother nature". The Sangiovese and one half of the Cabernet vines are head trained. The other half of the Cabernet vines are vertical cordon trained - no trellises.

From Hwy 101, exit at Templeton Rd east to the winery on your right.

Bianchi Winery

3380 Branch Rd

Paso Robles

805-226-9922

Tasting Daily 10-5

For Bianchi visitors, the sweeping vineyard, coastal mountain views, and a serene lake coupled with inspired wines offer a fulfilling wine country experience. The welcoming tasting room is an architectural feast for the senses. It blends modern elements - glass and contemporary lighting - together with earthen materials such as wood, stone and metal. A fireplace warms the tasting room in the winter, and cool breezes off the lake refresh the room in the summer. Whether enjoying the wines inside or outside, guests enjoy the relaxed, unhurried nature. It's how wine tasting should be!

Although the views are breathtaking, wines take center stage in the tasting room. The friendly and knowledgeable hospitality team is enthusiastic to present visitors with wines from the Bianchi Heritage and Signature collections. The Heritage Collection includes wines that bear the characteristics of the terroir of the estate ranches. Heritage Collection wines include Cabernet Sauvignon, Merlot, Syrah, and Zinfandel. The Bianchi Signature Collection is inspired by the unique complexities that come from an array of renowned vineyards throughout California's Central Coast. Prices range from $8-$25.

While visiting the tasting room, be sure to peruse their many unique gift items, wine accessories, books and apparel. Plan your picnic around their fine selection of imported gourmet foods. Or, for the more adventurous, try your skills with one of their remote control sailboats

Take Hwy 46 East 6 miles from Paso Robles and turn right on Branch Rd. Winery 1/2 mile on left.

Cass Winery

7350 Linne Rd

Paso Robles

805-239-1730

Tasting Mon-Fri 12-5

Sat-Sun 11-6

One hundred percent of the wines crafted at Cass Winery are Estate Grown. Their vineyard surrounds the tasting room and winery. You can literally touch, taste, see and smell the grapes from the block where they were harvested.

The Rhone varieties on the Cass Estate are genetically pure clones, having gone through 8 years of rigorous testing by an agency of the French Government (ENTAV) prior to being approved for sale in California in 1999. Cass Vineyard is among the first in California to offer Estate wines from these select vines.

Today, they offer Cabernet Sauvignon, Syrah, Viognier, Roussanne and a number of Rhone blends. Their *Rockin' One*, a blend of Grenache, Mourvedre and Syrah is designed to meet the need for an impeccably balanced, easy drinking wine. Bottles run $18 to $38.

Steve and Alice Cass believe the best wine drinking should always be accompanied by great food pairings, even if the wine is not opened at dinnertime. So they offer excellent gourmet palate cleansers with each wine tasting and encourage visitors to get comfortable at a table in the winery, under the trellis, or in their oak-shaded picnic area. One must be relaxed to truly enjoy! During the week, they offer picnic fare for your purchase and every weekend they offer gourmet lunch plates, such as award winning crabcakes from Alice's Kitchen , an Italian Focaccia Sandwich and other "Bites for Lunch" prepared by in-house chef Dustin Lehigh.

From Rt 101, take 46 East 7.2 miles to Geneseo Road. Turn right, go 4.2 miles to the stop sign at Linne Road. Turn right 100 yards and you are there.

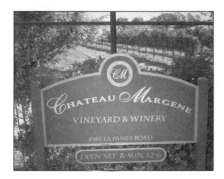

Chateau Margene

4385 La Panza Rd

Creston

805-238-2321

Tasting Sat-Sun 12-5

And By Appt

Michael and Margene Mooney dreamed of one day owning a winery. From their home in Southern California they would venture to Santa Barbara, Napa, Sonoma and Paso Robles to experience the wines from those regions and eventually, to look at property. The search began in 1990, but it wasn't until 1998 that they found the perfect site for growing Cabernet Sauvignon, in Paso Robles.

They planted their vineyard (with help from Jim Smoot, their vineyard consultant) and immediately put plans in motion to start a winery. For the first three vintages (1997–1999), local icon John Munch consulted on the winemaking process with Michael and Margene playing an active role in all phases, from crushing and pressing the fruit to lab analysis and bottling.

Chateau Margene is a small, family-owned and operated micro winery (3,000 cases) dedicated to the production of small lots of luxury, handcrafted Cabernet Sauvignon wines (and some other very limited production wines).

In fact, until 2006, they produced only three wines. A Cabernet Sauvignon at $42, a Reserve Cabernet Sauvignon at $60 and an Estate blend called *Beau Mélange* at $120 per bottle. The *Beau Mélange* is sold on an allocated basis in the years it is available and is designed for long aging – 12-15 years, the owners estimate.

The Mooney's two sons, Chris and Jon, are now actively involved in the vineyard activities, wine processing and caretaking of the property. With their parents, they are planning a second label, with a focus on Rhone blends (Syrah, Grenache & Mourvedre).

Located 13 miles east of Paso Robles or Atascadero, just off Highway 41 on La Panza Rd (2.2 miles east of Highway 41).

Christian Lazo Wines

249 Tenth St Suite A

San Miquel

805-467-2672

Tasting Sat-Sun 10-4:30

Or By Appt

In 1979 Doc McGillis, a thoracic surgeon from Los Angeles, decided to give up city life and move to the small town of Paso Robles. He purchased some land just west of town and built a barn.

Many an evening Doc and his wife Dale would sit in the hay loft of their barn house and watch the beautiful views of the town lights to the east and the mountain sunsets to the west. One such evening, with a cocktail in hand, Doc came up with a brilliant idea. "If we grew grapes, we could drink wine for free!" A dream was born and the next day a ten-acre vineyard was begun. Sadly, with the fruit of his first harvest safely in barrels, Doc suddenly passed away.

Steve Christian and Lupe Lazo bought the property in 2002 and started the long process of bringing the vineyard back to health. After more than two years of making every known mistake in farming, Steve was fortunate enough to meet one the original stars of the Paso Robles area, Richard Sauret. He is one those farmers that are organic to an area.

Most people in tasting the 2003 Zinfandel and the 2004 version comment on the difference in flavor and boldness. Some of this divergence is due to the long process of bringing the McGillis farm vines back into balance after years of neglect. Some is due to using the farming techniques of Sauret. The owners are just happy to have been blessed with the good fortune to become stewards to awesome Zinfandel vineyards and to have been taught by the best farmer ever to have farmed a head trained vine.

Today, the original vineyard along with a second they purchased, produce Zinfandel, Barbera and Petite Sirah. Pricing runs $16-$25 per bottle.

From Hwy 101, take the 10th St exit in San Miguel.

Chumeia Vineyards

8331 Hwy 46 East

Paso Robles

805-226-0102

Tasting Daily 10-5

For Chumeia Vineyards winemaker Lee Nesbitt, it started with a change in direction that grew into a passion. Upon graduation from high school, Lee accepted a college football scholarship to Cal Poly San Luis Obispo with the goal of playing professional football.

While at Cal Poly, Lee was exposed to an "on campus" viticulture enterprise project that quickly took up most of his spare time and began to detract from his desire to continue his pursuit of a football career. After two years of college football, Lee decided his future was going to be in a vineyard and not on the gridiron.

For partner Eric Danninger it all started on a beach in Maui, drinking a 1991 Cabernet Sauvignon that his good friend had created. Lee and Eric met through their wives, Kristen and Jennifer, who had known each other since they were children. It was on that fateful vacation, Lee and Kris shared their dream of building a winery and producing an even better Cab than what Eric and Jen had in their glass. That partnership was completed with the addition of Lee's father, Mark, who delivered a wealth of agri-business management expertise that was critical to managing the start up business.

Their reds include Cabernet Sauvignon and Cabernet Franc, along with a Barbera and a Port. White wines include Chardonnay and Viognier along with a blend called *Silver Nectar*. Prices run $10-$50 per bottle.

Exit Highway 101 at Highway 46 East travel 9 miles on Highway 46 East. Winery on your right approximately 1/2 mile past Geneseo Rd.

Clautiere Vineyard

1340 Penman Springs Rd

Paso Robles

805-237-3789

Tasting Daily 12-5

What can you say about a winery that describes its tasting room as "Edward Scissorhands meets the Mad Hatter at the Moulin Rouge"?

The vibrant colored atmosphere and the bold winemaking style reflect the owner's motto of "live the best life you can."

The creative forces behind Clautiere Vineyard are Claudine Blackwell and Terry Brady. Between them, they boast resume listings as varied as accountant, restaurant owners, fashion designer, welder, landscape designer and, lately, winemakers. Since moving to Paso Robles in July 1999, the couple has passionately rejuvenated and transformed a local ranch into a place of vibrant color and energy. The old farmhouse boasts a wild tasting room, gift shop, commercial kitchen and a theater space suited for special events. Outside are metal sculptures and 230 feet of metal fencing that Claudine has designed and welded to complete the ambiance. The property also includes vineyards that were planted in the late 1980s with Syrah, Mourvedre and Cabernet Sauvignon. They've added more clones of Syrah, as well as Grenache, Viognier and Counoise vines. Plus an acre of Portuguese varietals which they fashion into a classic vintage-style Port wine.

With an annual production rising to about 10,000 cases, Clautiere Vineyard's current releases of Estate wines include Viognier, Syrah, Cabernet Sauvignon, a Grenache-Counoise dry Rose, Port wine and three Rhone-style blends dubbed *Mon Rouge*, *Grand Rouge* and *Mon Beau Rouge*. Prices are $23 to $39 per bottle.

Be prepared for some serious fun when visiting Clautiere Vineyard.

From Hwy 101, take Rte 46 East to Golden Hill Road. Right on Golden Hill then left on Union Rd. Finally right on Penman Springs. Winery on the left.

Diamond Gem Winery

Paso Robles

805-237-1424

Tasting By Appt

Just fine Cabernet Sauvignon. That's the only wine Shirley Marshall produces and she takes great pride in each vintage.

The grapes are selected from a minute portion of the grapes produced on Justin E. Marshall's 14 acre vineyard. The vineyard is situated on a south facing limestone rich hillside approximately 10 miles east of Hearst Castle and west of Paso Robles.

The vines were planted in 1982 on their own root stock and enjoy very warm days tempered by afternoon ocean breezes which drop the low temperature by as much as 50 degrees. This weather pattern during the growing season extends the period during which the grapes mature. Harvesting most often occurs in early November. This long maturation period contributes to the complexity of the flavors and the intensity of the color and aroma of the wine.

After the grapes are crushed and fermented a second time (malolactic fermentation) in Diamond Jem's temperature controlled stainless steel tank, the wine is transferred by gravity to new French Oak barrels where they rest in Diamond Jem's cellar for 23 months prior to being bottled at the estate. Throughout the process the wine is never subjected to any pumping.

As an example of the small production and careful handling that the Cabernet Sauvignon receives, a total of 150 cases of the 2001 vintage were bottled in October 2003, benefited from further bottle ageing and were finally released for sale in August of 2005. Retail price is $40 per bottle.

Directions to the winery will be given when you make an appointment.

Eberle Winery

3810 Hwy 46 East

Paso Robles

805-238-9607

Tasting Daily 10-5

10-6 April thru Sept.

Thirty-some years ago, Gary Eberle had an epiphany. After achieving academic and athletic success at Penn State University in the 1960's – and while pursuing his doctorate in zoology at Louisiana State University – Eberle met a professor who introduced him to the world of wine, which significantly changed his life. In 1983, Gary opened the doors to his own Eberle Winery.

Today, Eberle handcrafts 25,000 cases of wine each year from surrounding vineyards. Wines like Viognier, Roussanne, Chardonnay, Syrah, Sangiovese, Barbera, Zinfandel and Cabernet Sauvignon with prices ranging from $12 to $65 per bottle.

The redwood building that houses the Winery and Tasting Room was built to be a natural extension of the vineyard and surrounding countryside. But in 1994, Eberle was seeking additional space for the red wine program and decided to go underground. Today, 16,000 square feet of underground caves located below the winery create the perfect place to age every bottle of wine they make. The exciting thing is, cave tours are offered daily.

The German name "Eberle" translates to "small boar." At Eberle Winery, a bronze boar greets every guest who visits the Tasting Room. The statue is the 93rd replica of the original bronze Porcellino cast by Tacca in 1620. And today, the original can be found in the straw market in Florence, Italy. It is considered good luck to rub the boar's nose and toss a coin in the water below. All money collected at the Eberle boar fountain is donated to local children's charities.

From Hwy 101, exit Rte 46 East 3.5 miles to the winery – on your left.

EOS Estate Winery

5625 Hwy 46 East

Paso Robles

805-239-2562

Tasting Daily 10-5

10-6 Summer Weekends

The EOS Estate Winery was established in 1996 and named after "Eos," the "Goddess of the Dawn" in Greek Mythology. At EOS Estate Winery, they harvest their wine grapes before, or right after the sunrise, to keep the fruit cool and help retain fresh varietal character.

The Estate Vineyards are planted with ten varieties in three large blocks totaling over 700 acres. The wine offerings include Chardonnay, Sauvignon Blanc, Fume Blanc, Cabernet Sauvignon, Syrah, Zinfandel, Petite Sirah, Merlot, Cabernet Franc and a number of dessert wines including their *Tears of Dew* – a late harvest Moscato. Wines are offered in three labels – the Novella wines price at $10-$15, the EOS line at $12-$20 and the Cupa Grandis line at $45-$60.

As you taste in their amazing 6,000 square foot Mediterranean Marketplace, you'll be captivated by the beautiful 50 foot mural of the award-winning EOS label art that surrounds the bar. That is if you can ignore the huge selection of handcrafted Italian pottery, elegant gifts, wine accessories and gourmet foods. Or the exciting Arciero Race Car exhibit, culled from winery partner Frank Arciero's long auto racing history. Or if you can leave their lovely rose garden or the spacious picnic area set among classical Italian architecture. In other words, the winery is a world unto itself, with lots to keep you intrigued, not the least of which is the opportunity to learn how their exceptional Estate varietals are grown and produced by taking an informative self guided winery tour.

From Hwy 101, take the Rte 46 East exit six miles. Winery on the right.

Falcon Nest Vineyard & Winery

5185 Union Rd

Paso Robles

805-226-0227

Tasting Daily 10-7:30

Falcon Nest is a family operated business started in 1993. Owners Francesco and Carolynn Grande purchased 149 acres of prime viticulture land in the appellation of Paso Robles and planted 53 acres in grapevines.

They believe in and practice meticulous vineyard management. The vines are planted from east to west direction to maximize exposure to the sun, thus achieving maximum ripeness. Vines are managed to produce small yields, small berries and intense flavors to make wines of distinction. All the grapes are hand-harvested to control quality. The grapes are fermented in small lots of 500 to 3,000 gallons.

Secondary malolactic fermentation is done in 59 gallon French Oak barrels and aged for one year prior to first racking. The wine continues aging in barrels for an additional year prior to filtering and bottling and is released 60 days after bottling. Total production is around 4,000 cases per year.

Falcon Nest offers Zinfandel, Syrah, Cabernet Sauvignon and Merlot, all in the $23 to $38 range.

From Hwy 101 take Rte 46 East to Golden Hill Rd, left on Union Rd for approximately 4 miles. Winery on the right.

Firestone Vineyard

2300 Airport Rd at Hwy 46 East

Paso Robles

805-591-8050

Tasting Daily 10-5

Firestone Vineyard's new Paso Robles winery opened in the fall of 2006, complementing the original winery in Santa Barbara County with a specific focus on small lots of Paso Robles-grown Bordeaux varietals, including Cabernet Sauvignon, Cabernet Franc and Merlot. "We have purchased Paso Robles fruit for several vintages, and we have long been impressed with the quality of the region's wines," says Andrew Firestone, who will manage the winery.

The new Paso Robles winery is an 8.5 acre estate at the corner of Route 46 East and Airport Road. It features a tasting room, barrel cellar, enclosed patio and nine pocket gardens with picnic accommodations. The remainder of the estate is planted to four individual clones of Cabernet Sauvignon, each trellised to optimize the hillside terrain and soils.

The winery is a two-level masonry structure inspired by the original Firestone Vineyard winery in the Santa Ynez valley. The Paso Robles winery is a fresh interpretation of the original. The interior offers a cave entrance into the barrel cellar, with elevator and stair access to the tasting area. The tasting area includes an island bar, merchandise displays and a balcony overlooking the barrel cellar.

Initial production will be 4,000 cases, featuring small lots of Bordeaux varietals and blends grown at select vineyards in Paso Robles. Wines from the 2004 and 2005 vintages are currently aging at the original winery in the Santa Ynez Valley, and will be available for tasting and purchase at the Paso Robles winery. Wines will be crafted on site in Paso Robles beginning with the 2006 vintage.

From Hwy 101, exit at Rte 46 East. Drive just a short distance to turn on to Airport Rd on your left and then make a right into the winery.

Fralich Vineyard

Paso Robles

805-434-1526

Tasting By Appt

In 1980 Harry and Ruth Fralich made their first move towards realizing Harry's dream of being a winegrower when they purchased a 20 acre property on the east side of Templeton. Though he still worked for Hughes Aircraft in Los Angeles until 1993, Fralich started his vineyard in 1989.

In 1992 Harry began planting the vineyard to Rhone varietals, which put Fralich on the front end of a Rhone Revolution, both locally and in the wine market as a whole. His attention to detail in the vineyard propelled him to the forefront of local growers, and he sought to work with winemakers and wineries that would put the same effort into crafting wines from Fralich Vineyard grapes.

For Fralich, establishing his own label was a natural progression from wine grower to winemaker who can offer a limited production of premium wines that showcase the very essence of his exceptional grapes.

Harry will continue to sell the majority of his fruit - about 80 percent - to other wineries that will handcraft his fruit into premium wines. The Fralich Vineyard label is a small project of less than 1000 cases annually aimed at improving its namesake vineyard and producing a unique selection of premium wines.

The Fralich line includes Viognier, *Harry's Patio White* blend, Syrah, Zinfandel, Harry's *Patio Red*, Claret of Syrah, a Port and a Late Harvest Verdelho. Prices fall between $26 and $42.

Directions to the Winery will be given when you call for an appointment.

Gelfand Vineyards

5530 Dresser Ranch Place

Paso Robles

805-239-5808

Tasting By Appt

Len and Jan Gelfand have been passionate about wines for many years. Having had the opportunity to travel and visit hundreds of boutique wineries around the world, their dream was to one day be the people standing behind the counter pouring their own wines instead of those doing the tasting.

That dream became a reality in 2000, when they purchased a 25 acre parcel in the rolling hills of Paso Robles. Situated a mere 25 miles from the Pacific Ocean, the area is influenced by tremendous fluctuations in the weather, where summer days regularly hit in the 100's and evenings dip down into the 40's, placing a great deal of stress on the vines. The swing in temperature only intensifies the flavor of the grapes creating the perfect environment for big earthy reds. So their first ten acres were planted with Cabernet Sauvignon, Zinfandel, Syrah, and Petite Sirah.

Those grapes, along with three or four red blends, make up the wines they offer. All are priced in the $20-$30 range. Their flagship wine, the dream they named *Quixotic* is a meritage, a blending of their best barrels, and will vary from year to year so as to achieve the most elegant style of wine they can make. In the two years it's been available, *Quixotic* has proven to be a favorite among their customers.

In fact, in their first vintage, their wines won many awards and sold out quickly. Their dream of creating memorable wines is now a reality. And they look forward to sharing their wines and memories with you.

From Hwy 101 take Rte 46 east towards Fresno. Turn right onto Union Rd and then immediately left to stay on Union Rd. Turn right onto Penman Springs Rd then slight left onto Harvest Ridge Way then slight right onto Sunny Ridge Place. Then slight left onto Dresser Ranch Place.

Graveyard Vineyards

6990 Estrella Rd

San Miguel

805-467-2043

Tasting By Appt

Rob and Paula Campbell-Taylor, owners and caretakers of Graveyard Vineyards, bought their beautiful hilltop property in 2003 when the vineyard was in its seventh year. They named the ranch Graveyard Vineyards for two good reasons. At least, they think they are good! See what you think –

The first and main reason is that their ranch is next to the historic Pleasant Valley Cemetery in San Miguel. When walking through this small country landmark, your imagination runs wild with stories that could be told of cowboys and life in the late 1800s. The second reason for choosing such a grave name (pardon the pun) is that they believe it is important to keep a fun, light-hearted attitude while working hard towards an important goal.

And Rob and Paula set their goals firmly in place to create wines that memories are made of. Paula says, "I want to know that our wine is served at memorable occasions with families and friends and enjoyed with the comfort foods of that occasion. Comfort food and comfort wine—a match made in heaven!"

A micro winery, or boutique winery, is one that produces no more than 10,000 cases of wine per year. Graveyard Vineyards produced about 350 cases of wine last year. Their wines include Cabernet Sauvignon, Syrah, Chardonnay, Sauvignon Blanc and a White Syrah (think Rose). Prices are $14-$18.

Make no bones about it, the challenge of developing wine grapes into the best tasting wine the Paso Robles region has to offer has been no easy task. Rob and Paula hope you'll find them up to the task.

From Highway 101, take Route 46 East 2.4 miles to Airport Rd. Turn left onto Airport Rd and drive to the end. Turn right onto Estrella Rd and go one mile to the Winery driveway.

Gremark Vineyards

Paso Robles

805-237-0154

By Appt Only

After working for Pacific Gas and Electric for 25 years, Greg Keezer earned a Bachelors Degree in Enology from Fresno State University and became a winemaker of some note, working for large corporate wine producers. His desire to create a better wine prompted him to have his own vineyard and create his own label, where he could have complete control over the final product.

In 1999, while searching for a suitable place to grow and produce premium quality grapes, Greg and his wife, Marina, came upon a 14 acre parcel in the Paso Robles area, fell in love with it, and bought it immediately. This was no easy task as neither party was employed at the time. The grapes were planted in 2000, consisting mostly of Cabernet Sauvignon and other varietals needed for producing Bordeaux style blends. A section of head pruned Zinfandel was added in 2004 to further enhance the product line. The Gremark Vineyards label was started in 2004 and all their wines are produced from estate grown grapes.

The winery will be producing from 500 to 1000 cases annually, made up of Viognier, Sauvignon Blanc, Chardonnay, Cabernet Sauvignon and *Mavelese*, an incredible blend of five varietals including Cabernet Sauvignon, Malbec, Cabernet Franc, Merlot and Tannat. Prices range from $14 to $33 per bottle.

Gremark Vineyards is located some 10 miles southeast of Paso Robles. By license, they are not allowed to have a public tasting room, but if you are going to be in the area and want to stop by, give them a call.

Directions to the Winery will be given when you call for an appointment.

Hansen Vineyard

5575 El Pomar

Templeton

805-239-8412

Tasting Fri-Sun 11:30-5:30

Or By Appt

As owners/winemakers of a small boutique winery, Bruce and Sheila Hansen offer ultra-premium hand-made wines, produced in small lots from their winery and vineyard.

Bruce grew up on a fruit farm in Michigan and remembers helping his father produce fruit wines – cherry, plum and others. As a general contractor in California, he built a number of the wineries to be found in the Paso Robles area. Now he can concentrate on producing his own fine wine, using the knowledge he gained from his father and his own experience.

Their vineyard has become so well known and respected among winemakers that much of their fruit is sold to other wineries and almost always vineyard-designated. But Bruce holds on to enough to bottle is own Viognier, Merlot, Cabernet Sauvignon, Syrah and Zinfandel. They sell for $28 to $48 per bottle.

You're invited to visit their uniquely rustic tasting room and experience some serious wine. Talk with the them while you picnic on the patio and enjoy the relaxing family atmosphere.

From Hwy 101, exit Vineyard Dr just north of Atascadero and drive east onto El Pomar Dr. Winery on your right just past the So El Pomar Dr intersection.

Hug Cellars

2323 Tuley Ct Suite 120D

Paso Robles

805-226-8022

Tasting Th-Mon 11-5:00

And By Appt

Hug Cellars is a small family owned winery specializing in limited production Syrah and Pinot Noir. Augie Hug's winemaking style is hedonistic, producing wines that are big and bold, rich and intense, while at the same time being complex and balanced.

Established in 1994 by Augie Hug and Raquel Mireles Rodriguez, Hug Cellars started conceptually during the mid 1980's while Augie was the chef of a small restaurant located in Northern California. Augie found that the union of food and wine came quite naturally to him, and it was during this time that he developed his love of wines.

A few years later, Raquel and Augie were owners of a wine shop and tasting room in Harmony, on the Central Coast, where they became known for their wide selection of Rhone varietals. In 1994, under the guidance of John Alban, Augie produced 87 cases of Edna Valley Syrah at Alban Vineyards. That was their first commercial release. Meanwhile, Augie continued his quest for knowledge by involving himself in the hands-on experience of making wine and participating in extension courses at the University of California, Davis. In 2000, they left the retail side of the business to focus on the production of Hug Cellars wine.

Hug Cellars' wines are truly "made in the vineyard." Each year, they bottle Pinot Noir and Syrah with grapes from a select number of growers – producing wines that reflect the stellar vineyards from which they came. Prices run $19-$60 per bottle.

From Hwy 101 take Rte 46 East for 1.3 Miles. At the 2nd Stop Light turn right onto Golden Hill Road then left onto Union Road and then left again onto Tuley Ct.

J. Lohr Vineyards & Wines

6169 Airport Rd.

Paso Robles

805-239-8900

Tasting Daily 10-5

The son of a South Dakota farming family, Jerry Lohr first began looking for vineyard land in the late 1960s. His California-wide search led him to Monterey County's Arroyo Seco appellation. One of Monterey's pioneers, Jerry planted his first 280 acres of grape vines in 1972-73. Enjoying one of the longest growing seasons for grapes in California, the original 280 acres of this vineyard flourished under Jerry's hands-on care, and have since been expanded to over 900 acres of cool-climate grapes including Chardonnay, White Riesling, Valdiguié and Pinot Noir

A firm believer in pairing the right grape with the perfect soil and climate, Jerry purchased property near Paso Robles in 1988. Impressed by the potential of a number of early Paso Cabernets, Jerry was convinced that the region's warm days and cool nights were ideal for red grapes. He planted Cabernet Sauvignon, Merlot, Syrah, and several other red varietals used for blending. Today, J. Lohr Vineyards & Wines cultivates over 2,000 acres of vineyards in Paso Robles.

From J. Lohr's diverse vineyards (which also include land in the Napa Valley) Jerry and longtime winemaker Jeff Meier strive to create lush, attractive and flavorful wines through a combination of cutting-edge viticulture and innovative winemaking. Offering an expressive range of styles, J. Lohr produces three tiers of wine from estate grapes – J. Lohr Estates, J. Lohr Vineyard Series and J. Lohr Cuvée Series. In addition, the winery makes an inviting array of vibrant wines suitable for every occasion, including Cypress Vineyards, ARIEL (non-alcoholic), Painter Bridge and Crosspoint labels. While a portion of J. Lohr's signature wines retail above $25, the heart of its portfolio is priced in the $10 to $17 range.

From Highway 101, take Route 46 East 2.4 miles to Airport Rd. Turn left 3.4 miles to winery on the left.

Laura's Vineyard

5620 Hwy 46 East

Paso Robles

805-238-6300

Tasting Th-Sun 10-5

Established in 1977 on what was once part of the original Estrella River Winery Vineyards, Laura's Vineyard traces its heritage to the very beginnings of Paso Robles wine country history. Cliff Giacobine and his half brother Gary Eberle named this vineyard after their mother Laura Eberle. During her retirement years and until her death in 1980, Laura lived and worked with personal dedication on this beautiful vineyard just east of Paso Robles. She spent long hours propagating rootings for planting, and dreaming of the time when her vines would be recognized as some of the best in the area.

After a successful career in manufacturing, Ray and Pam Derby made Cambria their full-time home in 1995. Discovering their interest in wine growing and production, they purchased the property that is now Derbyshire Vineyard (near Cambria) in 1998. Derbyshire is known for its Pinot Noir. They subsequently purchased Laura's Vineyard (planted in Zinfandel, Merlot, Cabernet Sauvignon, Syrah and Petite Sirah) in 2001 and the Westside Ranch (mostly Rhone varietals) in 2006. And Laura's Vineyard became the home of their tasting room.

Now they offer a wide range of reds, including Cabernet Sauvignon, Merlot, Cabernet Franc, Petite Sirah and Zinfandel. Their white wines include Sauvignon Blanc and Chardonnay. The wines sell for $8 to $22 per bottle.

In addition to their wines, Ray and Pam offer a nice selection of wine related gifts in the tasting room. And just outside the door, there's a cool, shaded picnic area available for relaxing or for a family picnic.

From Hwy 101, take the Hwy 46 East exit 6.2 miles. Winery on the left.

Locatelli Vineyards & Winery

8585 Cross Canyon Rd

San Miguel

805-467-0067

Tasting Fri-Sun 11-4

And By Appt

Locatelli Vineyards is family owned and operated, situated in a rustic ranch setting, overlooking the peaceful Salinas river valley, only two miles from the historic Old Mission San Miguel Archangel. You will not find a romanticized or glorified tourist version of wine culture at their facility - the entire winemaking process, from cultivating the grapevines to bottling the final product all takes place right there.

There are forty acres of vineyards on the ranch. Cabernet Sauvignon, Merlot, Petite Sirah, Malbec, Petite Verdot, Muscat Canelli, and Zinfandel are some of the wine grape varietals grown. Their bottlings also include Vigionier and a number of blends. Prices are in the $14-$30 range.

The family winemaking history dates back to great-grandfather Cesare Locatelli, who brought the art with him when he immigrated to California. Cesare was born near the border of Switzerland and Italy in the small village of Cerentino, in the Swiss Canton Ticino. Cesare taught his three sons to work the land, and each year they crushed the grapes. It is rumored that they sold quite a bit of wine during the period of Prohibition, but they never endeavored to open a legally recognized winery. Locatelli Winery would not come into existence until Cesare's great-grandson, Louis Gregory, together with his wife Raynette, decided to add life to the old tradition when they bought the ranch in San Miguel, which they chose for its strategic location, in anticipation of the supreme quality of the grapes to be grown. Today, they'll happily give you a tour of the winery during your visit.

From Hwy 101, take the 1st San Miguel Exit (Mission Street), turn east onto River Road, go over the Salinas River bridge & then immediately after the bridge, turn left onto Cross Canyons Road & proceed only 1/2 mile.

Madison Cellars

4640 Highway 41 East

Paso Robles

805-237-7544

Tasting By Appt

Madison Cellars Vineyard and Winery typifies the next generation winery. Owners Margie and Jon Korecki built their estate vineyard with the youthful exuberance of a Gen X family while maintaining respect for tradition and the land they are using.

The Koreckis grew up on the Coast of Connecticut near the town of Madison. The pure image of the quintessential rural New England town has remained with them and now lives on their label. They wanted those memories to be reflected in the new life that they were about to build and in the wines that they would create.

Jon, who studied at UC Davis and Cal Poly San Luis Obispo, has been making wine for more than 10 years. After evaluating many winegrowing regions Jon and Margie realized that Paso Robles would not only fulfill the conditions he wanted for creating great wines, but also the conditions they wanted for creating a great life.

This is why their mission statement and devotion to wine is written on the back of every bottle:

To work in harmony,
To forge the elemental union of man and nature,
To unveil the ultimate expression in man's hand,
This....is our passion.
What's yours?

Their wines consist of Syrah Rosé, Merlot, Roussanne, Cabernet Sauvignon, Syrah, Viognier and a Bordeaux blend they call *Maximus*. Prices are from $14 to $30.

From Hwy 101, take Hwy 41 East for 14 miles. Winery on the left side.

Maloy O'Neill Vineyards

5725 Union Rd

Paso Robles

805-238-7320

Tasting Fri-Sat 10-5

Sun 12-5 And By Appt

Shannon O'Neill likes to say that he and his wife Maureen are known for their "Enormous, inky black Syrahs. Unbelievably huge Zinfandels. Big concentrated Cal-Ital & Bordeaux-Style Blends." In addition, Maloy O'Neill produces Cabernet Sauvignon, Merlot, Petite Sirah, Pinot Noir and Chardonnay. Usually 30 some different bottlings per year, and all in the $16-$45 range.

Since 1982, the vineyards have been producing high quality grapes for some of the well-known local wineries as well as wineries in Napa Valley. In 1999, they began selling under their own label.

When they say they are a small, family owned and operated winery, they mean just that. Everything is done by hand – no pumps, no bottling lines. The wine is gravity fed and bottled one bottle at a time, with Shannon and Maureen doing all the work. That doesn't make for large production, but it makes for wines that are gently handled and produced in small quantities - usually 40-200 cases.

Last year, Shannon produced seven different Cabernet Sauvignon bottlings, each a little different, each handled separately. Only a small winery can make wine like that, and only at a small winery will you be able to taste the miniscule differences that result from grapes grown in different sections of the same vineyard. Maloy O'Neill would be a good place to start tasting the difference.

From Hwy 101, exit at Rte 46 East. Go east pass the redlight at Golden Hill and turn right onto Union Rd, then making an immediate left onto (another) Union Rd. The winery is on your right between Penman Springs and Branch Rds.

Martin & Weyrich Winery

2610 Buena Vista Dr

Paso Robles

805-238-2520

Tasting Daily 10-5

Martin & Weyrich Winery works hard to maintain its status as the premier winery in the United States experimenting with and producing Italian grape varieties.

Martin & Weyrich is proud to be the first grower and producer of Nebbiolo in the United States in recent history. They are also the first U.S. producer of a "Super-Tuscan" blend. This blend is 85% Cabernet Sauvignon and 15% Sangiovese. The wine, aptly named *Cabernet Etrusco*, has consistently been met with rave reviews. The estate has planted six clones of Sangiovese, and they produce a wine called "Il Palio," recognized as one of the most intense Sangioveses produced in California. Other Italian varietals produced include: Malvasia Bianca, Muscat Canelli, Pinot Grigio, Barbera, and Dolcetto. They are also known as the first and only winery in the country to ferment and age Chardonnay in chestnut barrels. The wines are available in the $8-$40 price range.

Your visit will also expose you to their award winning tasting room for a relaxed experience of Tuscany, with fine wine tasting, food sampling and unique gift shopping. Browse their many imported gift items, sample the white and red varietals or have a delicious gourmet coffee.

You can pick up some cheese and deli selections from the deli case, try some crackers and other snacks and sit out on their beautiful patio and enjoy!

Martin & Weyrich also offer their fabulous hotel, Villa Toscana, eight suites and a large vintner's residence, overlooking the rolling Paso Robles hills. Be sure to ask for information while you taste.

From Hwy 101, take Rte 46 East a short drive to Buena Vista Drive on your left. The tasting room is on the corner.

Jack Ranch, Edna Valley Chardonnay. VG.

Meridian Vineyards

7000 Hwy 46 East
Paso Robles
805-226-7133
Tasting Daily 10-5

Meridian Vineyards was established in 1988. The label was first created in 1984 by veteran winemaker Chuck Ortman, who spent the early part of his career as winemaker and consultant to several Napa and Sonoma wineries. Ortman was always intrigued by the emerging growing regions of Santa Barbara and San Luis Obispo counties, where vineyards in cool climates were yielding Chardonnay and Pinot Noir of phenomenal quality. In 1988, Beringer Blass Wine Estates invested in the four-year-old Meridian label and today, winemaker Lee Miyamura is responsible for every step of the winemaking process, using grapes grown in each of the different Central Coast growing regions.

Since its founding in 1988, Meridian has become synonymous with the California lifestyle and great-tasting, award-winning wines. Known for its bright, colorful labels and an uncomplicated view on life, Meridian produces wines in two different lines.

Meridian offers their Classic line of wines for everyday enjoyment, priced at $10 per bottle, and their Limited Release line, produced in small quantities and only available at the Winery or online. Wines including Zinfandel, Syrah, Petite Sirah, Sangiovese, Gewurztraminer, Pinot Noir, Cabernet, Pinot Gris, Chardonnay, Pinot Blanc, Merlot and Cabernet Sauvignon Blanc. Those wines run $12-$24 per bottle.

As you drive up their long driveway, past the sweeping vineyards, you'll find yourself surrounded by majestic oak trees over 200 years old, landscaped herb and flower gardens and beautiful picnic grounds. At the center is the natural stone winery building containing their tasting room and a lovely selection of wine and food related gifts.

From Hwy 101, take Hwy 46 East for 7 miles. Winery on the left.

Nichols Winery & Cellars

Paso Robles

888-278-9463

Tasting By Appt

Born and raised in the east, owner Keith Nichols came to California in a career move. Within a short time, he was invited to join a Gourmet Club where he developed his love for "Fine Food and Fine Wine" and in particular the marriage of the two.

To further develop his understanding of wine, and the winemaking process, he traveled to Bordeaux, France to visit various wine making establishments. Additional wine research was done during a trip to South Africa, which has a long history of winemaking dating back to 1659 near Cape Town. College classes followed in wine marketing along with a self taught, five-year Viticulture and Winemaking program from U.C. Davis.

The result, Nichols Winery is now a small winery which was established in 1991 to produce ultra premium wine with limited production of each varietal around the 1,200 case level. Chardonnay was the initial varietal to be produced while Pinot Noir followed in the 1993 vintage. In 1996 Cabernet Sauvignon, Zinfandel and Pinot Blanc were added.

Nichols bottles under two labels – Nichols – with wines aged in 100% French oak and Soleil & Terroir – wines aged in 70% French oak and 30% American oak. You'll find the difference very interesting. Prices range between $21 and $70 per bottle.

Directions will be given when you call for a tasting appointment.

Penman Springs Vineyard

1985 Penman Springs Rd

Paso Robles

805-237-7959

Tasting Fri-Sun 11-5:30

Closed January

Established in 1981, this artisan vineyard is 40 acres of beautiful hilltop over-looking the east side of Paso Robles. The property was previously home to two other premium labels; in 1996 Carl and Beth McCasland purchased the vineyard and began to make the changes that have allowed Penman Springs to produce the Merlot, Syrah, Petite Sirah, Cabernet Sauvignon and Chardonnay – and a number of blends - that they are known for today. Prices are in the $14 to $25 range.

In fact, if you're interested in knowing how farmers raise grapes that produce great wines, visit the Penman Springs website. Via video and photos, Carl shows how he trellises the vines to deliver the best juice.

But if you're interested in the tasting of great wine and the fun you can have while doing that, visit the Penman Springs tasting room. They pride themselves on having a small, but homey, relaxing room that invites you to stay and sip just one more tasting. There's always a jigsaw puzzle being worked on, and you're invited to help fill in the missing pieces. Along with the wine, Beth offers a small selection of the winery's logo merchandise and a wide selection of their oils and gourmet spreads.

And like many family-owned and operated wineries along the Central Coast, you'll be served by Beth or Carl or their one employee, Rosie. Hope that Rosie's there, because she often makes some of the best "tasties" that you'll find to go with wine. At Penman Springs, the conversation is usually lively, the wine lovely and the setting warm and friendly. You'll enjoy.

From Hwy 101, exit Rte 46 East past the redlight at Golden Hill and turn right onto Union Rd, then make an immediate left onto (another) Union Rd. Turn right onto Penman Springs Rd – winery on the right.

Pozo Valley Winery

2200 El Camino Real

Santa Margarita

805-438-5015

Tasting Fri-Sun 12-6

Or By Appt

The Arnold family first settled in the Pozo Valley in 1919, when Thomas and Josephine Arnold sold their farm in Nebraska and moved out west. For five generations members of the Arnold family have lived and worked on the original ranch land, raising beef cattle and farming a variety of crops.

The Pozo Valley is located approximately 28 miles northeast of San Luis Obispo and maintains a Coastal influence evidenced by the fog that can often be seen creeping through the mountain passes. The extreme fluctuation in daily temperature during the growing season has proven to be an ideal climate for growing flavorful varietals, resulting in some extraordinary wines.

The vineyard was planted in 1995 by Steve Arnold, with the help of his wife Debbie, and children Joey & Michelle. For years special attention has been given to producing grapes of the highest quality. Zinfandel, Cabernet Sauvignon, and Merlot were the varietals chosen for their suitability to the valley's soils and climate. The resulting wines are priced at $18-$20 per bottle.

The Arnolds are pouring their wines in Bonnie's Kitchen, the newest gift and gourmet shop in downtown Santa Margarita, and invite you to come and experience the small town atmosphere while you shop for unique gifts and taste great wines.

Tasting in Downtown Santa Margarita. Tasting at the Winery is by appointment only by calling 805-286-7172.

Pretty-Smith Vineyards & Winery

13350 N River Rd

San Miguel

805-467-3104

Tasting Fri-Sun 10-5

When Lisa Pretty and a partner purchased the estate in the sunny September of 2000, they brought with them the legendary figure of Kokopelli. Within the hump of his back, Kokopelli carries seeds of plants and flowers. The music of his flute creates warmth for germination. The presence of his Spirit in the vineyard assures a continuing life of balance and harmony.

Picnicking on the lawns and redwood decks, visitors to the tasting room can marvel at Kokopelli's colorful handiwork roundabout. The Pretty-Smith wines they sip are vibrant paintings of beauty and strength.

Pretty-Smith has 45 acres of estate grown grapes from 25+ year old vines, resulting in wines with solid character. Each Pretty-Smith wine is delivered with a front label displaying a unique piece of artwork with symbols from the Kokopelli era. The label reflects the individual attention given to each wine from the time the grapes are picked until the time the handcrafted wine is bottled.

This one-woman winery produces Sauvignon Blanc, Merlot, Cabernet Franc, Cabernet Sauvignon, a Zinfandel Port, a late-harvest Zinfandel and their signature wine – *Palette de Rouge* – a Bordeaux-style blend of Cabernet Franc, Cabernet Sauvignon and Merlot. Price range between $15 and $28 per bottle.

From Hwy 101, take the San Miguel exit and proceed onto Mission St. Turn right onto River Road (at the "Parkfield 23" sign). Stay on River Road after you cross the bridge and follow the road as it bends to the right. At the bottom of the hill you will see the Pretty-Smith gates on your left.

Rio Seco Winery

4295 Union Rd

Paso Robles

805-237-8884

Tasting Th-Mon 11-5:30

Long-time San Luis Obispo county residents Tom and Carol Hinkle began their wine adventure years ago. After successful teaching careers, the Hinkles began searching for vineyard property, looking at over two hundred parcels of potential vineyard land before they found the perfect spot in the spring of 1996.

Once owned by a Hollywood movie producer, the beautiful 63 acres nestled among rolling hills and the Huer Huero Creek was home to a big red barn, now the winery and tasting room building. It was originally constructed to accommodate the catering needs and food service for the actors on the set of a 1984 movie. After its film career, the barn was used for a large marijuana-growing operation. Bullet holes pock the side of the winery from the bust, and the CHP pilot who flew over to make sure nobody got away has dropped by the winery to do some tasting.

Rio Seco planted thirty-one acres in the spring of 1997 to traditional Paso Robles Zinfandel and Cabernet Sauvignon, but additionally planted Syrah, Cab Franc, Roussanne, and a test block of Viogner and Merlot...all in all, a winemakers delight! Their wines vary in price from $18-$30 a bottle.

Today, family and friends find Rio Seco the perfect place to picnic, explore in the creek bed, or walk through the 10-year-old vineyard. Enjoying sunsets across the river, music, laughter, shared stories, and fine wine are all the makings for a pleasant afternoon indeed!

From Hwy 101, exit at Rte 46 East approximately 2 miles - pass the stoplight at Golden Hill and turn right on Union Rd Make an immediate left for two more miles. Winery at the big red barn on your right.

RN Estate

7986 N River Rd
Paso Robles
805-610-9802
Tasting By Appt

Roger Nicolas started dreaming as a young boy growing up on his parents farm in a remote countryside village of Brittany, France.

When he landed in New York City at the age of 20 he believed dreams could come true. Ten years later, after working in some of the most prestigious restaurants in the United States, including La Grenouille in New York City, The Lodge at Pebble Beach and L'Etoile in San Francisco, Roger realized one of his first dreams of opening his own restaurant in San Francisco called La Potiniere.

Ten years later he gained international acclaim as the founder and owner of The Home Hill country inn and restaurant in New Hampshire, now a famous Relais & Chateaux - this had been another dream.

Ten years later, Roger thought it was time to play. In his restaurant career he developed a profound passion for wine. Another dream was being transformed. The search was on to find the perfect land for a vineyard.

Ten years later... In the fall of 2005, he released his first vintage of RN Estate Wines. Roger is still dreaming with passion and belief. You're invited to share Roger's dream by calling ahead to visit him for a private vineyard tour and tasting.

You'll find that his present offerings are very encouraging. In addition to a Zinfandel and a Mourvedre, Roger has a number of blends available. His various blends involve Cabernet Sauvignon, Merlot, Cabernet Franc, Syrah, Mourvedre, Zinfandel and Petit Verdot. And all of the wines are in the $25 to $35 price range.

From Hwy 101, exit Rte 46 East and turn left on N River Rd. Take N River Rd approx 6.4 miles to winery.

Robert Hall Winery

Photo by Fred Granzow

3443 Mill Rd

Paso Robles

805-239-1616

Tasting Daily 10-5

Summer 10-6

While living in Minnesota, Robert Hall and his family traveled to Southern France, Provence and the Rhone Valley - his family went to see the castles while Robert discovered the wines, "I started to drink Rhone wines and I fell in love with them," he says.

Traveling through the west, he began to develop his idea for a premium producing vineyard and winery, and in the mid-90's, Robert and Margaret discovered the perfect terroir in the Paso Robles appellation. "Home Ranch" was acquired in 1995 - soon after, the "Terrace" and "Bench" vineyards joined the Hall Ranch enclave. Almost all of the wine is estate grown.

Their modern facility includes 19,000 square feet of underground caverns. The naturally cool environment allows the wine to age gracefully in oak barrels at an even temperature of 55 degrees. Their grounds feature a 10,000 square foot tasting room with elevator to the caverns, a wine library, a full-kitchen with a dining room for special events, fountains, garden terrace and an amphitheater with fantastic 360 degree views of the area. And don't miss the two spectacular regulation Bocce courts in the old world style, with crushed oyster shells and a layer of oyster shell "flour."

Robert Hall wines are as all-encompassing as the buildings in which they're stored and served. Headed by their Reserve Cabernet Sauvignon, they include Merlot, Grenache, Syrah, Zinfandel, Chardonnay, Sauvignon, Viognier and a delightful *Rosé de Robles*. Prices are in the $12-$38 range. And unlike many wineries, Robert Hall offers many of their wines in magnum and double magnum-sized bottles.

From Hwy 101, exit Rte 46 East. Turn right on Mill Rd – winery on the right.

Scott Aaron Wine

422 S Main

Templeton

888-611-9463

Tasting Fri-Mon 11-7

And By Appt

Scott Aaron wines are handcrafted in very small quantities of just two to three barrels of each wine by winemaker and owner Scott Aaron Morgan. They are sold exclusively through their web site, wine club and tasting room in downtown Templeton.

Scott grew up learning about wine at his family's winery, Casa de Caballos Vineyards. There he learned all facets of the wine making process. "I am a farmer, a winemaker, a marketer, and a business person. It's funny but even with two degrees and years of Marketing and Business experience, my favorite job is still driving the tractor."

Scott used to go to seminars to learn more about the wine business. He remembers listening to growers talk about maximizing their yields and getting the most they possibly could from their grape vines and I always felt they were missing the point. "I believe great wine comes from minimizing yields and allowing your vines to thrive by growing less fruit on that vine instead of maximizing production. The result is better fruit which translates into better wine."

Cabernet Franc is one of Scott's favorite varietals and *Integrity* is the first wine under the Scott Aaron label. It's full of fruit and has the wonderful earthy characteristics of Cabernet Franc with Merlot and just a touch of Cabernet Sauvignon to add some complexity. His second wine was a Viognier and he just recently introduced *Nobility* - a beautiful blend of 68% Syrah, 20% Cabernet Sauvignon, and 12% Petite Sirah. Prices run in the $30 to $55 range.

If you're a chocolate lover, you have two reasons to visit the Scott Aaron tasting room. The wine, of course. But space is shared with Herrmann's Chocolate Lab – a landmark in downtown Templeton.

Tasting room in downtown Templeton

Sculpterra Winery

5125 Linne Rd

Paso Robles

805-226-8881

Tasting Th-Sun 11-5

Following his medical residency at U.C.L.A., and the opening of his medical practice in the San Fernando Valley, Warren Frankel began to take his desire for a simpler and more self-reliant lifestyle seriously. In 1979, Dr. Frankel moved his family and medical practice to a beautiful 90 acre ranch located in the Linne Valley of Paso Robles.

The Frankel family first planted 20 acres of pistachios on the ranch, followed by 20 acres of Cabernet Sauvignon grapes. After the initial success with the Cabernet Sauvignon vineyard, Dr. Frankel expanded his plantings in 1997, planting an additional 80 acres of Cabernet Sauvignon, 10 acres of Zinfandel and 10 acres of Merlot. Cabernet Franc, Mouvedre, Petite Sirah and Viognier are the most recent additions to the vineyard.

The Frankel estate grapes are cultivated to promote intense, varietal flavors that can then be sculpted in the cellar into a final artistic statement. The Sculpterra portfolio of premium wines is priced from $12 - $35 and includes Cabernet Sauvignon, Chardonnay, Pinot Grigio, Petite Sirah, Syrah and Zinfandel. A Merlot and a Bordeaux blend will be added to the collection in the future.

The Tasting Room and Sculpture Garden, scheduled to open in early summer 2007, will offer visitors an exceptional wine tasting experience. The Sculpture garden features larger-than-life sculptures by artist John Jagger. Sculpted from granite and bronze, the sculptures will amaze and inspire – as will the wines.

From Hwy 101 South, take the Spring St. exit, turn right on Niblick Rd. Go straight on Niblick Rd until it turns into Sherwood Rd. Travel straight until the road turns into a right hand turn on Fontana Rd. The road will then turn left and become Linne Rd, follow Linne Rd for 2 miles and then turn right at the Sculpterra Winery Signage.

Shadow Canyon Cellars

45 Main St

Templeton

805-781-9400

Tasting By Appt

Like many winemakers in the area, owner Gary Gibson attended Cal Poly in San Luis Obispo and, while there, grew to love wines. After graduation, he moved to Los Angeles, but the pull of the grapes was too strong, and he returned to the area in 1996, bought a 40 acre vineyard and harvested his first Syrah in 2000. That juice was sold to another winery, but his success brought him to the first Shadow Canyon bottling with the vintage of 2001. Bottles run $40 each.

Shadow Canyon is a mountain vineyard planted entirely to Syrah. Located in the middle of the east-west corridor known as the Templeton Gap, the vineyard lies at a 1600' elevation approximately eight miles from the ocean. The Gap allows cool marine air and fog to roll into the vineyard, which experiences daytime highs in the 80's and 90's, with nighttime lows in the 40's. This large temperature swing promotes a long growing season and balanced fruit development.

The York mountain terroir is ideally suited to growing Syrah. Five different Syrah clones were chosen to add complexity to the finished wines. The clones were matched with rootstock to ensure the highest quality fruit. Fruit is hand pruned and hand harvested.

When the grapes arrive at the winery, they use three sorting tables to help select only the best fruit. First, a vibrating table to sort imperfect clusters. Next they gently destem the clusters onto a "Le Trieur" vibrating screen, which eliminates stems and shot berries. Finally, the fruit is moved onto a belt table where the final hand sorting of individual berries occurs. Truly hand-crafted wines! And you'll see the difference when you taste.

Located in downtown Templeton off Hwy 101.

Silver Horse Vineyard & Winery

2995 Pleasant Rd

San Miguel

805-467-9463

Tasting Fri-Mon 11-5

And By Appt

Moving to the Central Coast in 1996, Jim and Carame Kroener operated Silver Horse from a converted barn for several years. In 2002, the family decided to embark on an extensive renovation. The result is a wonderful new facility; the winery includes a crush pad, production area, barrel storage, and case goods warehouse, while the stunning new tasting room is unlike any other in the Paso Robles area.

Situated on a hilltop overlooking hundreds of acres of vineyards, the tasting room features a sit-down bistro atmosphere, wood-burning fireplace, and elegant hacienda-style appointments such as 100-year-old ceramic roof tiles. Visitors are treated to breathtaking views of some of the Central Coast's most beautiful vistas, and — with bocce ball and horseshoes, outdoor patios and several elegant indoor facilities — the venue begs for your visit.

Winemaker Stephen Kroener describes his hand-crafted premium wines as, "100-percent food-friendly. As a family, we're always looking to combine our love of food with our love of wine. As a winemaker, I want to create wines, whether they're varietal-driven or blends, that have nice, bright notes and a well-balanced structure that's sturdy without being overpowering." It is in this spirit that each bottle of Silver Horse wine carries the inscription "NOT FOR US ALONE". They hope you'll enjoy their wines as you celebrate life with good food, family and friends.

Current offerings include a Spanish white called Albarino, Tempranillo, Syrah, Cabernet Sauvignon and a number of blends, all priced in the $24-$42 range.

From Hwy 101 in Paso Robles, take Rte 46 East exit to Airport Rd. Turn left onto Airport for 7 miles and turn right onto Estrella Rd for 1/2 mile. Then turn left onto Pleasant Rd. The winery is 1 mile on your right.

Still Waters Vineyards

2750 Old Grove Ln

Paso Robles

805-237-9231

Tasting Th-Mon 11-5

And By Appt

Still Waters Vineyards developed as a dream of Paul and Patty Hoover to own a small one-acre vineyard. "We were home winemakers," says Paul, "and we decided we wanted to do a small vineyard."

Their small dream grew into a large reality of about 60 acres producing ten varieties of premium grapes. Seventy percent of the two hundred tons of fruit produced is sold to exclusive wineries throughout the state. And mindful of their home-winemaker beginnings, Paul has created a Winemaker's Club, selling fruit (by the pound or by the ton) and offering consultation to those who like to "bottle my own."

The Hoover's commitment to producing only the finest quality fruit is reflected in the excellence of Still Waters estate wines, including Cabernet Sauvignon, Merlot, Syrah, Petite Sirah, Chardonnay, Pinot Gris, Sauvignon Blanc and Viognier. Their current offerings are in the $18-$28 range.

Also located on the vineyard is a 100 year-old olive orchard that yields Mission, Sevillano and Ascolano olives, pressed using an Italian mill that combines the best of traditional and modern methods. The resulting Extra Virgin Olive Oil is sold in their tasting room.

Their tasting room is the center of a beautiful yard and garden featuring numerous waterfalls and rippling brooks. The peaceful setting just calls out for you to relax and picnic.

From the beginning, the underlying concept the family has had was: "Be small, have fun and focus on quality!" They've done just that.

From Hwy 101 in Templeton, exit east on Vineyard Drive. After crossing the river, take the left fork onto El Pomar. Drive 6.7 miles. At the 4-way stop, turn left onto South El Pomar. Go 1.5 miles to Creston Road and turn right. Go 1.2 miles to the vineyard entrance on your left.

Sylvester Vineyards & Winery

5115 Buena Vista Dr

Paso Robles

805-227-4000

Tasting Daily 11-5

Summer 10-6

In the early 1960's, Sylvester Feichtinger purchased Rancho Robles, now the current home to Sylvester Vineyards & Winery. Originally used for beef cattle and hay production, Rancho Robles became a vineyard in 1982. After years of selling quality grapes to many of the premium wineries in the area, Sylvester Vineyards & Winery released its first wines in 1990. Their instant success prompted the building of Sylvester's modern winery and tasting room, which was finished in time for the 1995 harvest.

Amidst views of the beautiful rolling hills on the east side of Paso Robles, Sylvester Winery reminds visitors of a simpler time. Haflinger horses, imported from Austria, are harnessed to wooden carriages and travel the vineyard paths, reminding guests of a slower, more leisurely lifestyle. In the midst of the Cabernet Sauvignon vines, you'll want to explore their classic railcars, including 2 vintage Pullman sleepers and a dining car. These cars are a tribute to a bygone era of luxury rail travel. How did such elegant reminders of the past come to rest in the premium vineyards of Paso Robles? The answer seems to remain a secret to be known by only a few members of the Sylvester Winery staff.

But the experienced and knowledgeable tasting room staff will be happy to discuss the complexities of the Sylvester wines with you. Depending on availability, you'll explore their Chardonnay, Merlot, Sangiovese, Zinfandel, Cabernet Sauvignon, Cabernet Franc, Rhone Rosé, Pinot Noir and sparkling wines. And you'll be surprised to see many wines selling for $8.99 a bottle, with the new and more expensive reserves priced at $14.99 to $22.99.

From Hwy 101 exit at Rte 46 East. Travel east to Buena Vista and turn left. Go 4 miles to the winery on your left.

Tobin James Cellars

8950 Union Rd

Paso Robles

805-239-2204

Tasting Daily 10-6

It all started with an extra six tons of grapes that a winery could not accept and process. Tobin (Toby) James, a lowly assistant winemaker at the time, asked the owner of the winery if he could have the grapes and make wine out of them for himself. The owner replied, "Sure kid, knock yourself out". A year and a half later, gold medals began pouring in for Toby's first Zinfandel, the 1985 "Blue Moon" Zin.

After making his wines at another local winery for a few years, and tasting and selling them out of a local wine shop in town, Toby finally took the plunge and built Tobin James Cellars in 1994.

Built from the ground up on the site of an old stagecoach stop, it might seem more natural to stroll into the old-fashioned western-style saloon, place your booted foot on the brass rail of the bar and order a shot of whiskey from the bartender. However, in the Tobin James tasting room, award winning wines are poured from behind the grand, antique 1860's Brunswick bar shipped in from Blue Eye, Missouri where Jesse James himself would "belly-up."

Toby is famous for his spectacular Zinfandels. He creates as many as eleven different Zinfandel wines a year, all uniquely and incredibly wonderful. A huge following has developed for all of his reds; especially his Syrah, Cabernet Sauvignon, Merlot and the Late Harvest Zinfandel dubbed *Liquid Love*. Among their whites are Sauvignon Blanc and Chardonnay. Prices range from $11.50 to $55.

Toby and his partners, Lance and Claire Silver like to have fun with their wines which is why you'll often find them behind the bar pouring wine and socializing with guests. It is also very likely you'll discover them giving an impromptu tour of the winery. And they do enforce one rule; "Have fun." The party atmosphere proves visitors do.

From Hwy 101 take Hwy 46 East for approximately 8 miles. Winery on the right.

Via Vega Vineyard & Winery

2378 Adobe Rd

Paso Robles

805-238-0656

Tasting By Appt

The most often asked question that people put to owner/winemaker Larry Gomez is how he ended up in the wine business. "The easiest response that I can think of is that this is where I started. As kids, my brother Rick and I started hanging around my Uncle Tony's vineyard in Napa. Rick went straight to Uncle Tony's vineyard after high school and took over the farming. I went to Cal Poly to study Fruit Science so there would be a spot for me. We were producing Riesling and Pinot Noir on the Napa Valley floor, along with Chardonnay and Sauvignon Blanc. Between frost protection and harvest parties and Uncle Tony yelling at our mistakes, they were the best of times."

Larry purchased 20 acres in Paso Robles in 1998 and began planting his vineyard with 11 varietal blocks, each with clonal variations and began the long wait for fruit to reach harvest age. After four vintages with J.Lohr as red winemaker, then two as winemaker at Wild Horse Winery, Via Vega Vineyard and Winery was ready, and Larry crushed his first harvest in 2002.

Today, Via Vega produces Cabernet Sauvignon, Syrah, Zinfandel, Merlot and two red blends, *Bullpen* and *Bench Stars*. Then there's the October series, a tribute and celebration of the harvest season. With this red table wine, Via Vega invites you to share the lovely October glow of the harvest moon. Be sure to check out the October series label – the art was inspired by Keith Puccinelli's *El Dia de Los Muertos*. Via Vega's prices vary from $22 to $30.

For an appointment and directions to taste at the winery, call April at the phone above.

Victor Hugo Winery

2850 El Pomar

Templeton

805-434-1128

Tasting By Appt

Victor Hugo Roberts is the owner/winemaker of the small family operated vineyard and winery. The family legend has it that he was named after a great uncle and a great grandfather, with no influence accredited to any literacy connection.

In 1985, equipped with an enology degree (U.C. Davis, 1979), and 6 years of winery experience, Vic and his wife, Leslie planted 15 acres on the Templeton property which contains the family home and winery. The winery, officially established in 1997, is located in a picturesque, recently renovated 100 year old barn. The tasting area is nestled into a corner of a barrel-filled room.

More vineyards were added through the years, and the total stands at 78 acres planted to Chardonnay, Zinfandel, Syrah, Petite Sirah, Viognier and 5 Bordeaux reds - Cabernet Sauvignon, Cabernet Franc, Merlot, Malbec, and Petit Verdot.

Today, Victor Hugo is known for their intense hand-crafted reds including Cabernet Sauvignon, Zinfandel, Petite Sirah, *Hunchback* (a red table wine) and *Opulence*, their special blend of red estate grapes. Generally, the wines sell in the $12-$24 price range.

Victor Hugo Vineyards and Winery is one of Paso Robles' most exciting and innovative wineries. The winery is dedicated to producing elegant, rich wines exhibiting excellent longevity. You're invited to call and stop by to discover why Victor Hugo is, indeed, the promise of the Paso Robles area.

From Hwy 101 take the Vineyard Dr exit and head east 1/2 mile, make a slight left turn onto El Pomar Drive. Drive another 4 miles. Winery on the left-hand side just past Lupine Ln.

Vihuela Winery

995 El Pomar

Templeton

805-423-8423

Tasting Fri-Sun 11-4

Mon Appt call 805-239-8590

In the mid 1980s Matt Mikulics and his wife, Stefanie would travel to the Central Coast to enjoy the rolling hills, the friendly laid-back attitude and of course...the wines. Through the years Matt developed a greater thirst for the Central Coast and its wines than any weekend trip could quench. He wanted to become a winemaker and he wanted to run his own winery.

The next "logical" step for any Electrical Engineer was to acquire some formal training, so Matt enrolled in Fresno State's Enology program. According to Matt, Fresno State was a great place to learn because of the practical, hands-on experience and the next thing he knew he had graduated and was working for the likes of Geyser Peak and Rudd in Napa Valley. After several years of saving and searching for just the right place Matt located a property on El Pomar in Templeton. Ground broke in 2002 and Vihuela's first crush in 2003 produced just under 1000 cases.

So what about the name Vihuela Winery? Well, Vihuela Winery was not so much chosen as it chose Matt. A Vihuela can be roughly translated as a Spanish Guitar. In addition to Big Red Wines, Matt has always had a fascination with Classical and Spanish Guitar. Something about the music stirs the passions much as a spicy Tempranillo or a complex Cabernet Sauvignon. Currently, Vihuela Winery is producing Cabernet Sauvignon, Syrah, Zinfandel and Chardonnay. Prices run $16.99-$23.99. In the future plans include bringing some fine Tempranillos and Super Tuscans to the Central Coast.

Vihuela...it's music to your mouth!

From Hwy 101 take the Vineyard Dr exit and head east 1/2 mile, make a slight left turn onto El Pomar Drive. Winery on your right after about a mile.

Vina Robles

3700 Mill Rd
Paso Robles
805-227-4812
Tasting Daily 11-5

Vina Robles is a family-owned winery with a unique Swiss-European imprint and a vision for estate wines that express the excellence of their Paso Robles terroir. After an exhaustive search, owner Hans Nef purchased the oak studded land that would become the Vina Robles estate in 1996. After careful site studies and mapping, the appropriate rootstocks and varieties were chosen and a vineyard was planted the following year. The first estate wines were crafted by Swiss wine-maker Matthias Gubler in 1999.

Under the guidance of Hans and winemaker Mathias Gubler, Vina Robles specializes in Petite Sirah, Syrah, Cabernet Sauvignon and Zinfandel from its Huerhuero and Jardine vineyards.

There are two quality levels in the Vina Robles portfolio. The Estate label represents a blending of fruit from the three vineyards, chosen for their harmonious and complimentary flavors. The wines are priced $13-$19 per bottle. Vineyard Selections such as *Huerhuero* and *Jardine* are recognition of the unique characteristics of each site and the distinctive wines they produce. Vineyard label wines run $14-$34 per bottle.

Vina Robles has quickly found a comfortable home on the Central Coast. Their new hospitality center opened in 2007. This mission-style facility features a tasting room, retail shop and picnic grounds. A future phase will include a full-service inn to accommodate visitors from around the world.

From Hwy 101 exit at Rte 46 East and go east to Mill Rd. Turn right on Mill to enter the tasting room.

Wild Horse Winery & Vineyards

1437 Wild Horse Winery Ct

Templeton

805-434-2541

Tasting Daily 11-5

Located outside historic Templeton, Wild Horse Winery was named for the wild mustangs that roam the hills east of the vineyard estate. Descendents of the first Spanish horses brought to California, these mavericks suggest a free, noble spirit. They are the ideal symbol for the Wild Horse commitment to spirited winemaking.

The estate vineyard was planted in 1982; the first crush took place in 1983 with fruit from Santa Barbara and San Luis Obispo counties. Even then, founder Ken Volk recognized the synergism of blending grapes from the great vineyards of the Central Coast.

Wild Horse believes that while estate or vineyard-designated wines can be outstanding, they offer just one expression of the grapes from which they are produced. Growing the same variety in different terroirs, and then carefully blending the individual lots results in a wine which is extremely complex yet harmonious. With the exception of Pinot Noir, the winery's flagship varietal, fruit from the Paso Robles growing region is the cornerstone of the red wine program at Wild Horse including Merlot, Cabernet Sauvignon, Zinfandel and Syrah. Whites include Chardonnay and Viognier. Most wines sell at $16-$28.

In 2003, Volk was ready for a new challenge and made a personal and family decision to sell Wild Horse to Peak Wines International, now Beam Wine Estates, the wine division of Jim Beam Brands, Worldwide. That same year, Mark Cummins – Associate Winemaker under Volk since 1995, stepped into the role of winemaker, and now holds the reins on production of all the Wild Horse wines.

From Hwy 101 in Templeton, exit at Vineyard Drive. At the offramp stop, turn right and head east. Go through one traffic light, and over a small bridge. Take he first right immediately after the bridge onto Templeton Road. Travel 2.2 miles to the entrance to Wild Horse.

Winery Notes

Winery_____ **Date**_____

City or Area_____

Wine Comments

_____

_____

_____

_____

_____

_____

_____

_____

_____

_____

Winery_____ **Date**_____

City or Area_____

Wine Comments

_____

_____

_____

_____

_____

_____

_____

_____

_____

Winery Notes

Winery_____ **Date**_____

City or Area_____

Wine Comments

_____

_____

_____

_____

_____

_____

_____

_____

_____

_____

Winery_____ **Date**_____

City or Area_____

Wine Comments

_____

_____

_____

_____

_____

_____

_____

_____

_____

_____

Winery Notes

Winery_____ **Date**_____

City or Area_____

Wine Comments

_____

_____

_____

_____

_____

_____

_____

_____

_____

Winery_____ **Date**_____

City or Area_____

Wine Comments

_____

_____

_____

_____

_____

_____

_____

_____

_____

Paso Robles West

The Paso Robles AVA

There is a distinct difference in climate between the eastern and western portions of the AVA. The western end experiences temperatures in excess of 90 degrees F in the daytime and cool ocean breezes in the evenings. As a result, wines from the westside have more spicy, mineral-type flavors and tend to be more age worthy.

Cabernet Sauvignon, Chardonnay, Merlot and Zinfandel represent just under 80% of the planted acreage and some thirty-seven other varieties, lead by Syrah making up the remainder.

The York Mountain AVA

Just 7 miles from the Pacific Ocean, the York Mountain AVA is cooler than the adjacent Paso Robles AVA and receives more moisture than most of the adjoining area.

There are five or six vineyards in this small AVA growing Cabernet Sauvignon, Chardonnay, Grenache, Pinot Blanc, Pinot Noir and Syrah

Sorry We Missed A Few

We believe the following wineries do offer tasting, but for some reason they chose not to respond to our requests for information. If you visit them, we hope you'll let them know what they missed.

Changala, Donati, Fratelli Perata

Adelaida Cellars

5805 Adelaida Road

Paso Robles

800-676-1232

Tasting Daily 11-5

The winery, which originated in 1981, is located 15 miles east of the Pacific Ocean at an elevation of 1,800' in the Santa Lucia mountains.

Adelaida's wild and rugged mountainside vineyards are loaded with limestone and calcareous shale. According to winemaker Terry Culton, "these characteristics cause the vines to strengthen. This results in added stress on the vines, which lowers the yields but produces more intensely flavored fruit."

Adelaida is best known for big red wines with bold fruit flavors and spice. Although most wine lovers come for the Cabernet Sauvignon, old vine Zinfandel, and Pinot Noir, Adelaida is just as proud of their Syrah, Rhone style red wines, Chardonnay and Rhone whites.

Their wines are categorized by 4 labels. The Reserve wines range from $35 to $75, and are made from the best barrel selections, hand selected by the winemakers. Adelaida wines fall in the $20 to $30 range, and are made from their best non-reserve barrels. The SLO wines (named after San Luis Obispo County), fall in the $15 to $20 range, and are blends made from barrels that stylistically, did not meet their premium requirements. The Schoolhouse wines fall in the $13 to $15 range, and are blends of declassified estate grapes and non-estate grapes.

The new tasting room provides a comfortable, living room atmosphere. Stop in for an enjoyable visit.

Exit Hwy 101 at Hwy 46 East and go west on 24th St and Nacimiento Rd For 1 mile then turn left onto Adelaida Rd Winery on left after 5.3 miles.

AJB Vineyards

3280 Township Rd

Paso Robles

805-239-9432

Tasting Sat-Sun 12-5

For A. John Berardo, growing grapes and making wine are a celebration of his Italian heritage. He has fond childhood memories of his father and uncles making wine and storing barrels under his family's home. He hopes to continue the richness of that family tradition with AJB Vineyards.

The winery and vineyard are located on Township Road just five miles west of Highway 101. The property has a rich local history as part of the Mennonite community that had settled there over a century ago. The original house still exists and all of the new structures are built to reflect the original farm style.

The first blocks of AJB vineyards were planted in 1993 and consisted of Viognier and Syrah. The remaining acreage was planted from 1994 to 1996 and include Nebbiolo, Sangiovese and Zinfandel. Beginning with the 1999 harvest, all of AJB Vineyards' wines are estate grown and produced. Prices range in the $13-$19 area.

A unique feature of the winery is a vacation rental program. Their Hilltop Hacienda is across the street from AJB Winery on the AJB Vineyards property near the vineyard and winery, with views of surrounding vineyards and the Santa Lucia Mountain Ranges. The Vineyard Suite is located directly above the AJB Winery and Tasting Room. It boasts lovely vineyard views from every window. What an idea — a few days relaxing at a working winery!

Exit Hwy 101 onto Hwy 46 West. Turn right onto Oakdale Rd then right onto Creek then right onto Township.

Anglim Winery

740 Pine St

Paso Robles

805-227-6813

Tasting Th-Mon 11-5:30

And By Appt

Anglim Winery is a small, family-owned label focused on producing vineyard-designate Rhône varietals with grapes from some of the finest growers in California. Their limited case production of 3,000 to 4,000 cases a year allows them to handcraft wines in small lots with a combination of tradition and innovation. They use 100 percent French oak, but manage the new oak percentages to create wines with a balanced style, and enough character to be cellared but enough elegance to be enjoyed now.

Partnering with some of the best growers in California, including Bien Nacido, Fralich, Fiddlestix and French Camp Vineyards, Anglim has produced Viognier, Roussane, Syrah and Grenache wines that have constantly received accolades beginning with the 2002 vintage. Their wines sell in the $15 -$40 per bottle price range.

Along with tasting Steve Anglim's wines, you'll enjoy their unique tasting room located in the historic Paso Robles train depot at 8th and Pine streets. In the late 1800s, with the rapid development of major commercial centers in San Francisco, Sacramento, and Los Angeles, stagecoaches and overland mail companies were being quickly replaced by the rail. Construction began on the Paso Robles station in December 1886, just two months after the arrival of the first train to Paso Robles. Retaining the original floors and windows, and rebuilding the interior to retain the original look and feel, Anglim Winery opened at the location in 2005.

Located in Downtown Paso Robles at 8th and Pine.

Arroyo Robles Winery

739 12th St

Paso Robles

877-759-9463

Tasting Wed-Mon 11-7

The Shore Family started making wine in 1998, sharing equipment with three other wineries in a converted apple barn in See Canyon above Avila Beach. Since then they've shared winemaking facilities in San Luis Obispo, Santa Maria and now Paso Robles.

And now they proudly announce the acquisition of their new vineyard, 64 acres north of Paso Robles on San Marcos Road, with 24 planted acres of Cabernet Sauvignon, Syrah, Syrah Noir, Mourvedre and Tempranillo. This will be the home of their estate winery, opening in 2007. In the meantime, visit their tasting room to discover their hand-crafted wines made from estate vineyard Syrah, Mourvedre, Tempranillo and Cabernet Sauvignon. And their Cabernet Sauvignon, Merlot and Zinfandel from select vineyards on the west and east sides of Paso Robles as well as Chardonnay from the Arroyo Seco area in Monterey County. If you're a sparkling wine lover, ask about their grand cuvee sparking wine and their unusual almond sparkling wine. They've just recently added two ports to their list of dessert wines. Their wines cost between $12-$24 per bottle.

You can enjoy tasting their wine at their tasting room in downtown Paso Robles (at 12th and Park Street in the historic Mastagni Building), shop for gifts and picnic supplies or let them make a gift basket for you. Allow a little extra time to take a short class on wine tasting, food pairing, sensory tasting or grape growing.

Downtown Los Robles at the corner of 12th and Park.

Bear Cave Cellars

1227 Park St Suite B

Paso Robles

805-238-4329

Tasting By Appt

And When the Flag is Flying

Bear Cave Cellars is the creation of Barry Kinman and Marilyn Curry who are husband and wife as well as partners in the law firm, Kinman & Curry. In a unique melding of two distinctly different businesses, the law office is also the legal tasting room of Bear Cave Cellars. Whether you want legal advice or to try wines, call their office.

While living in Sonoma county, Barry had access to top quality fruit from winery clients of his law office, including Kunde Vineyards. Focusing on Cabernet Sauvignon and Zinfandel, Barry had the opportunity to work with top quality fruit in what may be the greatest decade of California grape growing - the 1990's. Barry produced excellent wines from Napa in 1994, Sonoma in 1997 and the Sierra foothills in 2000. Now, with the outstanding fruit available from Paso Robles he is developing his own style of wine that he calls "Paso Extreme!"

By using a cool fermentation with extended time on the skins their wines all provide a softness and full mouth feel. The Cabernet Sauvignon and Cabernet Franc will both age well and will be good for many years to come. The Zinfandel and Syrah should be consumed within the first 1 to 5 years. Their wines run $18-$40 per bottle.

More than anything else, they entered into this venture to meet new friends through the production of wine. Call for an appointment, or, if the welcome banner is hanging, drop right in.

Located in their law office – downtown Paso Robles.

Brian Benson Cellars

2985 Anderson Rd

Paso Robles

805-296-9463

Tasting Sat-Sun 10:30-5

Being run exclusively by owner/winemaker, Brian Benson Cellars is truly a one man army. From hanging out in his grandparent's vineyard and later his father's winery, Dark Star, Brian started to learn about the winemaking process and business before he was out of elementary school. In 1995, when Brian's father Norm Benson bought 10 acres in Westside Paso Robles, Brian worked part time on the weekends learning the ins and outs of the business and in 1997, at the ripe age of twelve, made his first wine, a Cabernet.

In 2001, at age 19, Brian decided he wanted to start making his own wines. His father was supportive, but made it clear Brian had to do it all himself; come up with a label, buy his corks and bottles and make the wine. Starting with a little less than $2000, Brian worked deals with local Paso Robles growers and made his first commercial vintage, a Cabernet and a Zinfandel, totaling 147 cases. He's added a Merlot, a Syrah and a couple of Rhone blends. Prices run $20-$25 a bottle.

In 2005, Brian, a huge custom car and hot rod addict, decided he needed a winery truck. Brian contacted famous designer Jimmy Smith to design and render the truck – a '35 Ford. Brian found a shop that agreed to get the project rolling and teach Brian how to chop and channel the truck. Meanwhile, Brian met world famous pin striper Doug Dorr and they decided to collaborate on a limited production run of custom pinstriped bottles to go along with the truck. The Brian Benson Cellars Kustom Series of wines was born. Brian will build a custom car or hot rod every year and create a special custom blended wine and bottle to match the design of the vehicle.

From Hwy 101, take Rt 46 West. Turn right on Anderson Rd. Winery on the left, shared with Dark Star.

Calcareous Vineyard

3430 Peachy Canyon Rd

Paso Robles

805-239-0289

Tasting Daily 11-5

The vision of three motivated people helped make Calcareous Vineyard a reality. Lloyd Messer sold his wine and beer distributing business in Sioux City, Iowa, to search for the ideal growing region for his vineyard. He recognized Paso Robles as an emerging premium wine producing area. Daughter Dana Brown sold her Iowa wine distributing business to partner with Lloyd and shape the dream with her passion and classic style. Erika Messer, Dana's younger sister, seized the opportunity to be involved in the winery from the ground up with a hands-on approach.

Their search for the perfect combination of terroir, climate and varietal selection brought them to the Central Coast of California, and more specifically to the rare and unique calcareous soils of West Paso Robles. Their goal is to produce the finest Rhone and Bordeaux blends and distinctive Burgundies this region will allow. The benefit of the Westside of Paso Robles is that the terrain allows for the production of Bordeaux, Rhone, and Burgundy varietals virtually side-by-side.

Established in 2000, Calcareous Vineyards is a 442-acre estate that begins about one mile west of town and stretches for several miles towards the beautiful Pacific Ocean. The expanse of this land offers many opportunities for optimal vineyard sites and varietal selections.

Today, Calcareous produces Chardonnay, Roussanne, Viognier, Syrah, Zinfandel and Pinot Noir in the limestone soils derived from the sea-life once covering those hills in pre-historic times; creating the foundation for great vineyards. Prices run $20-$28.

From Hwy 101 take the Spring Street Exit and head straight into town. Head west on 6th Street. That's a right turn if you coming south, and a left turn if you're coming north. Turn right on Olive then a quick left on Pacific. Pacific becomes Peachy Canyon Road. They are four miles out on Peach Canyon Road, on the right.

Caparone Winery

2280 San Marcos Rd

Paso Robles

805-610-5308

Tasting Daily 11-5

This winery is truly a father-and-son operation. All Caparone wine is made by Dave and Marc Caparone, without any employees. One of the most experienced winemakers in Paso Robles, Dave has made wine every year since 1973. In 1979, he founded Caparone Winery to focus on the wines he loved best: full-bodied red wines, made in a classic style, producing small amounts of Cabernet Sauvignon, Merlot, Zinfandel, Sangiovese, Nebbiolo and Aglianico. All are $14 a bottle.

Caperone Winery has been a California pioneer in the production of premium wine from the "noble" Italian varietals. Dave began working with Nebbiolo in the mid '70s. He obtained some Sangiovese vines from one of the best producers of Brunello di Montalcino and planted them in 1982. In the late '80s, Dave established the first American planting of Aglianico, a grape legendary as one of Italy's "archaeological varietals" with a history going back to ancient Rome. Caperone Winery produced the first American Aglianico in 1992. Caperone's Italian varietals have shown exceptionally well in tastings with the great red wines of Italy.

The Caparones are especially proud of their vineyards. The Estate vineyard is located next to the winery and was chosen by Dave in 1978 based on 6 years of careful research of the many microclimates of the Paso Robles region. Initially selected as a good site for Zinfandel, experience over the last 28 years confirms this and shows that all three of the Italian red varietals planted there consistently produce quality fruit.

From Hwy 101 exit at Hwy 46 East but turn left (west) towards Paso Robles. You are on 24th Street. Head west on 24th (which becomes Nacimiento Lake Drive) 5.5 miles, then turn right on San Marcos Road. The winery is located 1.5 miles from Nacimiento Lake Drive on the left.

Carmody McKnight Estate Wines

11240 Chimney Rock Rd

Paso Robles

805-238-9392

Tasting Daily 10-5

More than thirty years ago, Gary and Marian Conway purchased land in Adelaida, west of Paso Robles. Gary first beheld the idyllic beauty of the area aboard a helicopter moments before it crashed. Emerging from the wreckage, Gary exclaimed to the still stunned real estate broker, "I'm going to buy this place!" This is the stuff of legends; and indeed, in the ensuing years the land and its soils and textbook microclimates are fast becoming legendary.

But how they got to this place makes for more great stories. Gary was an actor (where his name changed from Carmody to Conway - starring in numerous movies and in TV series Burke's Law and Land of the Giants), writer and painter. Today, Carmody McKnight labels depict Gary's intense vineyard landscapes. Marian discovered wine on her initial journey to France, which began another journey in becoming a wine and food authority. You may remember Marian McKnight (her maiden name) when she was crowned Miss South Carolina and then that same year, Miss America.

In 1995, the Conways produced their first wine in the cellar of their 130-year old farmhouse. Now they offer hand-crafted, 100% estate blends of Cabernet Sauvignon, Merlot and Cabernet Franc along with Chardonnay, Pinot Noir and a one-of-a-kind dessert wine, *Kathleen*. Wines run $16.50 to $38 per bottle.

Their shaded lake offers the perfect relaxing or picnicking point.

From Hwy 101, exit Rt 46 East and go west along 24th St. and Lake Nacimiento Dr for 7 miles, then turn left onto Chimney Rock Rd. Winery on the right.

2004
Faantasy Riesling

Casa de Caballos Vineyards

2225 Raymond Ave

Templeton

805-434-1687

Tasting Daily 11-5

Casa de Caballos Vineyards started out as Morgan Farms. While in residency at Orange County Medical Center, Dr. Tom Morgan experimented with fruit and berry wines. Upon graduation he purchased the property on the west side of Templeton that is now known as Casa de Caballos (House of Horses).

What started out as just one acre of grapes slowly expanded to just over six acres, which is just perfect for a small family operation. In 1984 the first foal was born on the farm and for Tom and his wife Sheila, the Arabian business was off and running. Over the years both the Arabian business and the winery have prospered. Today Morgan Farms Arabians is known nationally and internationally for producing award winning Arabians. Casa de Caballos Vineyards has also established itself as making award winning wines.

Casa de Caballos offers seven different wines. Almost all feature their Arabian horses on the label and are sold 99% out of the tasting room and wine club. The wines include Merlot, Cabernet Sauvignon, Pinot Noir and a Bordeaux blend named *Forgetmenot*. Prices fall in the $26-$38 range.

Total case production runs about 1100 cases per year. All the wines are grown, produced and bottled on the estate.

Each year several new foals are born in the spring and visitors are welcome to come see the new additions, picnic on the patio, and taste their award winning wines.

From Hwy 101 take the Vineyard Dr Exit and go left. Follow on Vineyard to Bethel Rd and go left. Bethel Rd turns into Santa Rita Old Creek Rd. Follow the blue winery signs to Raymond and make another left. Follow Raymond to the top of the hill.

Castoro Cellars

1315 North Bethel Rd

Templeton

888-326-3463

Tasting Daily 10-5:30

Castoro Cellars was founded by the husband and wife team of Niels and Bimmer Udsen. The winery was named after the Italian translation of Niels' long-time nickname, "Beaver," prompting the motto "Dam Fine Wine."

One of the oldest wineries in the Paso Robles AVA, Castoro Cellars is said to have taken the backwards approach to developing a brand. They began making wine in the early 1980s, and, over the course of the next ten years, bought equipment and opened a tasting room. The winery site was purchased in 1991, and within the past decade, existing vineyards were purchased and new vineyards planted. Today, they produce a wide range of both reds and whites, ranging in price from $7 to $36 per bottle. Obviously, Castoro holds strongly to the belief that high quality wines should be accessible to all consumers.

Uniquely, the working winery is open to the public, although tasting is not available. Located at 6465 Von Dollen Road in San Miguel, it's open during the week from 10 to 4 and gives visitors the opportunity to see what can be accomplished when the winemaker is never satisfied with the status quo. The winery phone number is (805) 467-2002.

At the tasting room, visitors are led under a 100 ft. long grape arbor into an attractive, Mediterranean style room, where the resident tasting room cat can be found lounging in front of the large stone fireplace. A spacious art gallery exhibiting local talent is next to the tasting room, and outside, a large picnic area and gazebo invite visitors to enjoy lunch while relishing views of the sprawling Cobble Creek vineyards.

From Hwy 101, take Hwy 46 west towards Cambria, turn left on N. Bethel Rd.

Cayucos Cellars

143 N Ocean Ave

Cayucos

805-995-3036

Tasting Wed-Mon 11-5:30

History, tradition, and curiosity have always been an important inspiration to Cayucos native Stuart Selkirk. In the early 1980's, curiosity caused him to ask a neighbor of Swiss decent what the heck he was doing with a load of grapes in the back of his truck?

In response to his question, neighbor Paul soon had Stuart turning the handle on an old hand-crank grape crusher. The next few days brought the job of punching down the fermenting grapes in a large wooden vat and moving the finished wine from the vat to the cellar via a bucket brigade. This was Stuart's introduction to the historical art of family wine making.

Today, from the small vineyard he planted on his ranch, Stuart has added grapes from the Templeton Gap area, the Adelaida and a small amount from the Paso east side. Now producing 600-800 cases per year, Stuart, with wife Laura, sons Clay and Ross and daughter Paige has created a small family operated winery atmosphere with excellent hands-on quality winemaking for your enjoyment and satisfaction. After all, everyone has to get something out of this experience.

Wines include Chardonnay, Zinfandel, Cabernet Sauvignon, Syrah and Pinot Noir. Per bottle prices run $18-$35.

From seed to fruit to wine. Enjoy!

Downtown Cayucos on Ocean Ave. (Business Rte 1) between C and D Sts.

Dark Star Cellars

2985 Anderson Rd

Paso Robles

805-237-2389

Tasting Fri-Sun 10:30-5

"Many wineries will tell you that they are a small family winery. In their minds a staff of fifty producing 100,000 cases is small. At Dark Star it's Me, my son Brian, my daughter Nicole, and my wife Susan. That's it. Some days we make wine, some days we sit on tractors, and not often enough, some days we watch sunsets, but everyday it's just us. Every single bottle we produce has our finger prints on it. If we don't do it, it doesn't get done. When you serve a bottle of our wine at your table you are serving a beverage we hand made, wine that we are tremendously proud of." A quote from Norm Benson, Dark Star's owner and winemaker.

The wines he's speaking of are all reds, priced in the $10-$26 range and include Zinfandel, Merlot, Syrah, Cabernet Sauvignon, a blend called *2004 Anderson Road* and *Ricordati* (always remember), a complex Bordeaux-style blend of Cabernet Sauvignon, Merlot, and Cabernet Franc which is produced to celebrate the memory of their friends and family. Ricordati began as a tribute by Norm to his father. It has now evolved into a wine that celebrates the memory of all of the friends and family who have passed away.

Their focus is on producing small lots of ultra-premium hand crafted red wines. They feel their success comes from a gentle treatment of the wines from harvest to bottling.

From Hwy 101, take Hwy 46 West to Anderson Rd. Turn right onto Anderson Rd – winery on the left.

Denner Vineyards & Winery

5414 Vineyard Dr

Paso Robles

805-239-4287

Tasting Sat-Sun 12-4

Or Fri By Advance Appt

Ron and Marilyn Denner had always dreamed of returning to their roots in California after a long and fruitful career owning and operating numerous Ditch Witch equipment dealerships in Colorado, Utah and Idaho. After a patient and exhaustive search of California that lasted for years, they founded Denner Vineyards in 1997 in Westside Paso Robles on what was formerly 156 acres of rocky, rolling hills covered with barley.

Three years of careful planning and preparation went into the design and layout of the 105 acre estate vineyard before planting in 1999. In 2005 Denner Vineyards completed construction of a state-of-the-art, gravity flow winery for the production of estate wines. The Denners' single-minded goal since day one has been to produce individualistic, expressive, premium wines.

The winery was completed in time for the 2005 harvest. Their wines include Syrah, Viognier, *Theresa,* a Roussanne/Viognier blend and *Ditch Digger*, a blend of Grenache, Syrah and Mourvedre. Bottles are priced between $29-$36.

Their son Brian earned his enology degree from Fresno State and immediately joined Williams-Selyem Winery, one of the most esteemed pinot noir producers in California. After three years as Cellar Master, he worked for three years as "Enologo," at Kingston Family Vineyards in Chile. Brian took over as Denner Vineyards' winemaker with the 2004 harvest.

From Hwy 101, take Hwy 46 West to Vineyard Dr. Turn right on Vineyard Dr.

Doce Robles Winery & Vineyard

2023 Twelve Oaks Dr

Paso Robles

805-227-4766

Tasting Daily 10-5:30

The path to Doce Robles started several years ago when Maribeth and Jim Jacobsen visited the Paso Robles area to taste wine. They were hooked! Not only did they love the area, but they immediately recognized the incredible potential that Paso Robles has as a premium winemaking area.

Jim and Maribeth purchased the magnificent 40 acre property that became their vineyards, winery, tasting room and home. Around the hilltop grounds were a dozen beautiful, stately oaks that inspired the name "Doce Robles." The estate's vineyards consist entirely of red wine grapes – Syrah, Zinfandel, Cabernet Sauvignon, Merlot and Barbera. With careful buying of wine grapes from other premium vineyards, they've added Sauvignon Blanc to their offerings. Prices are in the $15 to $28 range.

Arriving at the tasting room, you may have to step over the lazy German Shepherds, Duchess, Syrah, Ava and Ellie. Inside you'll likely find other family members – Slobaby or Coco - cats who often spend the daylight hours curled up on the end of the tasting bar. Doce Robles encourages a very casual approach to wine tasting. Belly up to their long bar and feel free to stay a while, shoot the breeze and ask about their wine making philosophies. Or check out the eclectic range of gifts they offer while good ol' rock and roll plays on the radio.

Around here, they're known as the "party winery", and they're happy with that! Stop by.

From Hwy 101, take Hwy 46 West 3/4 of a mile. Twelve Oaks Drive on your right.

Donatoni Winery

3225 Township Rd

Paso Robles

805-226-0620

Tasting Sat-Sun 12-5

And By Appt

Established in 1979 by runway 2.5 right at LAX, Hank Donatoni and Sandi Baird have always used Paso Robles grapes to make their wines. Now located on the Westside of Darn Near Paradise, they invite you to come enjoy Hank's handcrafted, full- bodied, well-balanced wines in their tasting room where they mix skill and humor.

This is their logo. They use it on their glasses, t-shirts, wine club pins and have stickons of it to give to tasting room guests.

Hank and Sandi both retired off of the 747-400. Hank was a captain and flew for 36 years for the airline. Sandi retired as purser and flew for 37 years. The corkscrew has a dual meaning. Yes, they have a winery and yes, the airline they worked for cancelled their pensions

Donatoni wines include Cabernet Sauvignon, Sangiovese, Syrah, Petite Sirah, Zinfandel and blends. Prices are in the $14-$32 range.

From Hwy 101, take Rte 46 West to Oakdale Rd. Right on Oakdale Rd then right again on Willow Creek Rd then right on Township Rd.

Dover Canyon Winery

4520 Vineyard Dr

Paso Robles

805-237-0101

Tasting Th-Sun 11-5

Dan Panico's wine style reflects his individualistic approach to life and wardrobe. His wines have a distinctive silk and smoke profile, and his cheerful label has been described by wine critic Robert Parker as "dog-gone cute." (You'll have to read the story of "Blue" on the Dover Canyon website.) Dan has been making wine in Paso Robles for 15 years, with six of those years as winemaker for Gary Eberle of Eberle Winery.

Dover Canyon's total production hovers around 2,500 cases a year of vineyard designated wines and special blends. Most releases sell out within months of release. Hopefully, you'll be able to taste Viognier, Roussanne, Cabernet Sauvignon, Zinfandel, Syrah and a number of Rhone blends. Prices are in the $10 to $35 range.

"Blockbuster wines are just not Dan's style," says partner Mary Baker. "He uses neutral oak, carefully selected yeasts, and sometimes native yeasts. We are really pleased when a vineyard produces a signature flavor profile year after year, because the expression of Paso Robles terroir is still a mystery and a challenge. It's exciting to reach for that."

Before you visit Dover Canyon, try to visit their website. It's entertaining, informative and unique. Not much telling you how great their wine is, more about how much they enjoy what they're doing. And full of useful information, like how long to hold onto a wine before you drink it, copies of news articles on wines, etc. It's also a way to access their blog – one of the most respected winery blogs in the country.

From Hwy 101, take Rte 46 West and turn right onto Vineyard Dr. Winery on the left.

Dunning Vineyards

1953 Niderer Rd

Paso Robles

805-238-4763

Tasting Th-Mon 11-5

And By Appt

Robert Dunning came to the Paso Robles area from Malibu, California. In 1960 his family purchased 80 acres in the hills west of Paso Robles where the vineyard and winery are now located. Robert, his wife Jo-Ann and son Garrett live on the property. Located on the property is also a building aptly named the "Vintage House" — once a limestone cellar that served as the wineries' first barrel room. This structure was built in the early 1900's and is pictured on every bottle of Dunning Vineyards Estate Wine. It has now been converted into a beautiful Country Inn containing two suites available for travelers to the area.

The inspiration to establish a small, family-owned winery came after 15 years of successful experimental home winemaking with local grapes. Robert Dunning had been producing great wine from Paso Robles vineyards non-commercially for years. But grapes were getting harder and harder to find and Robert was quickly outgrowing his sources. He wanted complete control from the vineyard to the bottle in an effort to produce only the finest wines. In 1991 he began planting his own vineyard with Chardonnay, Merlot, Cabernet Sauvignon, Syrah and Zinfandel. Bottles currently run $16-$28 each.

The small intimate winery currently produces less than 2000 cases annually, with expectations to grow to about 4500 cases as the new vineyards begin bearing fruit. Robert prefers to remain small so he can retain the closeness with his visitors.

Take Hwy 46 West from Hwy 101 just over three miles to Oakdale Road. Turn right onto Oakdale and drive one-half mile. Turn right onto Las Tablas/Willow Creek Road and drive about 1.2 miles. Bear right onto Niderer Road and continue about one mile. Turn left up the path to the winery.

Eagle Castle Winery

3090 Anderson Rd

Paso Robles

805-227-1428

Tasting Daily 10:30-5:30

Bet you never expected to cross a moat before you could taste wine. At Eagle Castle, you not only cross a moat, you enter a "real" castle. Once you're inside, you'll experience the Old World feel that owners Gary and Mary Lou Stemper have designed to make tasting a bit merrier. As you taste, you'll be guarded by a Knight in full body armor and watched over by Renaissance and Celtic mementos.

Nestled in the majestic hills of west Paso Robles, Eagle Castle offers a magnificent eagle's eye view of the surrounding vineyards and rolling hills, allowing visitors the opportunity to feel like King or Queen of the land. You're able to sample the fine wines in the Hospitality Center and gain an understanding of operations in the winery through guided tours.

The Stempers have been growing grapes in the Paso Robles region for many years. They have been an integral part of the growth of Paso Robles both in relation to the Wine Industry and the township of Paso Robles. Both are involved in the partnerships of Mill Road and Treana Wineries. Their belief in the region as a quality grape growing and wine producing area led them to start up their own company - Eagle Castle – with the belief that combining quality vineyards, winemakers and the environment of Paso Robles this project has 'wings to fly'.

And of course, wine is the real reason for visiting Eagle Castle, and with over 900 acres of premium vineyards to work with, they offer a full range of wines – Chardonnay and Viognier along with Merlot, Syrah, Cabernet Sauvignon and Zinfandel. In the dessert wine area, they offer a Zinfandel Port, Muscat Canelli and Late Harvest Viognier and Zinfandel. All are priced at under $20 except for the Port at $28 per bottle.

From Hwy 101, take Hwy 46 West to Anderson Rd. – winery on the right.

Ecluse Wines

1520 Kiler Canyon Rd

Paso Robles

805-238-4998

*Tasting Room Open

In 2007

Ecluse is French for the locks on the canals that gently carve their way through the remarkable French wine country. In Paso Robles Ecluse is the winery of Lock Vineyards, the creation of Steve and Pam Lock, known for producing some of Paso Robles most sought-after grapes. The Locks have provided fruit to and created relationships with some of the Central Coast's best known wineries including Talley Vineyard and Winery for their Bishop's Peak label, SummerWood Winery, Chateau Margene, Linne Calodo Cellars, Four Vines, Cellars, Norman Winery, and Vina Robles Winery. It was a natural progression from grower to winemaker for the Locks who now create a limited production of hand-crafted award winning wines.

Planted in 1998 on approximately 30 acres of gently rolling hillside terrain of Westside Paso Robles, Lock Vineyard offers exposures to the northeast, the southeast and south and their plantings of Zinfandel, Syrah and Cabernet Sauvignon take advantage of the varied sun and wind patterns of those exposures.

In addition to the Zinfandel, Syrah and Cab, they produce a blend they've named *Ensemble* – a red blend they describe as "all the parts of something put together that are in harmony." Pricing is in the $28 to $38 per bottle range.

Contact in advance for tasting information. Directions will be given when you call for an appointment.

Edward Sellers Vineyards & Wines

1220 Park St

Paso Robles

805-239-8915

Tasting Th-Mon 12-7

And By Appt

Edward Sellers Vineyards and Wines began in 2004 from the lifelong dream of Ed Sellers. Yes, that's his real name. Born on a farm in Upstate New York near the Finger Lakes wine region, Ed migrated to California in 1977. Armed with a microbiology education and a boundless entrepreneurial drive, Ed chose a career in business. All along, Ed yearned to make his own great quality wines. Coming full circle, back to his roots, Ed decided to change careers mid-life to try his hand at grape growing and winemaking. After lots of research, Ed found the ideal location to grow and produce world class Rhône style wines in Paso Robles. He bought a vineyard, planted Rhône varietals, hired a talented UC Davis-educated winemaker by the name of Amy Butler, sourced great fruit from local vineyards and started a new wine label. Now he combines his desire to be "on the land" with his love of business and his passion for wine.

Edward Sellers is a boutique winery specializing in small lots of handmade Rhône-style blended wines. Although modeled on the great Châteauneuf-du-Pape wines from the Rhône Valley of France, their ultra-premium wines speak distinctly of contemporary Central Coast origins. Grapes for the wines are grown and handpicked from the finest vineyards found on the cool limestone hillsides of Paso Robles. This rich ripe fruit has produced a wine with an elegant structure, an intense fruit concentration and a luscious mouthfeel.

In addition to Syrah, Grenache, Roussanne and Viognier, Sellers produces a number of red and white wine blends, all in the $18 to $42 price range.

From Hwy 101 take the Paso Robles St exit and turn left onto 13th St. then turn left onto Park St.

Four Vines Winery

3750 Hwy 46 West

Templeton

805-237-0055

Tasting Daily 11-5

First there was One. Winemaker Christian Tietje is a hedonist. He is passionate about wine: making it, drinking it and bringing people together to enjoy it. He fell head over heels for old vine Zinfandel, and began planning for bigger things.

Then there were Two. In 1994, Christian met Susan A. Mahler, a brainy and beautiful scientist and pilot, whom he nicknamed "Sam." It was love at first sight, and a partnership was formed. Armed with a degree in Earth Science, Sam took an immediate interest in vineyards.

Together they created Four Vines Winery featuring eclectic, appellation-specific Zins, and one no-oak "Naked" Chardonnay. They named their Zins *Biker*, *Sophisticate* and *Maverick*. Rich, succulent, fruit-generous wines that pair incredibly well with food. They relocated to Paso Robles where they began experimenting with Rhone varietals; bigger, headier wines that are positively explosive in flavor and form, as in the rogue Rhone blend *Anarchy*.

Now there are Three. Christian and Sam worked hard to grow their winery to 14,000 cases, but they needed someone to help share the load. They connected with an old friend, Bill Grany, a successful entrepreneur and financier. Bill joined the partnership in 2004, helping it grow to approximately 40,000 cases and introducing new blends named *Heretic* and *Phoenix*. Wines run $14-$30 per bottle

Makers of fleshy, seductive wines for aficionados and hedonists alike, Four Vines brings a refreshing, playfully irreverent attitude to the industry.

From Hwy 101, exit Hwy 46 West. Winery on your right just before Vineyard Dr.

Grey Wolf Cellars

2174 Hwy 46 West

Paso Robles

805-237-0771

Tasting Daily 11-5:30

Wolves were always a fascination to the Barton family, especially the animal's affectionate nature with it's family – the pack of mother and father, uncles and aunts and siblings. Today, Grey Wolf is a small, family operated winery, and proud of that.

Joe and Shirlene Barton established Grey Wolf Cellars in August 1994. Since then, the Barton's have made their winery a family-run business. Joe Sr. had a vision and a dream to create great wine and do so with his family. He put on his wine labels, *"A family is a circle of caring, strong and eternal."* Every bottle of Grey Wolf wine is their signature of a fine, hand-crafted product for their own family and yours. The Barton's style has always been to create wines that have depth and complexity for superior aging potential yet are also approachable and enjoyable when young.

The Barton's son, Joseph, a Fruit Science Graduate from Cal Poly, S.L.O., is the current winemaker at Grey Wolf Cellars. He credits local winemakers for providing friendly support and advice towards his ability to continue to craft premium quality wines.

Their specialty is red wine, including Cabernet Sauvignon, Zinfandel, Syrah and a specialty blend they call *The Lone Wolf*. They've recently introduced an Estate Zinfandel and a Barton Family Estate Blend. You'll always find a few other blends and some white wines being tasted. In general, prices are in the $12-$50 per bottle range. Annually, they produce about 3,500 cases.

From Hwy 101, exit at Hwy 46 West and drive 2.5 miles west. Winery on the right.

Halter Ranch Vineyard

8910 Adelaida Rd

Paso Robles

805-226-9455

Tasting Th-Mon 11-5

And By Appt

Halter Ranch is a new winery with a rich history. Located on the west side of Paso Robles, the property dates to the 1880s, when it was part of a 3,000-acre ranch owned by Paso Robles pioneer Edwin Smith. The beautiful Victorian farmhouse Smith built in 1885 remains a Westside landmark.

In 2000, Swiss-born businessman Hansjörg Wyss fell in love with the Paso Robles area and purchased 900 acres of the original ranch, intent on producing the best grapes and wines possible from the ideally situated site.

Fervently committed to quality, Wyss spent the next five years developing a 250-acre vineyard, renovating the historic farmhouse, and laying the ground-work for a new, state-of-the-art winery.

They have 15 grape varieties planted in 42 separate vineyard blocks delineated primarily based on soil types, which range from calcareous clay to clay loam with shale and sandstone deposits. Sixty percent are Bordeaux varieties and 40% Rhone varieties, plus Zinfandel. The varieties grown in the vineyard affords them the opportunity to produce not only world-class varietal wines, such as Syrah and Cabernet Sauvignon, but also creative blends like their *Ranch Red* and *Ranch White*. Prices are in the $18-$34 area.

With an advance appointment, your visit can include a 45 minute tour which begins with a walk around the beautiful, historic 19th-century Victorian Farmhouse. You'll learn about the history of the area, the renovation of the farmhouse, and their plans for the restoration of the old barns. You'll tour the vineyard and the winery. Remember, though, an advance appointment for the tour is required.

From Hwy 101 and downtown Paso Robles exit 24th St./right (west) continue on 24th St. 2.0 miles. 24th St. becomes Lake Nacimiento Rd then turn left onto Adelaida Road and go 9.0 miles on Adelaida Rd to Halter Ranch on right.

Harmony Cellars

3255 Harmony Valley Rd

Harmony

805-927-1625

Tasting Daily 10-5

Nestled in the hills overlooking the quaint, artisan town of Harmony, just off Highway 1, Harmony Cellars Winery produces award-winning wines and offers a remarkable view of the coastal countryside. Owners Chuck and Kim Mulligan built their winery in 1989 to reflect the unique country atmosphere of the surrounding area. Roam the gardens, lounge in the gazebo, wander the gift shop or pack some goodies to enjoy with Harmony Cellars wine in the picnic area.

The Mulligan's founded Harmony Cellars with the idea that wine needn't cost a king's ransom. Therefore, 20 year winemaking veteran Chuck strives to make the best possible wine at the best possible value.

Popular wines include Chardonnay, Merlot, Cabernet Sauvignon, Pinot Noir and Zinfandel. Harmony Cellars often produces reserve bottlings of especially good vintages. And like many winemakers, Chuck often produces very small quantities of blends like the very popular *Harmonie*, a delicious summer sipping wine marrying Chenin Blanc with other crisp white wines. Prices range $8-$38 per bottle.

Unique at Harmony Cellars are their holiday wines. *Christmas Blush*, *Snowflake* and *Santa's Reserve* wines are available after September. You can customize your Noel Vineyards wines with your personal message and create a special, unique holiday gift.

The town of Harmony is located between Cayucos and Cambria on Route 1, one mile south of Highway 46. Take the Harmony turnoff, stay right and go up the hill to the winery.

Hice Cellars

821 Pine St. Unit D

Paso Robles

805-237-8888

Tasting Fri-Sun 12-5

Summer Th-Mon 12-5

Eric Hice strongly believes that winemaking is a true form of art; some artists paint on canvas, some with food, and yet others with wine! The greatest compliment to Eric and his wife Bettina, is that their wine is welcomed at your table and enjoyed with good food and good friends!

Their ultra premium wines are hand crafted in a style long forgotten by modern day wineries; almost every wine they produce is un-fined and un-filtered. Wines are made in small lots, from grapes selected from organically grown vineyards, and hand harvested to ensure top quality is maintained.

In addition to their *Vintner's Blend*, Hice produces Syrah, Cabernet Sauvignon, an Old Vine Zinfandel, Port and a specialty – Alicante Bouchet (and they are one of only four wineries bottling this varietal). For white wine lovers, they offer Chardonnay and a blend they call *Tre Blanc*. Prices range $15-$36.

Shoppers will enjoy the Hice Cellars tasting room. As you taste, be sure to look over the gourmet corner where they stock some of the finest gourmet cheese & meats, local & international oils, vinegars, mustards, pasta and much more. Their gift shop has great gifts for everyone, including Bettina's fine crafted silver jewelry, and everything at incredibly affordable prices.

Located in beautiful downtown Paso Robles.

Hunt Cellars

2875 Oakdale Rd

Paso Robles

805-237-1600

Tasting Daily 10-6

Winter Hours 10:30-5:30

When The Hunt Family decided to pursue their wine dream they were uncertain where to build their vineyard. They spent exhaustive days and weekends traveling to various premium wine regions from Oregon, Washington, and throughout the State of California. They finally narrowed their decision down to the Central Coast. Paso Robles was selected because of its rich diversity in soils, superb growing climate and unique styles of winemaking along with the spirit of graciousness and traditional American values.

Today, as you enter The Hunt Cellars tasting room, the fun wine experience begins, as you are greeted with either live music or music from the white grand player piano, which can play any song. Stroll up to the Cabernet Bar, where the warm and friendly staff leads you through a sampling of wines. Generally, the price range is $23-$75 per bottle.

You'll find Chardonnay and Sauvignon Blanc, as well as Barbera, Zinfandel, Petite Sirah, Cabernet Sauvignon, Merlot and a number of blends for every taste. In all, some 20 wines crafted by a man – David Hunt – who feels his way around the winery and the tasting room, because he really can't see. He had to stop driving 25 years ago, but he feels much of his winemaking ability comes from increased senses of taste and smell. When he learned that Dom Perignon was blind, he felt he was in fine company. Now, as he says, he enjoys making wine for people who "really enjoy wine."

The Hunts promise you'll enjoy your visit to Hunt Cellars. If you're lucky, David might be playing that white grand.

From Hwy 101, exit on Hwy 46 West about 3 miles to Oakdale Rd.

Jack Creek Cellars

5265 Jack Creek Rd

Templeton

805-226-8283

Tasting By Appt

Doug Kruse, like many winery owners along the Central Coast, started his career in an entirely unrelated field. His first career was in grain science – developing and producing feed for animals. His plants were in Northern and Southern California, which meant he traveled through the area regularly, and watched the developing wine industry. When he sold his company in the mid 1990's, he was ready for a change.

After visiting the Central Coast for many years and falling in love with the area, Doug and Sabrina Kruse began "the search." And after many weeks of searching for the right piece of land they were blessed to be led to the JRK Ranch. After meeting and immediately loving the owner, they bought the front 75 acres of JRK Ranch... now Kruse Vineyards and Jack Creek Cellars.

Located about 7 miles from the coast and on the southern end of the Santa Lucia Mountain Range, Kruse Vineyards is located in the "Templeton Gap" as the locals call it. Secured in a unique micro-climate the vineyard receives heavy coastal influence: cool morning fog burning off to early afternoon sun which ripens the fruit, followed by coastal breezes rushing through "the Gap" which cools the fruit down and maintains the integrity of the varietals they've planted.

The vineyard consists of 40 acres of Pinot Noir, Syrah and Chardonnay. These varieties were selected to fit the unique micro-climate of the vineyard's location. Bottles of the three Estate wines, and sometimes an Estate Pinot Noir Reserve, run $28 to $42each.

From Hwy 101 exit Rte 46 West for 7 1/2 miles. Turn right on Jack Creek Rd. Winery 1/2 mile on the left.

JanKris Winery

1266 Bethel Rd

Templeton

805-434-0319

Tasting Daily 11-5

JanKris Winery & Vineyards is a family owned estate winery located on the west side of the Paso Robles appellation in the area called "The Templeton Gap." Established in 1990 by Mark and Paula Gendron, daughters January and Kristin are both the company's namesakes and successors.

JanKris wines are 100 percent estate grown, blending the subtle differences of East and West side Paso Robles grapes, grown on the three JanKris properties. With 170 acres under vine, and duplicate varieties on 2 or 3 of the ranches, lots of exciting choices exist for crafting lots of moderately priced wines.

JanKris grows Merlot, Zinfandel, Cabernet Sauvignon, Syrah, Sangiovese, Petite Syrah, Petite Verdot, Cabernet Franc, Mouvedre, Chardonnay, and Viognier. The label is known for its mastery of unique blends such as the *Picaro*, *Riatta* and *Crossfire*, a signature blend of Cabernet, Merlot and Syrah. Deemed "fruit-forward" wines, JanKris wines exemplify the result of hand crafted expertise from planting and grafting, to growing and finally, bottling. And all of their wines sell for under $20.

Their modern tasting facility includes a nice selection of food items – especially chosen to compliment the JanKris wines.

From Hwy 101, take the Hwy 46 West exit, then turn left at Bethel Road (about 1 1/2 miles from Hwy 101).

JUSTIN Vineyards & Winery

11680 Chimney Rock Rd

Paso Robles

805-238-6932

Tasting Daily 10-5

Deborah and Justin Baldwin founded JUSTIN in 1981. Their dream of a family-owned, estate grown and produced winery became a reality when 72 of their 165 acres were planted as vineyards.

Their focus is on Sauvignon Blanc, Chardonnay, Syrah, Cabernet Sauvignon, *JUSTIFICATION*, a blend of Cabernet Franc and Merlot, *ISOCELES*, a Cabernet Sauvignon, Cabernet Franc and Merlot blend and *Obtuse*, their dessert wine. Prices vary from $14.75-$60 per bottle.

JUSTIN offers daily winery tours at 10:30 and 2:30, detailing the wine-making process while touring their production facilities and underground caves. In addition, they offer a vineyard tour (weekends only), an ever-changing season-al experience where guests are able to see and touch the vines as they walk along our vineyard hillsides. Reservations are strongly suggested for both tours, and there is a small fee.

Unique among Central Coast wineries, JUSTIN keeps a full-time Executive Chef employed in their renowned Deborah's Room, where nightly dinners are served. Saturday and Sunday lunches are also served on their Wishing Well Patio. Reservations are required for dinner and suggested for lunch. And you can make your visit complete by reserving one of the four suites available in the JUST Inn, where you'll rest and relax in sumptuous style.

What a nice way to tour the Paso Robles area – a stay and dinner at JUSTIN.

From Hwy 101, exit Hwy 46 East and travel west on 24th St and Lake Nacimiento Dr for 7 miles, then onto Chimney Rock Rd for 8 more miles. Winery on the right.

L'Aventure Winery

2815 Live Oak Rd

Paso Robles

805-227-1588

Tasting Th-Sun 11-4

And By Appt

Stephan Asseo, owner and winemaker at L'Aventure Winery, began making wine in 1982, following his education at L'Ecole Oenologique de Macon, Burgundy, France. In that same year, he established Domaine Courteillac in Bordeaux. He and his family later purchased Chateau Fleur Cardinal, Saint-Emilion Grand Cru, and Chateau Robin, in the Cotes de Castillion, Bordeaux. Over the next 15 years, Stephan developed into an artisan winemaker, and gained a reputation as a maverick vigneron. However, his true desire was to be more innovative than AOC law would allow. In 1996, this led him on a quest for a great terroir, where he could pursue his ideal as a winemaker. After searching for over a year among the world's great wine fields, Stephan found Paso Robles and immediately "fell in love" with the unique terrior of the west side. It is here, in Paso Robles, that Stephan began his adventure, "L'Aventure".

The "tasting salon" is a small, intimate space where guests can taste currently available wines. The "degustation" experience at L'Aventure is for wine aficionados - no gift shop or gimmicks here. The emphasis is on learning about the west side terroir, and understanding Stephan's winemaking and grape growing philosophies.

L'Aventure sells out of their wines quickly, but hopefully you'll be able to taste their Roussanne, Syrah, Rosé, Cabernet Sauvignon and *Optimus* - Stephan's signature Paso blend, consisting of Syrah, Cabernet Sauvignon, and Petit Verdot. You'll find prices ranging from $15 to $75.

From Hwy 101, exit Hwy 46 West. Continue to Arbor Rd and Turn right on Arbor, then left onto Live Oak Rd.

Linne Calodo Winery

3845 Oakdale Rd

Paso Robles

805-227-0797

Tasting Fri-Sun 11-5

Linne Calodo is a family-owned and operated winery, focused on the production of unique and exceptional, hand-crafted wines. The name, Linne Calodo, describes the distinctive limestone soils of the west side of Paso Robles where their vineyards are located. They're proud to be creating unfined and unfiltered wines balanced through the blending of Rhone and Zinfandel varietals.

Presently, they bottle around ten blends each year. Mostly red with an the exception of *Contrarian*, a Viognier/Roussanne blend and an occasional other white blend when owner/winemaker Matt Trevisan finds just the right grapes. Prices are in the $40 to $70 range.

"I want to make wines that are regionally distinctive," Trevisan says, "and have fun making the best wines possible from the region." As part of that philosophy, he works closely with winegrowers from noted local vineyards. "What's important," he notes, "are the vineyard practices, the location, and working with good people."

Since the tiny Linne Calodo label is still very much a family affair, either Matt and/or his wife Maureen (and often their 2-year-old daughter as well) will greet you on arrival. Matt handles all of the winemaking duties, while Maureen handles the operations.

The Trevisans approach their wines as if going on a journey, about learning, about enjoying the adventure. "It's all about the learning process," said Trevisan. "You're never at the pinnacle. You're always looking for something down the road, and there's always something more you can do to push the envelope of quality. It's kind of like searching for the Holy Grail."

From Hwy 101, exit at Hwy 46 West, then turn right on Vineyard, then right at the first entrance on Vineyard. Please drive slowly up the dirt road, the winery and parking will be on your left.

Lone Madrone Winery

2485 Hwy 46 West

Paso Robles

805-238-0845

Tasting Daily 11-5

Neil Collins is the founder and winemaker of Lone Madrone. He's also been making the wines and tending to the vineyard operations for Tablas Creek Vineyards since 1998. The wines he produces for Tablas Creek are among the best Rhone varietals produced in California, and he brings this same passion and quest for excellence to his own Lone Madrone wines.

Neil honed his craft in the cellars and vineyards of two prestigious California Central Coast operations, Wild Horse Winery and Adelaida Cellars, where he served as winemaker for five years.

Prior to joining Tablas Creek and starting his own wine label, Neil worked for Chateau de Beaucastel, one of the most highly-regarded estates in the Chateauneuf-du-pape, southern Rhone region of France. His experience in French winemaking complemented his earlier training as a French chef in his hometown of Bristol, England.

His experience spans 14 harvests and four wineries producing highly acclaimed wines every step of the way. Now, with partners Tom Vaughn and Jackie Meisinger, he's offering Cabernet Sauvignon, Syrah, Barbera, Nebbiolo, Tannat (the prominent grape of Uruguay), Mourvedre, Rousanne and Picpoul Blanc along with an occasional blend. Prices are in the $18-$50 range.

In addition to tasting wines, you'll enjoy the unique pieces of artwork created by many talented local artists. Come enjoy all of this amidst the beautiful Sycamore Farms gardens.

From Hwy 101, exit Hwy 46 West towards Cambria for 2.5 miles. Tasting room on the left in Sycamore Farms.

Midlife Crisis Winery

1244 Pine St. Suite A

Paso Robles

805-237-8730

Tasting Th-Mon 10:30-6

The Midlife Crisis Winery is a very small family operation. It is owned and operated by Kevin and Jill Mittan. They get to be the winemakers, the cellar workers, the bottling line and the marketing mavens.

How did they decide to start a winery? The truth of the matter is that they are a DINK (dual income no kids) couple at the midlife crisis stage of their lives. They married later in life and developed a mutual passion for Australian Shepherds and wine and winemaking. When they combined these passions with all the associated midlife concerns about what they have done with their lives, dreams deferred, workplace stress, etc., and a booming real estate market in LA, the stage was set for them to start a winery.

And the list of wines they produce is surprising...Pinot Grigio, Chardonnay, Syrah, Zinfandel, Sangiovese, Barbera, Merlot and *Roo Boy Red* – their big red blend; plus two sparkling wines. Not bad for solving a crisis, huh? Prices fall in the $12-$22 range.

They still have to keep the day jobs for a while longer. They climb in the car after work every Friday with two Australian Shepherds and enjoy the four-hour drive to Paso Robles. Weekends and free days are spent at the winery or working on establishing the vineyard.

Oh, if you join their wine club, you become a member of the Crisis Management Team, named because they have discovered that a glass of wine can help manage many of life's small crises and make bigger ones a little easier to handle.

Tasting room located in Downtown Paso Robles at the corner of Pine and 13th St.

Midnight Cellars Winery & Vineyard

2925 Anderson Rd

Paso Robles

805-239-8904

Tasting Daily 10-5:30

Every winery has a story, and Midnight Cellars is no different. In 1994 a dream began when members of the Hartenberger family were on a wine tasting vacation. Sitting out on the patio overlooking the Napa Valley, eating toasted almonds and sipping fine sparkling wine, Rich Hartenberger uttered those fateful words: "Dad, why don't you take some of your money and buy a winery, and Michele and I will run it for you?" It seemed like such a good idea that Rich's brother Mike soon joined the bandwagon. Robert, Mary Jane, Michael, Richard and Michele Hartenberger founded the Midnight Cellars Winery and Vineyard in March 1995.

In the years since, they have held true to their single goal... to produce consistently fine wine... and have developed the two critical assets required to accomplish this goal... a Vineyard and a Winery.

The Midnight Vineyard is 25.5 acres in size and is planted to Chardonnay, Cabernet Sauvignon, Merlot, Zinfandel, and Petit Verdot.

The first Midnight Winery was located in a horse barn but is now located in a new 10,000 square foot building adjacent to the tasting room. This state-of-the-art facility allows the winemaker to produce ultra-premium wines from vineyard to bottle. Visitors are welcome to take a tour with the winemaker whenever he is available. Spontaneous barrel tastings are known to occur as Rich is always eager to show off upcoming releases.

Wines include Chardonnay, Sauvignon Blanc, Pinot Noir, Cabernet Franc, Cabernet Sauvignon, Syrah, Zinfandel, Port and a number of blends and run $7-$40 per bottle.

From Hwy 101, take Hwy 46 West about 2.2 miles. Turn right on Anderson Rd. Winery is the second one on the left.

Minassian-Young Vineyards

4045 Peachy Canyon Rd

Paso Robles

805-238-7571

Tasting Fri-Sun 11-5

And By Appt

Minassian-Young Vineyards opened its doors in the summer of 2005. The winery and tasting room are situated on a ridge with views that unfold to the Santa Lucia Mountains and beyond. The panorama of head pruned vines is framed by beautiful walnut trees that give visitors a true sense of place.

Located on a hillside is this small winery with a killer view. Small? Basically it's a one man operation. David Young is the winemaker, tasting room manager, and owner of this gem. You'll be greeted by an energetic young man passionate about growing grapes and making wine.

On the estate is a twenty-five year old dry farmed Zinfandel vineyard with new plantings of Syrah and Counoise grapes. The Zinfandel grapes reflect the strong heritage the west side of Paso Robles is known for, and the new plantings are typical of Rhone varietal grapes that are coming of age in the area. The wines include Chardonnay, Merlot, Estate Zinfandel, Muscat, and a blend of Syrah, Mourvedre, and Grenache. Future releases will include Viognier, Mourvedre, and Marsanne/Roussanne blends All the grapes used in their wines are either estate grown, or carefully selected from other estates and sought after vineyards. His pricing is in the $16-$24 range.

It is David's goal to create wines you will enjoy and share with others. He invites you to visit his tasting room and share the vision. Bring a picnic and have an adventure of food and wine in the beautiful setting of "far out" Paso Robles.

From Hwy 101 exit Hwy 46 West. Turn right on Vineyard Dr, then right on Peachy Canyon Rd. Winery on the right.

Nadeau Family Vintners

3860 Peachy Canyon Rd

Paso Robles

805-239-3574

Tasting Sat-Sun 12-5

Nadeau Family Vintners is an estate microwinery located in the Santa Lucia Mountains four miles west of Paso Robles, producing small lots of genuinely hand-crafted wines, carefully guided through their development by owners/vintners Robert and Patrice Nadeau.

The Nadeaus' ranch is a no-nonsense vineyard planted primarily to Zinfandel, with a small amount of Grenache and Petite Sirah. The fact that their tasting room is also their laboratory emphasizes the utilitarian nature of their winery. In fact, while picnicking on their deck visitors are surrounded by grapevines and processing equipment.

They specialize in huge, mountain-grown Zinfandel wines, and the more austere red Rhone varietals, like Syrah, Mourvedre, and Grenache. White wines include Roussanne and Viognier. Further, they're not afraid to be mavericks, so each vintage they source a small lot of an unusual variety which may be new to many wine enthusiasts ...a Nebbiolo one year, a Petite Sirah the next...just a barrel or two of something different. Prices are in the $18-$28 range.

Due to the small quantities of wine they produce, most of their wines are only available at the tasting room. And because this is truly a family operation, you'll usually be greeted by Patrice or Robert.

"Our wines are hand-made...and taste that way" says Robert Nadeau when asked about their winemaking style. Robert quips "We start with stellar fruit...our job, simply, is to not goof it up!"

From Hwy 101, exit at Spring St. Travel west onto 6th St, then onto Pacific Ave. Pacific becomes Peachy Canyon. At Merry Hill Ln. Go 4.5 miles on Peachy Canyon. Road. Winery on the right.

Nerelli Wines

3730 Highway 46 West

Paso Robles

805-238-0959

Tasting By Appt

At ZinAlley

Fourth generation winemaker Bryson Nerelli is carving a name for himself, following a family tradition. You can read the family background under the listing for ZinAlley in the Paso Robles West section.

Bryson is specializing in limited production dessert wines and is sourcing grapes from some of the most prestigious vineyards in the Santa Maria Valley.

With a wine making heritage and a passion for excellence, Bryson is hand-crafting wine for your and his enjoyment. His *After Hours Proprietor's Choice*, a 100% botrytis late harvest Pinot Noir, can be tasted in the family tasting room at ZinAlley. Retail price is $40 per bottle.

From Hwy 101 take the Hwy 46 West exit towards Cambria. Winery is about 3 miles on the right.

Norman Vineyards

7450 Vineyard Dr

Paso Robles

805-237-0138

Tasting Daily 11-5

Norman Vineyards was started in 1971 when Art and Lei Norman were looking for a place to realize their dream of growing grapes and making wine.

Art recalled what drove him to found Norman – his memories of his father and grandfather making wine in the home when he was a child. They spent weekends searching out a site in the cooler, coastal climates of California before settling on their Adelaida site in the westside appellation of Paso Robles.

After twenty years of grape growing, and with the encouragement of various local wineries, they decided to start their own winery. At the time, Paso Robles was a relatively new player in the wine industry; a virtually unknown place on the map, just starting to become the major player that it is today. And so the winery was founded with the help of Robert Nadeau and the first wine was produced from the 1992 vintage.

Today, their wines include Chardonnay, Cabernet Sauvignon, Merlot, their Mediterranean Collection of Pinot Grigio, Syrah, Barbera and Petite Sirah, their wide line of Zinfandels and a number of popular blends. Prices are in the $8-$36 range.

On their label, you'll notice the vineyard's mascot, the California Puma. Art said the Puma "showed up in the vineyard one year and kept the deer away." Scaring off the deer meant an increased yield of 10 tons for the 1992 Chardonnay. Now, he's honored everyday for his role as Protector of the Vineyard.

From Hwy 101, take Hwy 46 West to Vineyard Dr. Turn right onto Vineyard Dr 5.2 miles. Winery on your right.

Opolo Vineyards

7110 Vineyard Dr.

Paso Robles

805-238-9593

Tasting Daily 10-5

Opolo Vineyards is located on a beautiful 70 acre mountain site, west of Paso Robles. All of their wines are estate grown, produced and bottled, and production is typically less than 500 cases per varietal. Specialties include big mountain Zinfandels, classic Zinfandels, full bodied Pinot Noirs, Merlots, and Syrahs, as well as an 'easy going' Sangiovese. They also have other great varietals, including Chardonnay, Cabernet Sauvignon, Cabernet Franc, and a delightfully sweet and fragrant Muscat Canelli. Prices are in the $14-$45 range.

Be sure to taste their estate blend of Cabernet Sauvignon and Syrah – a wine they call *Fusion*. The 20 months of aging in oak barrels has given this wine flavors that are truly unique. And the reviews it's receiving may mean they'll soon be out of stock.

Partners Rick Quinn and Dave Nichols began business growing grapes for a number of local wineries. Of course, there were always a few grapes left over, so they started making small amounts of wine at home. Friends liked the wines, so in 1999 the inevitable occurred. "Let's get a license and make 1000 cases." The wines sold out in three months. Today, Opolo Vineyards bottles 40,000 cases a year.

The tasting room has a real "winery" feel, as it is located in their "cellar". You'll soon realize that the "cellar" is really an old tractor barn, dressed up with photos and posters of past Opolo parties. Especially interesting are the photos of the damage Opolo suffered in the 2003 earthquake. And the tasting bar is really typical of many small wineries – wood planks neatly attached to old wine barrels. A tasting room like Napa wineries had 40 years ago, and one that makes wine tasting on the Central Coast so much fun today.

From Hwy 101, take the Vineyard Drive Off Ramp west. The winery is just 8 miles from US 101 at the junction of Peachy Canyon Road and Vineyard Drive.

Orchid Hill Vineyard

1140 Pine St.

Paso Robles

805-237-7525

Tasting Th-Mon 11-5:30

And By Appt

Orchid Hill is a 51 acre vineyard located on sloping limestone hills in the Templeton Gap area of the west side of Paso Robles Wine Country. The low-vigor vineyard enjoys ideal southeast facing sun exposure and cooling afternoon breezes. The vines are meticulously hand tended and harvested and this environment provides wines with exceptional bouquet, depth of color, and impressive ripeness of flavors.

Recognizing Paso Robles' potential for growing quality grapes, Mike Schenkhuizen evolved from a "serious wine hobbyist" to an owner of a professional-grade vineyard. In the late 1990s, he and his wife Estrella looked around the Paso area for five acres on which to build a home. After falling in love with the Paso Robles countryside, Mike became determined to put Orchid Hill on the winemaking map – the home could wait for a few years. That's how 5 acres turned into 51 acres. Buoyed by the natural beauty of the land and with the help of his wife, he assembled a first-rate winemaking team and began nurturing the land, resulting in great wines.

Along with his winemaker, Dan Kleck, Mike is producing estate-grown Pinot Noir, Syrah, Zinfandel and Viognier. Wines are priced from $19-$27 a bottle. Soon they'll introduce a Grenache and a red blend to take advantage of the estate grapes.

Mike still is proud of his wine hobbyist days – the wines he produced and enjoyed in those days. But the hobbyist in the family today is Estrella. Mike smiles as he relates that the "dozens, maybe hundreds" of her prized orchids led to the name of the winery; the orchids and the hill their vineyard occupies.

Located on the square in beautiful downtown Paso Robles.

Peachy Canyon Winery

1480 N Bethel Rd

Templeton

805-239-1918

Tasting Daily 11-5

*Note Second Location Below

At Peachy Canyon they believe that great winemaking begins in their four estate vineyards; Mustang Springs, Old School House, Snow, and Mustard Creek. The Beckett Family labors to ensure the highest quality fruit from their nearly 100 acres of winegrapes. The estate-grown varieties include Zinfandel, Cabernet Sauvignon, Cabernet Franc, and Petite Sirah.

The Peachy Canyon label began in 1988 with a load of Zinfandel grapes from Benito Dusi's vineyards. Amounting to two hundred cases, that first release was produced in the small winery adjacent to the Becketts' family home on Peachy Canyon Road on the Westside of Paso Robles, a facility that could easily handle the 500 cases the family produced in 1990. However, demand for the label's wines quickly outgrew the original winery capacity, so in 1999, the Becketts purchased a 20-year-old winery on Nacimiento Lake Road. Now, some 15 years after the first release of Peachy Canyon wines, the label produces some 45,000 cases annually

Peachy Canyon Winery consistently produces some of California's better premium wines, including: Cabernet Franc, Cabernet Sauvignon, Merlot, *Para Siempre* (Bordeaux-style blend), Petite Sirah, Non Vintage Port, *Vesuvio* (Tuscan-style blend) and an amazing number of Zinfandels. Their pricing is from $12 to $50 per bottle.

Unlike many wineries, the Becketts feel that by releasing Peachy Canyon wines at the "peak of their youth," they give the consumer the opportunity to enjoy a young wine at its most vibrant state or hold on to it for several years for a more mellow style.

*From Hwy 101, take Hwy 46 West towards Cambria. Go 1.5 miles to the corner of Rte 46 W and Bethel Rd. *Their new "Peachy Too" tasting room is located at 2020 Nacimiento Lake Dr, Paso Robles 805-237-7848 and is open Sat and Sun, 11am to 5pm, except major holidays.*

Pianetta Vineyards & Winery

829 13th St

Paso Robles

805-226-4005

Tasting Th-Mon 12-6

11-6 on Sat-Sun

The Pianetta farming family spans four generations. John Pianetta Jr. and his daughter, Caitlin, continue this legacy today. Their vineyard is located in the southern Monterey County near Paso Robles on the eastern slopes of Indian Valley. Warm days combine with cool central coast nights to produce a premium red wine grape. The views from the vineyard are refreshingly breathtaking and the oak trees among the vineyard add to its aesthetics.

The first planting, in 1997, was 34 acres of Cabernet and the second planting, in 1998, consisted of 19 acres of Cabernet and 5 acres of Syrah. The first crop was harvested in 1999. The third and final planting was in 2000 with 5 acres of Syrah, 5 acres of Shiraz, and 1 more acre of Cabernet. These 11 acres completed the vineyard.

The grapes used in Pianetta wines come from the terraced slopes of the vineyard, and are picked by hand. The grapes are then de-stemmed and lightly crushed and fermented. After the wine is drained and pressed, it is aged in predominantly French oak barrels for 18 months, then bottled by hand.

They offer Syrah, Sangiovese, a Cabernet/Shiraz blend, Cabernet Sauvignon and *Bilancio*, a Cab/Syrah blend. The prices fall between $24 and $28 each.

Tasting Room in Downtown Paso Robles.

Pipestone Vineyards

2040 Niderer Rd

Paso Robles

805-227-6385

Tasting Th-Mon 11-5

Tues-Wed By Appt Only

Pipestone Vineyards is dedicated to producing handmade estate grown Rhône-style wines from Syrah, Viognier, & Grenache. They also offer Zinfandel, Mourvedre and a Rhone red blend. Prices vary from $16 to $38 per bottle.

Jeff Pipes left a career in Environmental Law and Environmental Engineering in Minnesota to come to Paso Robles. Florence Wong had a much more unlikely road. She grew up in Hong Kong and "never" had the dream to plant a vineyard or to live on a farm! She spent her career in the garment industry as a designer and importer after college.

But now, combining Eastern and Western traditions, Jeff and Florence strive to manage Pipestone sustainably and organically. In fact, Pipestone may be the only vineyard in California that is laid-out and constructed based on the principles of *Feng Shui* (wind and water).

During your visit, find time to relax and enjoy the quiet surroundings, tour the vineyard and visit their farm animal petting zoo. And you may see more than farm animals. Pipestone has a goal to be easy on the critters that share their little neighborhood. Much of the property is unfenced and they maintain areas for the deer to pass through. Owls and other raptors are encouraged with housing and perches (they eat the ever present gophers – yum, yum). And you may see everything from ladybugs and butterflies, to a diverse number of small birds, rabbits, squirrels, raccoons, bob cats, mountain lions and even a tarantula or two!

Betsy and Bobby (pictured above) will be happy to explain how they are much gentler on the vineyard than Jeff's tractor. Just ask!

From Hwy 101, take Hwy 46 West. Drive 3 miles to Oakdale Rd and turn right 1/2 mile to Las Tables Rd/Willow Creek Rd. Right again 1 mile and turn right on Niderer Rd. Winery about 0.8 mile on the right.

Poalillo Vineyards

1888 Willow Creek Rd

Paso Robles

805-238-0600

Tasting By Appt

Owned by Charles and Joyce Poalillo, Poalillo Vineyards is one of California's smallest wineries, but as winemaker Charles Poalillo says, "The winery may be small, but the wines are big!"

The westside vineyard produces intensely flavored wines due to the near-dry farmed vines lovingly tended by the Poalillo family. The minimum irrigation causes the grapes to grow slowly, retaining the flavor bursting intensity so sought after by premium wine lovers.

Poalillo Vineyards wines are in limited production and only available at the winery and one wine shop in the area. Wine lovers are invited to taste a gamut of whites including Chardonnay and Sauvignon Blanc and reds that include Syrah, Cabernet Sauvignon and Zinfandels at the winery's humble tasting bar, which is open by appointment and all holiday and wine festival weekends. Retail prices vary from $15 to $34 per bottle.

All winery visitors are invited to have their picnic on the charming tree-lined redwood deck overlooking the vineyard and surrounding hills.

From Hwy 101, exit Rte. 46 West. Turn right onto Vineyard Dr. then right onto Willow Creek Rd. Winery on the left.

Rabbit Ridge Winery

1172 San Marcos Rd

Paso Robles

805-467-3331

Tasting Daily 11-5

Founder and winemaker Erich Russell earned his nickname *"The Rabbit"* as a world-class runner in college. After graduation he took a teaching job, making wine in his spare time. His winemaking talents were unmistakable and his entry into an amateur winemaking contest in 1979 won him a job at Chateau St. Jean. In 1981, Erich opened Rabbit Ridge Winery in Healdsburg, becoming one of the top wineries in Sonoma County.

In an effort to continue Rabbit Ridge's commitment to producing high quality wines at affordable prices, Erich began looking for prime vineyard land elsewhere. His travels took him to Paso Robles where he spent a week viewing the area and tasting wine. He soon realized that this area had something that neither Sonoma nor Napa had - limestone soil just like the best vineyards of Italy and France.

As Erich and his wife Joanne started spending more and more time in Paso Robles they fell in love with the area and decided they would make it their home and new winery site. In 1996, Erich began buying land on the west side of Paso Robles and in 1997 his first vineyards were planted.

Today, the Rabbit Ridge family of wines includes Sauvignon Blanc, Viognier and Chardonnay among the whites, and a long list of reds including Pinot Noir, Sangiovese, Syrah, Cabernet Sauvignon, Merlot, Zinfandel, Petite Sirah and a number of custom blends. In keeping with their goal of affordable pricing, wines are in the $8-$30 range.

From Hwy 101, exit at San Marcos Rd. and drive west about 2 miles. Winery on the right.

Rotta Winery

3750 Hwy 46 West

Templeton

805-237-0510

Tasting Daily 11-5

Rotta Winery, founded in 1908 by the Rotta Family, is the only remaining family owned "original" winery in San Luis Obispo County. Mike Giubbini and Steve Pesenti have combined their talents to "bring back to life" the historic and rustic winery.

To longtime fans of this wine region, the name Rotta Winery might ring a few bells, but only if you were familiar with Paso Robles' wines before the rest of the country barely knew where Paso was. In fact, you have to go back several decades to discover the beginnings of Rotta Winery, which was one of the first three wineries established in Paso Robles - the others were York Mountain and Pesenti.

Today, the Rotta label is being revived by one of their grandsons, Michael Giubbini, who remembers long, happy days of working in the vineyard as a child when he visited his grandparents from his home in Menlo Park. He fell in love with the area, so after graduating from high school, he attended Cal Poly in San Luis Obispo, and has been there ever since.

In reviving the Rotta label, Giubbini is also re-establishing a link with history by working with winemaker Steve Pesenti, whose grandparents founded Pesenti. For now the Rotta label is focusing on Cabernet Sauvignon, Cabernet Franc, Zinfandel, Merlot, Chardonnay and Black Monukka - a dessert wine. Prices are in the $10-$27 range. All of the fruit for the winery will be sourced from local vineyards, especially those from the Westside.

One thing from the past that's definitely staying is the old redwood sign with "Rotta Winery" neatly hand stenciled in white paint. "I painted that sign when I was ten years old," remembered Giubbini.

From Hwy 101, exit Hwy 46 West. Tasting room at Cider Creek on your right.

San Marcos Creek Vineyards

7750 N Hwy 101

Paso Robles

805-467-9260

Tasting Daily 11-5

In the early 1990s, Fling and Annette Traylor began considering retirement on the scenic Central Coast; not a lazy retirement, but something that would get them involved with the community and provide some fun and excitement. They knew about the area's growing, reputation for quality winegrapes, and planted 40 acres on property they had purchased just north of Paso Robles.

San Marcos Creek Vineyard was established in 1992, and successfully developed contracts with several local premium wineries to supply them with grapes. However, as the Traylors became more involved with the Paso Robles wine industry, their plan for a quiet retirement of growing winegrapes gradually evolved into plans for a winery and a tasting room – producing their own wines under their own label.

Today, you can visit their beautiful French Country tasting room and enjoy their wines, picnic on the scenic terrace that overlooks the vineyard and roam through their small but elegant gift shop. The list of current wine releases includes Cabernet Sauvignon, Zinfandel, Merlot, Shiraz, Nebbiolo, Viognier, and Late Harvest Zinfandel. All of the wines exhibit the bold fruit and elegant balance for which Paso Robles' wines are known. The price range is from $12-$30.

With the success of their "retirement" dream, Fling and Annette were also able to realize another dream, that of developing a family business. Daughter Catherine Winter and her husband Brady came on board, and are now full partners in San Marcos Creek Vineyard. And plans for a Bed and Breakfast are being discussed. So much for retirement!

Located directly on Hwy 101, 7 miles north of the Rte 46 East exit.

Silver Stone Wines

827 13th St

Paso Robles

805-226-2788

Tasting Wed-Sat 12-7

Sun 12-4

Silver Stone Winery was founded on the premise of selecting the finest varietals and vineyard sites within key growing regions of California's cool coast. Their motto: "All Central Coast all the time. Except the Napa Cab."

Owner and winemaker Dan Kleck has been producing premium wines for the past 30 years. He began his career in the mid-1970's, on Long Island in New York, where he was involved with Chardonnays, Merlots and other varietals.

He and wife Debra migrated to California in the late 1990's, when Dan joined Jess Jackson at Kendall-Jackson Winery in Monterey, managing its Monterey winery. There he discovered the enormous potential of the outstanding vineyards stretching down California's Central Coast.

So when Silver Stone was born in 1997, Dan made it his mission to hand-craft wines from key coastal appellations, focused on uniquely-suited growing sites tended by astute vineyardists. And so his Pinot Noir and Sauvignon Blanc have origins in Monterey County, his Cabernet Sauvignon grapes come from Napa, another Pinot Noir and his Chardonnay come up from the Santa Maria area, and the Syrah, Zinfandel and Tempranillo are grown in Paso Robles. Prices run $15-$38 per bottle.

You'll enjoy Silver Stone's wines in their unique wine gallery, where the winemaker and his wife display fine custom hand-crafted jewelry as well as vivid, original oil paintings in a stylish, relaxed tasting atmosphere.

Located in beautiful downtown Paso Robles

Stacked Stone Cellars

1525 Peachy Canyon Rd

Paso Robles

805-238-7872

Tasting Sat-Sun 11-5

And By Appt

Stacked Stone Cellars began in 1998 when owner Donald Thiessen united his love of fine craftsmanship to his love of winemaking. With a reputation for crafting the finest woodwork available, Donald knew the commitment it takes to create a world class product.

Donald worked with many of the finest grape growers in the Paso Robles Appellation to grow grapes capable of producing world-class wines. Stacked Stone has also taken full advantage of its westside Paso Robles soil by planting a head-trained, dry-land farmed Estate Zinfandel Vineyard, producing a low yield of highly concentrated fruit.

Their first commercial vintage occurred in 2002, producing nearly 1000 cases. Today, they produce approximately 2000 cases per year – a nice volume that allows them a completely hands-on approach to small barrel production of hand-crafted wines.

Although Stacked Stone's primary focus is Zinfandel, other wines also produced include: Cabernet Sauvignon, Merlot, Bordeaux blends, Syrah, Petite Syrah, Sauvignon Blanc, Chardonnay, and two different fortified Port-style wines. The price range is $13-$40.

Stacked Stone was named after the elaborate stacked stone landscaping adorning the grounds where his wines are made. Nestled within their surrounding vineyards and rolling hills is a beautiful ancient oak studded dining area and tasting room.

So stop by Stacked Stone Cellars on the weekend from 11-5, and enjoy a complimentary tasting of their currently released wines, or talk owner Don Thiessen into sharing, from the barrel, what's to come.

From downtown Paso Robles, take 6th St west which turns into Pacific Ave. Follow Pacific Ave until it turns into Peachy Canyon Road. Stacked Stone Cellars is located on the left, about 1.5 miles from Spring Street.

Stephen's Cellar

7575 York Mountain Rd

Templeton

805-238-2412

Tasting By Appt

In late 2002 Stephen and Lori Goldman started construction on Stephen's Cellar. A new vineyard was planted spring 2002, devoted entirely to Pinot Noir. It is situated on a northerly slope 1,500' above the Pacific in the York Mountain Viticultural Area. Goldman and his father Max gained AVA status for the York Mountain area in 1983, and the region has proved it was worth the trouble. With significantly higher rainfall and cooler overall climate than nearby areas, wines from the York Mountain area exhibit much different characteristics than those grown even a mile to the east.

Goldman believes that the short distance from York Mountain to the ocean has a huge maritime influence on his vineyard. There's a lot of fog due to the 1500 feet elevation, and they're classified as a cool Region 1, something that is unique to the northern part of San Luis Obispo County. The resulting wines are lower in pH and higher in total acids, and tend to have brighter, fresh fruit aromas as compared to the jammier fruit flavors typical to most Paso wines. Because of its cool temperatures, Goldman believes York Mountain is a perfect spot for Pinot Noir, which is just fine, because Pinot Noir is his favorite wine.

Until the new vines are producing, wines will be made, as previously, from neighboring vineyards that have proven to be exceptional. Though Pinot Noir is the focus, a Bordeaux variety blend, Chardonnay, and Dry Sherry will be made in limited amounts. Prices are in the $9-$36 area. Stephen has also maintained a library of some of his older Pinot Noirs, priced between $30 and $60 each.

From Hwy 101 take Hwy 46 West to York Mountain Rd. Turn right to the winery.

Summerwood Winery

2175 Arbor Rd

Paso Robles

805-227-1365

Tasting Daily 10-5

Summer 10-6

Summerwood Winery is located on a picturesque 46 acres in the gentle rolling hills of West Paso Robles.

Their elegant tasting room captures views both inside and out. The welcoming interior boasts a bar of beautifully polished marble and slate floors laced with African mahogany. Relax in oversized plush chairs in front of the fireplace and enjoy a taste of their premium wines. For guests interested in sitting and sipping outside, French doors open to an expansive brick deck overlooking the vineyards.

While tasting, you can also witness the winemaking process. The tasting room features large picture windows that look out into the winery's production facilities.

The wines you'll enjoy include Cabernet Sauvignon, a red Rhone-style blend, Syrah, Rose, a red Bourdeaux Blend, Chardonnay, Riesling, Sauvignon Blanc and a Late Harvest dessert wine. Prices are in the $29-$115 price range.

But to taste these great wines, you must visit the tasting room, because Summerwood sells everything they make through their estate. No wine stores, no restaurants. And Summerwood likes it that way; it allows them to concentrate on small volumes of individual wines…they don't want to ever consider mass production.

An added feature of Summerwood Winery is the Summerwood Inn, located across Arbor Road from the winery. The Inn invites you to a luxurious retreat offering magnificent views of the Summerwood Vineyard and estate. With only nine rooms and innkeepers working 24 hours a day, all guests receive the attention required, while peace and tranquility are maintained. Each guest room is elegantly decorated and includes a fireplace and private balcony overlooking the vineyards.

From Hwy 101 take exit Hwy 46 West. Travel one mile west, turn right on Arbor Rd.

Tablas Creek Vineyard

9339 Adelaida Rd
Paso Robles
805-237-1231
Tasting Daily 10-5

Tablas Creek Vineyard was founded by the Perrin family of Château de Beaucastel and Robert Haas, longtime importer and founder of Vineyard Brands. They had since the 1970's believed the California climate to be ideal for planting Rhône varietal grapes. In 1987, they began the lengthy process of creating a Châteauneuf-du-Pape style vineyard from scratch in the New World. They chose the hilly Las Tablas district of west Paso Robles for its similarities to Châteauneuf du Pape: limestone soils, a favorable climate, and rugged terrain.

The partners imported the traditional varietals grown on the Perrins' celebrated estate, including Mourvèdre, Grenache Noir, Syrah, and Counoise for reds, and Roussanne, Viognier, Marsanne, and Grenache Blanc for whites.

The "Tablas Creek Vineyard" label debuted with the construction of the estate winery for the 1997 vintage. Beginning with the 2001 whites and the 2000 reds, the wines were named *Esprit de Beaucastel* and *Esprit de Beaucastel Blanc*, blended for richness, balance, and ageability. The *Cotes de Tablas* and *Cotes de Tablas Blanc* wines are designed to be clean, bright expressions of fruit, ready to drink younger and very approachable in price. Tablas Creek also produces single varietal and limited release wines. Their wines are priced $22-$95 per bottle.

Tablas Creek offers one of the region's most interesting tours, covering the organic estate vineyard, grapevine nursery and winery twice daily at 10:30am and 2:00pm. Please reserve space on these tours in advance by calling the winery.

From downtown Paso Robles, take Spring St north to 24th St. Turn left on 24th St which curves to the right and becomes Nacimiento Lake Drive. Continue on Nacimiento 1.5 miles and turn left on Adelaida Rd. Travel 9.3 miles along Adelaida Rd. Tablas Creek Vineyard is on your left, still on Adelaida Rd, 3/10 mile past the intersection with Vineyard Dr.

Terry Hoage Vineyards

870 Arbor Rd

Paso Robles

805-238-2083

Tasting By Appt

Terry Hoage Vineyards is a small, family owned vineyard that is dedicated to producing the finest grapes and wine. The John Alban designed vineyard is planted with Rhone varietal grapes on 26 acres of a southwest facing hillside in Paso Robles. Blessed with hot summer days and cool evenings, a fifty degree temperature difference between night and day is not uncommon. The special climate, terroir and fastidious farming practices produce exceptional fruit. The small clusters have tiny berries that are intensely dark in color and rich in flavor. Every aspect of the vineyard's farming is done by hand. Each and every vine is touched and babied many times during the growing season. Terry and Jennifer Hoage produce minimally processed wines that show intense fruit and complexity showcasing their passion for excellence.

Terry and Jennifer purchased the vineyard in July of 2002. It consisted of 5 acres of Estrella Syrah. They immediately enlisted the help of friend and wine master guru Justin Smith (Saxum) to help with not only the viticulture but also the winemaking. Justin continues to help in the viticulture (they have two blocks planted for Saxum) and Jennifer and Terry have taken over the wine making.

Current offerings include Syrah, a Grenache Rosé and two Rhone blends – *The Pick* made of Grenache, Syrah, Mourvedre and Counoise, and *The 46*, a Grenache/Syrah blend. Prices are from $16 to $60 per bottle.

The winery was built by Terry and his parents, Terry and Mary Lee, from three historic barns rescued from destruction in southeastern Iowa.

From Hwy 101, exit at Hwy 46 West. Turn right on Arbor Rd and go 1.7 miles to the winery on your right.

Thunderbolt Junction Winery

2740 Hidden Mountain Rd

Paso Robles

805-226-9907

Tasting Fri-Sun 11-5

And By Appt

Dr. Stanley Hoffman is considered the godfather of the modern Central Coast wine industry, laying the groundwork for generations of winemakers. His Hoffman Mountain Ranch Winery was the first large-scale modern facility in the area. To those who know the history of winemaking along California's Central Coast, the Hoffman Mountain Ranch wines are something of a legend. His wine put Paso Robles on the map, when they entered it in a blind tasting in Europe in the late '70s and it beat Romanée-Conti. People from all over the world started coming to see the winery.

In 2005, Richard and Aurora Gumerman purchased the property and the Gumermans plan to revive the winery to its glory days. The new owners will share their passion for food and wine pairings making your visit educational and fun. The winery and grounds will be undergoing intensive rebirth. Respect for the land and nature are primary goals for this renovation and beautification. Richard has planned for replanting the vineyard, five acres per year up to 60 acres. So drive down to where history was made.

Thunderbolt Junction Winery will offer a number of Rhone varietals as well as Cabernet Sauvignon, Zinfandel, Merlot, Chardonnay, Viognier and Muscat Canelli. Wine prices will be in the $10-$22 range, with their premium Port *Mundo Viejo* selling at $50.

Their motto is simple: "Rain or Shine Always Great Wine!"

Exit Hwy 101 at Hwy 46 East/24th St. exit. Drive west on 24th Street through town past Spring St for 1.5 miles until you reach Adelaida Rd. Turn left onto Adelaida Rd from 24th St/Nacimiento Lake Dr. Follow Adelaida Rd for 5.1 miles until you reach Hidden Mountain Rd. You will see the big Thunderbolt Junction signs at the entrance.

Tolo Cellars

9750 Adelaida Rd. #1A

Paso Robles

805-226-2282

Tasting Fri-Mon 11-5

In the far west of Paso Robles there's a little red farmhouse, home to Tolo Cellars. Josh Gibson, proprietor and winemaker, offers a sumptuous array of wines, all sourced from vineyards tucked away in the rustic hills, where once farmed the pioneers of the Adelaida township. This historic area, marked by rugged terrain, offers ideal hillside conditions for vines bearing hardy and distinctive wine grapes.

Josh's goal in winemaking is to allow these vineyards, each with its own "flora and fauna," to express themselves in glorious harmony. Thus, all his wines are fermented on native yeast, allowing the robust and wild flavors of the vines to exude in the wines. The results are wines of uncommon depth and character – much like the surrounding hillsides.

Josh opened his tasting room doors in December 2005, though he was well-versed in the Far Out lifestyle long before that. As assistant winemaker at Le Cuvier Winery for several years, Josh learned the art of crafting high quality wines in small lots. He continues that practice today, limiting production to just around 2500 cases.

The Tolo wines include Chardonnay, Syrah, Cabernet Sauvignon, Zinfandel and, for now, two red blends, Aria and Leros. Retail prices run $24 to $28 per bottle.

The little red farmhouse, built in the 1880s, doubles as a tasting room and a showcase for exclusive Provencal linens, pottery, tablecloths and cookbooks, selected especially for the discerning wine enthusiast. Experience the best of Westside Paso Robles wine country at Tolo Cellars.

From Hwy 101 and downtown Paso Robles exit 24th St./right (west) continue on 24th St. 2.0 miles. 24th St. becomes Lake Nacimiento Rd then turn left onto Adelaida Road and go about 10 miles on Adelaida Rd. Tasting room on the right.

Venteux Vineyards

1795 Las Tablas Rd

Templeton

805-610-9293

Tasting Fri-Sun 10-5

Or By Appt

On a family vacation to the Central Coast, Scott and Bobbi Stelzle visited the Paso Robles wine country. While they had read and heard positive things about the region, they had doubts about the quality of the wines. What an eye-opening day that was! Scott and Bobbi instantly fell in love with the natural beauty of the area and the friendly small-town atmosphere. When they tasted the excellent Zinfandels and Rhone varietals, they were inspired! After a few visits to the region, they were convinced that the area known as the "Templeton Gap" had the ideal soil and climate for growing premium grapes. They soon returned and made an offer on the ten acres known as Rancho Las Tablas, right in the heart of the Templeton Gap.

On the way to their first bottling, they needed a name for their wine. What would describe this special property? Suddenly it came to them... Venteux Vineyards. This French word meaning "windy" was perfect. The hot dry days are cooled each afternoon by the coastal breezes that make this region similar in many ways to the Rhone Valley.

Their 2004 vintage is now available – a Cabernet Sauvignon, a Syrah and a Petite Syrah, priced at $36 to $38 per bottle. From soil to bottle, their hands-on approach allows them to uphold the highest level of care in all aspects of the wine-making process. They are continually working to improve and maintain a healthy and beautiful property for neighbors, wine-country visitors and themselves.

And be sure to check out *V*entuex Vineyards Bed & Breakfast, a luxury inn that features Americana farm style. The three rooms offer the appeal of fine country elegance once so prominent along California's Central Coast.

From Hwy 101, exit at Vineyard Dr and go west to Bethel Rd. Turn right on Bethel Rd then left on Las Tablas Rd. Winery will be on your left.

Villicana Winery

2725 Adelaida Rd

Paso Robles

805-239-9456

Tasting Fri-Sun 11-5

And By Appt

Villicana Winery produces fewer than 1,800 cases per year in a family owned and operated winery, which allows proprietors Alex and Monica Villicana to handcraft each vintage and create a superior wine.

The Villicana label owes its existence to an unsuccessful culinary school. After college, Alex decided to pursue his interest in food and wine and enrolled in a culinary program. When the school failed to open, he turned his attention to winemaking and took a job working the harvest at a local Paso Robles winery in 1990. He also began taking viticulture and enology classes at U.C. Davis.

In 1995 they purchased 72 acres on the westside of Paso Robles and personally planted their 10 acre vineyard in Cabernet Sauvignon, Zinfandel, Merlot, Mourvedre, Syrah, Grenache, Petit Verdot and Cabernet Franc. This wide selection allows them to offer wonderful varietals as well as unique blends. Their wines retail $14-$32.

Their tasting room is nestled in the corner of a working winery so bring a sweater; they keep the temperature cool. It's a great place to beat the heat during the summer. You will more than likely find Alex or Monica behind the bar, and if you're are looking to picnic, they have a peaceful setting for you to enjoy.

Basically, what started as a small, unimaginable dream has turned into their reality and continues to be their labor of love. They invite you to come be a part of their dream.

From Hwy 101 exit at Hwy 46 East and head west onto 24th St. Veer right onto Naciamiento Lake Dr, then left on Adelaida Rd. Winery approximately 7 miles down Adelaida Rd.

Vista Del Rey Vineyards

7340 Drake Rd

Paso Robles

805-467-2138

Tasting Most Sundays 11-5

And By Appt

Translated in Spanish, Vista Del Rey means "King's View," which is an apt description since its founder's name is Dave King. Vista Del Rey Vineyards consist of two sites: Hacienda (Home) Vineyard and Colina de Roble (Oak Knoll) Vineyard.

Currently, Dave and his wife, Carol, offer Zinfandel (using their 25 year old vines), Barbera, and Pinot Blanc. To their knowledge, they are one of only six wineries offering a Barbera Port. Their wines run $16-$22 a bottle, the Port retails for $25.

And in their rustic tasting room, you'll also find homegrown dry-farmed walnuts and pistachios, a selection of gourmet items and Carol's carefully chosen local wine country items.

If you happen to be a Navy veteran, be prepared to share some great stories. After earning his degree in Agricultural Engineering from Oregon State University, Dave pursued a 22 year US Navy career which included five ship tours, teaching geology, oceanography and chemistry at the Naval Academy, and tours with two high technology Navy laboratories, specializing in state-of-the-art undersea warfare systems.

The Kings acquired Vista Del Rey Vineyards in 1994 and produce less that 1000 cases per year. Dave truly wants to keep the small-volume approach to wine making that has served him so well.

Their motto says it all – "Get off the beaten path; experience the difference!"

From Hwy 101, take the Wellsona Rd exit west and turn left onto San Marcos Rd. From San Marcos Rd, turn right onto Mahoney Rd which turns into Drake Rd. Winery on the right.

Whalebone Vineyard

8325 Vineyard Dr

Paso Robles

805-239-8590

Tasting Fri-Sun 11-4

And By Appt

In 1989, well ahead of the Paso Robles vineyard boom Bob and Jan Simpson decided to plant a small vineyard. Ten acres were ripped down four feet yielding large calcareous rocks laden with whalebones and other marine mammal fossils. On this hillside reminiscent of a moonscape, the Simpson Family planted exclusively to Cabernet Sauvignon. Today the vines have lost their youthful exuberance and are gracefully transforming into a harmonious, low vigor vineyard, which needs little manipulation to produce low yields and high concentration required for quality wine.

Whalebone Vineyard and Winery started with the bones and a homemade wine called *BOB WINE*. This original wine had a pedestrian label made out of duct tape. Traveling to various hunting and fishing spots, Bob always brought along a bottle or two of BOB WINE. Many of Bob's friends with refined pallets were reluctant to try the garage wine but it soon became a prized gift and a mini cult favorite.

Through a process that was more whimsical and meandering than purposeful, a colorful history has evolved, on this coastal cattle ranch in the Santa Lucia Mountains not far from Hearst Castle. The surprisingly wonderful fruit and wine produced from vines growing on a rocky hillside led to more ambitious plans, coming to fruition over a decade later with the first vintages of Whalebone Cabernet Sauvignon.

Their estate Cabs retail for $28 per bottle. And for the sake of nostalgia, or because it's a darn good red table wine, the Simpsons still offer *BOB WINE* (with a nice label) – a blend of Cabernet Sauvignon, Zinfandel, Merlot and Syrah at $25.

From Hwy 101, exit at Hwy 46 West and turn right onto Vineyard Dr. Stay on Vineyard - winery on the left.

Wild Coyote Estate Winery

3775 Adelaida Rd

Paso Robles

805-610-1311

Tasting Daily 11-5

Owner & Winemaker Gianni Manucci grew up in California, became an architect, and pursued a more creative balance to his life through stone sculpturing. But, his true roots in grape farming began in Europe over three generations ago which inspired him to get back to his roots in 1995. His hands-on personal skills shine in this beautiful 40-acre hillside vineyard, and his UC-Davis viticulture education has gained him many winemaking awards. Gianni's unique sense of balance has also transformed his vineyard with an ancient adobe style of architecture, an art colony, and winemaking, all harmoniously created in balance at his winery.

His philosophy is to be a small estate winery, but be the best at what he does. If that means that he should stay at the vineyard production capacity of 3,000-5,000 cases per year, then so be it. To him, quality is more important than quantity, and it's all about pounds of grapes per vine not tons per acre.

The tasting room is a one-of-a-kind adobe with a genuine tipi and artifacts. You can picnic by the pond, meet the winemaker, see his personal stone sculpture creations & eclectic art collection. As best whispered by one of their visitors "it is like a piece of heaven on earth"

Wild Coyote produces Zinfandel, Merlot and Syrah, along with a number of blends and dessert wines using those varietals. Bottles run $18-$55.

In 2005, Manucci added five "Bed & Breakfast" casitas, perfectly carved out of the mountain-side atop the vineyard, between the tasting room and the winery. These Casitas' original designs were inspired from Taos New Mexico's Pueblo Native American reservation. A retreat…a hideaway…with great wine!

From Hwy 101 exit Hwy 46 East and travel west on 24th St. (Lake Nacimiento Rd) about 2 miles. Turn left on Adelaida Rd for 2.2 miles.

Windward Vineyard

1380 Live Oak Rd

Paso Robles

805-239-2565

Tasting Daily 11-5

Pinot Noir is the driving passion of Marc Goldberg and Maggie D'Ambrosia, husband and wife owners of Windward Vineyard. Windward Vineyard is dedicated exclusively to producing Burgundian style Pinot Noir.

Marc and Maggie purchased and planted the vineyard in 1989 based upon the terroir and microclimate of the Paso Robles Westside. Today, the 15 acre vineyard is planted in four notable French closes. The combination of the cooling Pacific breezes, the calcareous soil and the 50 degree daily drop in temperature produce exemplary Pinot Noir.

Since their debut in 1995, each of Windward's sold-out vintages have achieved inspiring acclaim, particularly within the community of wine aficionados who appreciate the layered complexity of Burgundian styled Pinot Noir.

The annual vintage is named "Monopole" – a Burgundian French term that expresses the vision of total control over both the vineyard and the winemaking. Following his instincts, Marc often chooses from among his favorite barrels for a select bottling – his Barrel Select Gold Pinot Noir. The Gold reflects the inner core of the vintage with an intense Burgundian profile of ripe bing cherry and wild strawberry. The velvet texture whispers the long cellar life anticipated. Prices can vary from $30 to $60.

Windward Vineyard produces only, on the average, 1400 cases per year. Given the small production, Windward Pinot Noir does not enjoy wide distribution. So you can assure yourself a taste by visiting their tasting room.

From Hwy 101 exit at Hwy 46 West for one mile to Arbor Rd. Turn right on Arbor for 1/4 mile to Live Oak Rd. Winery on the right.

York Mountain Winery

7505 York Mountain Rd
Templeton
805-238-3925
Tasting Daily 11-4

At the end of a sun-dappled roadway, nestled among old arching oaks and thick Spanish moss, you'll discover a Central Coast treasure called York Mountain Winery. In 1882, apple farmer, Andrew York, discovered his soil and climate were ideal for growing grapes — thus York Mountain Winery was born.

After nearly 90 years, the Yorks sold the winery in 1970 to winemaker Max Goldman. The Goldmans continued the family winemaking tradition for more than three decades. The family transitions in ownership have made York Mountain Winery the oldest winery in continuous operation.

In 2001, the local landmark was purchased by David and Mary Weyrich, owners of the award winning Martin & Weyrich Winery & Tasting Room. Their appreciation of York Mountain's heritage and their knowledge of the local wine industry helps ensure the wineries continuance and hopefully their plans will even improve upon the winery's venerable winemaking tradition.

Plans for the facility include a complete restoration of the rustic tasting room and the creation of a wine museum. In addition, the original farmhouse located on the property will be transformed into a romantic bed & breakfast retreat, perfect for special occasions and weekend sojourns into wine country. The Weyrichs also plan to expand the vineyards at York Mountain and will start by planting 30-40 acres of grapes, mostly reds, including Pinot Noir and Cabernet Sauvignon.

York Mountain produces small lots of Rhone varietals, including Viognier, Roussanne and Syrah, as well as vineyard-designated Chardonnay and Pinot Noir. Prices are $10-$35.

From Hwy 101 take Hwy 46 West towards Cambria. Turn right onto York Mountain Rd.

Zenaida Cellars

Photo by Mike Larson Photography

1550 Highway 46 West
Paso Robles
805-227-0382
Tasting Daily 11-5

Eric Ogorsolka, the owner/winemaker of Zenaida Cellars has been growing and making wine since 1994. In 1988 the family purchased the west Paso Robles property and began planting the estate vineyard. After earning a Bachelor of Science degree in biology from Cal Poly at San Luis Obispo, Eric began working the vineyard and making small lots of experimental wines.

Eric feels that wine is the perfect culmination of science and passion, and he draws on his scientific background every day. When he set out to name the winery, he returned to the roots of his academic study. "In Biology, I studied quite a few Latin names," he says, "Zenaida Macroura is the Latin name for Mourning Dove. The man who named them, thought they were beautiful birds, so he named them after his wife, Zenaida. I always liked the story and the name."

His winemaking philosophy is fairly simple. He believes: That you must know the vineyard; this is where great wines begin. It's crucial to understand your soil and how each varietal interacts with it to express its true character. And lastly, try your best not to get in the way and screw it up!

Currently on their home vineyard, they produce Zinfandel, Syrah, Petite Syrah, Viognier, Cabernet Franc, Cabernet Sauvignon, Merlot, Pinot Noir, and Chardonnay. Wines run $15 to $30 each.

The design of the winery reflects the Ogorsolka's love of the region. It's set in the rolling, oak-studded hills, and is designed with a rustic mission theme. "The atmosphere is very low key and relaxing," says Eric. "The patio overlooks the vineyard and the winery is set right in the midst of 100 year-old mature oaks."

From Hwy 101 exit at Rte 46 West towards Cambria. Drive for 1 1/4 miles. Winery on the right.

ZinAlley

3730 Highway 46 West

Paso Robles

805-238-0959

Tasting By Appt

Owner/winemaker Frank Nerelli has a standard greeting for visitors to ZinAlley. "Do you like Zin?" Depending on the answer he gets, his response is "Good" or "Too bad. Because that's all we've got." That's right, because following in the footsteps of his father Al and grandfather Frank Pesenti, Frank and his wife, Connie continue the heritage of producing fine Zinfandels. Specifically, an Estate Zinfandel and an Estate Zinfandel Port. Either sells for $42.

ZinAlley is a small family-owned and operated winery nestled in the heart of the Central Coast's famous Templeton Gap and was once part of the old Pesenti Estate. Frank and his wife Connie bought the property from his uncle in the early 1970's. Until 2000, when the winery was sold to Turley Wine Cellars, Frank crafted wine for the Pesenti Family Winery. Now he's putting all his energy and passion into hand crafting world class wines for his own label.

The design of the label was a story in itself. While traveling through Italy in 2001, Connie came across an artist in the little town of Greve, in Tuscany, who had the same talent and passion toward art as Frank has for wine. With a small deposit and a handshake, a deal was struck: he will paint a different alley picture each year to grace ZinAlley's label. The first two years depicted alleys in Florence, the next two, Venice. And at the bottom of each label, the gold-embossed mountain lion remains – the lion that roams free in the Templeton Gap and serves as ZinAlley's "alley cat."

From Hwy 101 take the Hwy 46 East exit towards Cambria. Winery is about 3 miles on the right.

Winery Notes

Winery_____ **Date**_____

City or Area_____

Wine Comments

_____

_____

_____

_____

_____

_____

_____

_____

_____

_____

Winery_____ **Date**_____

City or Area_____

Wine Comments

_____

_____

_____

_____

_____

_____

_____

_____

_____

Winery Notes

Winery_____ **Date**_____

City or Area_____

Wine Comments

_____

_____

_____

_____

_____

_____

_____

_____

_____

Winery_____ **Date**_____

City or Area_____

Wine Comments

_____

_____

_____

_____

_____

_____

_____

_____

_____

Winery Notes

Winery_____ **Date**_____

City or Area_____

Wine Comments

_____

_____

_____

_____

_____

_____

_____

_____

_____

Winery_____ **Date**_____

City or Area_____

Wine Comments

_____

_____

_____

_____

_____

_____

_____

_____

_____

Winery Notes

Winery_____ **Date**_____

City or Area_____

Wine Comments

_____

_____

_____

_____

_____

_____

_____

_____

_____

Winery_____ **Date**_____

City or Area_____

Wine Comments

_____

_____

_____

_____

_____

_____

_____

_____

_____

San Luis Obispo Area

The San Luis Obispo County AVA

There is a significant maritime influence of Pacific winds and coastal fogs on this region's climate. Cooling marine air enters through the east-west running valleys and leads to a long growing season resulting in intense, complex flavors. This puts San Luis Obispo wines in the company of the world's greatest.

The Edna Valley AVA

Frequent summer fog and afternoon winds act as a natural cooling system keeping Edna Valley's temperatures far below the averages found in some of the more inland growing regions of the Central Coast. These climatic conditions are ideal for growing concentrated Chardonnay and Pinot Noir.

The Arroyo Grande AVA

The western part of the area has a long cool growing season, but the eastern part of the area is warmer. Chardonnay is the most popular variety by a considerable amount, followed by Pinot Noir and other grapes like Cabernet Sauvignon, Sauvignon Blanc, Sémillon and Zinfandel.

Sorry We Missed A Few

We believe the following winery does offer tasting, but for some reason they chose not to respond to our requests for information. If you visit them, we hope you'll let them know what they missed.

Rancho Arroyo Grande

Alapay Cellars

415 First St.

Avila Beach

805-595-2632

Tasting Daily 10:30-6

Alapay Cellars debuted their first wine in the fall of 2001 and have expanded to include Viognier, Syrah, Pinot Noir, Chardonnay, Zinfandel, a Rosé and the occasional surprise that the owner/winemaker, Scott Remmenga is experimenting with. Bottle costs range $14-$50.

Alapay Cellars maintains no vineyards; instead Scott has contracted with a number of well-known vineyards to supply fruit; vineyards like Edna Ranch, Zaca Mesa, Stolpman and Bien Naciedo. A good move on his part, because it allows him to concentrate his time where he shines - winemaking.

The tasting room is a experience in itself, with two huge salt water fish tanks, custom tile art calling attention to their nearby beach and a staff that finds joy in their work. You'll often be served by Scott or his wife Rebecca who keep in constant touch with their customers' tastes. And as you see in the picture, they're one of the few wineries with seats at the tasting bar - making for a warm, friendly visit.

Like a lot of wineries, Alapay Cellars maintains a small gift shop, but their offerings tend toward the fun side of wine rather than the large gift baskets and expensive serving pieces found elsewhere. Many of the items feature the winery's motto: "Come on in....the water's wine."

In the native Chumash language, Alapay means "a world above" or heavenly" and one visit will convince you the name is appropriate.

From Hwy 101, Take Avila Beach Drive exit west four miles to downtown.

Baileyana Winery/Tangent Winery

5828 Orcutt Rd

San Luis Obispo

805-269-8200

Tasting Daily 10-5

Photo by Marya Figueroa

Catharine and Jack Niven moved to the Edna Valley in the early 1970's. Pioneering the planting of the first winegrapes in the area, Jack focused on the larger market while Catharine worked diligently on a small 3 1/2 acre vineyard in her front yard. Her study drew her to Burgundy and Burgundian methods of planting and trellising. Although "the experts" advised her that the then "California" methods were best, she stuck to her guns and proved she was right. Thus Catharine founded Baileyana.

Today, her grandsons, John and Michael, along with their French wine-maker, Christian Roguenant are meeting the challenge of taking her winery to the next level.

Baileyana focuses on Chardonnay, Pinot Noir and Syrah from their estate Firepeak Vineyards and invites you to experience Catharine's legacy in their historic tasting room, the old Independence Schoolhouse. Wines run $15-$40 per bottle.

The sister winery - Tangent - was begun to focus on clean, lively wines with good acid structure, wines that cried out to be served with food; wines like Sauvignon Blanc, Pinot Gris and Pinot Blanc. Pricing runs $13-$20 per bottle.

When you visit, you'll also be entranced by their well-stocked line of gifts as distinctive as their wines. And enjoy their large patio that would be perfect for a picnic, with spectacular views of the Seven Sisters (nearby ancient volcanos).

From San Luis Obispo, take Broad St south, left on Tank Farm Rd, onto Orcutt Rd. Schoolhouse on left.

Cerro Caliente Cellars

831-A Via Esteban

San Luis Obispo

805-544-2842

Tasting Fri-Sun 12-5

Possibly you've read stories about the "garagiste" of France. They're vintners who make minuscule quantities of high quality wines in their home garage.

Don Peters, the owner/winemaker of Cerro Caliente has gone them one better. He's a certified mechanic, the owner of Peter's Automotive in San Luis Obispo, and Cerro Caliente Cellars' tasting room occupies space in that garage. His daughter – Mitzi – a local school teacher, runs the tasting room.

In 1990, his love for fine wine drew him to making wine in his basement. And he hasn't stopped yet. After winning two gold medals at the Indy International Wine Competition in 1997, Cerro Caliente was born in 1998. The first year, he produced 320 gallons of Chardonnay and Cabernet Sauvignon. He's expanded to include Syrah, Pinot Grigio, Merlot and a Bordeaux-style blend he calls *Multi-Viscosity* (get it?).

Production is still relatively small; Don plans to limit his annual production to 1000 cases. Prices run $7 (for his "garage sale" Syrah) to $33. And now the Peters Family has added a line of "good things" to taste at the garage – chocolate cordials filled with their award-winning Merlot and a line of premium ice cream made with their wines.

Don offers his description of Cerro Caliente: "The place where Cabernets and Cadillacs are at home, Merlots and Mercurys mix, Chadonnays and Chevrolets play and hydraulic presses and wine presses work side by side. The only winery where, it is told, 30 weight is converted to wine."

From Hwy 101, Take Broad St south. Left on Capitolio Way, left on Sacramento, right on Via Esteban.

Claiborne & Churchill Winery

2649 Carpenter Cyn Rd

San Luis Obispo

805-544-4066

Tasting Daily 11-5

Founded in 1983, Claiborne & Churchill is a small, family-owned winery specializing in hand-crafted, Alsatian style wines. Their special focus is on dry Gewurztraminer and dry Riesling, modeled on the fruity but dry dinner wines of the French province of Alsace. A variety of other wines are produced in small lots, including Chardonnay, Pinot Noir, some interesting blended wines and a number of sweet dessert wines, including their Port Obispo. With the exception of Pinot Noir, these other wines are not widely distributed but are available directly from the winery. Prices range $12-$25 per bottle.

In 1995, construction was completed on their new and permanent winery building. This structure, a noteworthy example of environmental architecture, is a "straw bale building," the first of its kind in California. With sixteen-inch thick walls made of bales of rice straw, the winery is so well insulated that it maintains a constant cellar temperature, without the need for mechanical cooling or heating.

And that's the exciting building where you'll be tasting the Claiborne & Churchill wines - right among the barrels of aging wines. And because they're a small winery, you'll be served by a tasting room staff that works with the wines daily - they know their wines and will be proud to share them with you.

Claiborne & Churchill also has a pleasant picnic area and garden for your use. Stop by and enjoy.

Located on Rte 227 just south of Price Canyon Rd intersection.

Domaine Alfred Winery

7525 Orcutt Rd

San Luis Obispo

805-541-9463

Tasting Daily 10-5

Domaine Alfred is a young winery, built on their first vintage in 1998. Most of their wines are estate bottled with grapes from their Chamisal Vineyard. Chamisal was the first vineyard in the Edna Valley, planted in 1972. Purchased by winemaker Terry Speizer in 1994, the vineyard has been replanted based on its nearly 30 year history of producing world-class wines.

Domaine Alfred Winery offers both Califa and Estate styles of it's Pinot Noir, Chardonnay and Syrah wines and has recently introduced other new wines including Pinot Gris, Vin Gris and Rosé. The Califa bottling is a bolder reserve style wine with more oak and tannin built for aging. Prices range $18-$90 per bottle.

In 2005, Domaine Alfred was honored to be selected the San Luis Obispo Vintners "Wine of the Year" for their 2002 Califa Pinot Noir.

Recently, Domaine Alfred has built a large state-of-the-art winery which has allowed them to rebuild their tasting room to add space for an exciting revolving exhibit of local artists and their work.

So your visit will allow for tasting fine wine, viewing great art, breathtaking scenery and a close-up view of the vineyards.

Located on Orcutt Rd south of San Luis Obispo.

Edna Valley Vineyard

2585 Biddle Ranch Rd

San Luis Obispo

805-544-5855

Tasting Daily 10-5

At the heart of Edna Valley Vineyard's winemaking is the idea that wine should be as pure an expression of the place and the grape as possible. They handle the fruit gently and treat the wine with respect, minimizing pumping, fining, and filtration.

They focus on estate-grown Chardonnay and have a strong commitment to producing Pinot Noir and Syrah using new varietal clones. They also craft a variety of limited production wines that are sold exclusively in the tasting room. Prices fall in the $15-$50 per bottle range.

One of the unique features of your visit to the Edna Valley Vineyard is the opportunity to walk through the demonstration plantings just outside the tasting room. Using the easy to follow guide provided, you'll be able to note the differences between the different grapes used in their wines.

Edna Valley Vineyard is open to visitors year round for wine tasting, tours and special events. The Hospitality Center is consistently rated Best Tasting Room in San Luis Obispo by locals. The spectacular views overlooking the vineyards are among the most photographed in the valley. And the choice of wine and culinary gifts are so plentiful and beautifully arranged that you'll be highly tempted to take something home.

You can also see the winemaking process in action during a tour that is designed to highlight the activities going on at the winery at that moment. Tours are given weekends from 11 a.m. to 3 p.m., on the hour.

Take Broad St south from Hwy 101, turn left on Biddle Ranch Rd. Winery on right.

Kelsey See Canyon Vineyard

1947 See Canyon Rd.

San Luis Obispo

805-595-9700

Tasting Most Days 11:30- 5:30

Welcome to the beautiful Avila Valley, apple country on a small scale - a narrow creek-sculpted canyon just inland from Avila Beach. But wine in apple country? That's right. The same soil that produces those crisp, delicious apples is responsible for some pretty amazing wine.

Owners Dick and Delores Kelsey are your hosts as you taste from an array of wines. They often serve Sauvignon Blanc, Chardonnay, Pinot Grigio, Merlot, Pinot Noir and Cabernet Sauvignon, and a monster Zinfandel that Dick takes particular pride in producing. And if you're an apple fan, you'll look forward to their best-selling Apple Chardonnay, along with an Apple Merlot. Port and a sparkling Syrah are often on the tasting list. Prices range $17-$35 per bottle.

This small family-owned and operated winery takes pride in producing wines of quality, not quantity. So you may find them sold out of your favorite on occasion. Just another reason to return.

To make the one-mile drive up picturesque See Canyon Road even more worthwhile, we'd suggest purchasing some cheese and crackers in Pismo or Avila Beach, a bottle of cool wine from the Kelsey's and relax under the ancient oaks next to the babbling creeks.

Wine tasting just can't get any better.

From Hwy 101 take San Luis Bay Dr west to See Canyon Rd. Turn right for 1 mile. Winery on right.

Kynsi Winery

2212 Corbett Canyon Rd

Arroyo Grande

805-544-8461

Tasting Th-Mon 11-5

Kynsi is a small family winery. Don and Gwen Othman, the winemaker/proprietors, focus on producing vineyard designated wines, sourcing their grapes from select coastal vineyards.

The winery resides in a charming renovated 1940's dairy - one of the few reminders of Edna Valley's days of vast cattle herds. The old milk processing room is the entrance and the setting for the tasting room. High coved ceilings and the original cold room door leading into the wine vault contribute to the unique character and cozy ambience.

Their labels features the resident barn owl that roosts in the old barn adjacent to the winery. The Kynsi owls have been "working partners" for more than 10 years, keeping the vineyard gopher population under tight control.

1995 was their inaugural vintage. Currently they produce 3000 cases of single vineyard Pinot Noir, Syrah and Chardonnay along with *Merrah*, a Merlot/Syrah marriage, and Zinfandel from the Barn Owl Vineyard in Adelaida on the west side of Paso Robles. Pinot Noir, Pinot Blanc and Syrah from the Bien Nacido Vineyard were added in 2002. Estate Pinot Noir from their Stone Corral Vineyard that was planted on the ranch in 2001 rounds out their offerings. Production goals are not to exceed 4500 cases. Bottles run $22-$46.

Come relax. Picnic in their beautiful garden with tile tables, benches and umbrellas. The perfect pairing with Kynsi wines!

Located at the north end of Corbett Cyn Rd just off Rte 227.

Laetitia Vineyard & Winery

453 Laetitia Vineyard Dr
Arroyo Grande
805-481-1772
Tasting Daily 11-5

Laetitia has long been known for its warm hospitality. Located just off Highway 101 near the village of Arroyo Grande, Laetitia offers tastings of Laetitia, Barnwood and Avila wines at a beautiful hilltop visitor center that features commanding views of the vineyards, the Arroyo Grande Valley, and the Pacific Ocean.

Laetitia's wines include Chardonnay, Pinot Noir, Pinot Blanc and Syrah. The winery also produces a number of highly prized single vineyard pinot noirs. In tribute to Laetitia's French heritage, they continue to produce premium sparkling wines from estate grapes in the time-honored Methode Champenoise. Offerings include brut, extra dry, brut rose and Cuvee M. Laetitia. Pricing runs $16-$60.

Nestled in the Sierra Madre Mountain range and unique in its 3,200' desert elevation, Barnwood Vineyard's terroir offers growing conditions ideal for Petite Sirah, Cabernet Sauvignon, Sauvignon Blanc and Tempranillo. They also offer a Reserve Cab called *South Mesa* as well as *TRIO*, a Merlot, Cab and Syrah blend. Bottles range from $14-$35.

Avila Winery offers a line-up of Chardonnay, Merlot, Syrah, Cabernet Sauvignon and *Cote d'Avila*, a blend of Syrah, Mourvedre and Grenache - all with knock-out flavors at affordable prices, $10-$13.

So Laetitia truly offers an unmatched choice in great tasting. And visitors are invited to use the scenic picnic area and explore the ever-changing items in their gift shop.

Located on Hwy 101 between Arroyo Grande and Santa Maria.

Ortman Family Vineyards

3080 Biddle Ranch Rd

San Luis Obispo

805-473-9463

Tasting Daily 10-5

Closed Tues-Wed, Jan-Mar

Ortman wines are founded on two generations of winemakers and family roots that reach deep into California agriculture. Wines are crafted by the father and son team of Chuck and Matt Ortman. Long recognized as one of California's most accomplished winemakers and the founder of Meridian Vineyards in Paso Robles, Chuck Ortman has returned to the accountability of a limited-production family winery.

Just as Ortman Family Vineyards was being launched, Matt apprenticed at Italy's famed Castello di Gabbiano winery, bringing a European influence to his winemaking approach and inspiring the addition of Sangiovese to their small family of wines.

By the end of 2001, all of the inaugural releases of Ortman Family Vineyards were in the barrel. And in 2003, their first wines were released. They specialize in varietals that excel in the local areas, working with a small "family" of premium winegrowers whose vineyards are distinguished by progressive viticulture, exceptional terroir and world-class fruit.

Perhaps best known for their distinguished Pinot Noir, the Ortman Vineyards offerings include Chardonnay, Cabernet Sauvignon, Sangiovese, and Syrah. Pricing is $16-$40.

Ortman Family Vineyards shares space in the tasting room of another family winery - Saucelito Canyon Vineyard. An opportunity for you to enjoy two of the areas leading wineries in one visit.

Take Broad St south from Hwy 101, turn left on Biddle Ranch Rd. Winery on the left.

Per Bacco Cellars

1850 Calle Joaquin

San Luis Obispo

805-787-0485

Tasting Th-Mon 11-5

Marco Rizzo, owner of Café Roma Restaurant in San Luis Obispo and Craig Shannon, a third generation vineyard manager, had long spoken about making wine together. They had dreams of putting together the best possible fruit with solid winemaking in order to produce wines of distinction.

Opportunity struck when an older Chardonnay vineyard in the southern portion of Edna Valley came up for lease, and they jumped at the chance to farm it.

They contracted with John Alban of Alban Vineyards to act as their consulting winemaker, and began making wine at John's facility across the valley from the vineyard. Currently, Per Bacco Cellars produces Chardonnay, Pinot Grigio and Pinot Noir and occasionally makes small barrel batches of Rosé and Petite Sirah.

Per Bacco Pinot Noir is sourced from four separate blocks in the Laetitia Vineyard, located at the south end of the Arroyo Grande Valley, less than a mile from the Pacific Ocean. The cool vineyard site combined with the unusually high incidence of limestone and chalk in the soils make for nearly perfect Pinot Noir territory. Wines cost $18-$50 per bottle.

After tasting the wines, experience more of the Per Bacco spirit by trying your hand on their bocce court or horseshoe pit. A short hike will take you to any one of a number of picnic sites, offering panoramic views of the vineyards and surrounding area.

Exit Hwy 101 at Los Osos Valley Rd. Start to enter south bound Hwy 101, but stay to the right to drive onto Calle Joaquin. Winery straight ahead.

Piedra Creek Winery

6425 Mira Cielo Dr

San Luis Obispo

805-541-1281

Tasting Appt arranged by Phone or e-mail to margaret@digitalputty.com

If you ask Romeo Zuech, with his wife Margaret, co-owner of Piedra Creek, the secret of making high quality wine, he answers "One, I make sure the grape grower is a good friend and, two, I use flawless procedures because I don't want to drink my mistakes."

Piedra Creek Winery, one of the smallest bonded wineries in the state, was born in 1983. It's a family owned and operated facility from crush through sales. In fact, you'll taste their wines on the patio of their home in the Edna Valley. And Margaret, or Romeo, or both will be serving you. What better way to taste wine?

The San Floriano Vineyard is the culmination of the Piedra Creek dream. The miniscule vineyard of 2 acres producing Pinot Noir, Lagrein and Teroldego surrounds the home of Romeo and Margaret, allowing them a "hands-on" experience from bud break to harvest.

The yearly production of Piedra Creek is approximately 700 cases, with Zinfandel as the predominant grape. Their *San Floriano*, a blend of Lagrein, Teroldego, Petite Syrah and Merlot was first released in 2000. A major procedure used in producing this blend is the crushing and fermenting of all the grapes together, achieving maximum amalgamation of flavors. Their third wine is an Estate grown Pinot Noir. Bottles range in price from $17-$24.

San Floriano Vineyard and *San Floriano* blend are both named in honor of the patron saint of Romeo's native village, Brez, Italy – where he visits each summer. His old neighbors love his wine!

From Hwy 101 in Pismo Beach, take Price Canyon Rd to Edna Rd. (Rt 227). Go straight through the red light onto Twin Creeks Rd and turn left onto Mira Cielo. Their home – and tasting room – is on the left. Appointments are necessary for tasting.

Salisbury Vineyards

6985 Ontario Road
San Luis Obispo
805-595-9463
Tasting Daily 11-6

The historic Santa Fe School of Avila Valley was dedicated in June of 1907 and served the youth of the area until 1964 when it was closed. Travelers on Route 101 watched as it slowly deteriorated until the Salisbury Family began its renovation in 2000. Today the two-roomed schoolhouse serves as the tasting room for their estate wines as well as the home of Salisbury Fine Art, their gallery which features the works of nationally and internationally recognized artists.

The Salisbury-Rucks family has been farming in California since 1850, and through seven generations they've developed a deep understanding of fruits and the microclimates in which each does best. They began planting grapes on their Sacramento Delta property in the mid 1990's and began their central coast vineyards in 2000.

Taking advantage of Avila Valley's unique climate, with fog most nights followed by clear, mid-70 degree days, they've come to be known for their exquisite Pinot Noir, Chardonnay and Syrah. Their warm weather vineyards in Paso Robles provide luscious Zinfandel and Cabernet Sauvignon. Prices range from $20 to $35 per bottle.

On scheduled weekends, Salisbury Vineyards takes visitors on trolley tours through the vineyards, serves barbecue sandwiches on the patio and introduces new art in the gallery. Call for tour schedules and dates of events.

Winery located between San Luis Obispo Bay Dr. and Avila Beach Rd. off Hwy 101.

Saucelito Canyon Vineyard

3080 Biddle Ranch Rd

San Luis Obispo

805-543-2111

Tasting Daily 10-5

Closed Tues-Wed, Jan-Mar

With Vineyards hidden away in a remote canyon off Hi Mountain Road, west of Arroyo Grande, Saucelito is what you might call "off the beaten path" from where you would expect a vineyard and winery to be located. Owned and operated by Bill and Nancy Greenough, Saucelito Vineyard utilizes three acres of some of the oldest Zinfandel vinestock within the entire Central Coast, dating back to the early 1880s. The vineyard is recognized both as a U.C. Davis Heritage Vineyard and as the oldest producing vineyard in San Luis Obispo County.

The vineyard had been completely deserted since the early 1940s, and by the time Bill took over the property in 1974, there were only three acres of the original Ditmas vineyard remaining. After long hours and careful grafting, Saucelito today produces a Zinfandel the Wine Spectator calls "one of California's greatest Zins, bar none." They also produce Cabernet Sauvignon and limited production wines available only in their new tasting room. Bottles vary from $20-$36.

You'll find a small picnic area with a view of newly planted vineyards. And inside the tasting room, you'll see stock from that old 1880 vineyard as well as be able to read the entire story of how the vineyards was started, fell into neglect until it was completely abandoned in the early 1940's and how Bill, while camping out in the canyon, found the traces of vineyard that led him to purchase and eventually bring life back to the old stock. As you taste the resulting wine, you'll marvel at the love winemakers bring to the grape.

Tasting room located between Rt. 227 and Orcutt Rd.

Sextant/Windemere Wines

3536 S Higuera #240B

San Luis Obispo

866-833-9463

Tasting Sat-Sun 11:30-5

The story begins with proprietors Craig and Nancy Stoller who were born, raised and currently reside in Bakersfield. Craig is the CEO at Sunridge Nurseries Incorporated, a company founded by Craig's parents Glen and Terrie Stoller.

In 1982 Glen, a Soil Scientist and alumni of Cal Poly, and Terrie, a former teacher, developed Sunridge Nurseries. The company specializes in grape root stock and provides the beginning fruits to many wineries around the United States. As the company slogan goes, Sunridge Nurseries is "Where the Vintage Begins".

Craig joined the team in 1992 upon graduating from Cal Poly where he studied horticulture and has been very instrumental in taking the company to new heights. One of his major steps was the establishment of their estate vineyard. RBZ Vineyard was developed with Sunridge Nurseries as the only commercial vineyard in the Paso Robles AVA that is also a State of California registered nursery block. All material planted is the first of its kind in the United States after being imported from France through the French Entav-Inra program. All vines can be traced back to ONE original mother plant in France.

And in 2007, Windemere became part of the family when the Stollers purchased Cathy MacGregor Wines. With the winery came the MacGregor Vineyards in the Edna Valley – one of the vineyards planted by Cathy's father, who was among the very earliest to recognize the grape-growing potential of the region.

Winery plans are not complete, but expect to find Zinfandel, Chardonnay, Pinot Noir, Merlot, *Beachcomber* - a white Rhone blend and *Night Watch*, a Zinfandel/Petite Sirah blend. Prices are not set – possibly in the $15-$49 range.

Located in an industrial park off Broad St near Tank Farm Rd.

Talley Vineyards/Bishop's Peak

3031 Lopez Dr

Arroyo Grande

805-489-0446

Tasting Daily 10:30-4:30

The Talley family farming tradition began in 1948, when Oliver Talley started growing specialty vegetables in the Arroyo Grande Valley. Talley Vineyards produced its first wine in 1986 with the bottling of 450 cases. The winery's first five vintages were produced in a small winery adjacent to one of Talley Farms' vegetable coolers. Talley Vineyards currently produces about 18,000 cases annually.

Talley Vineyards seeks to create wines that consistently reflect the unique character of the vineyard, the terroir, rather than changing trends in winemaking fashion. They're especially known for their estate grown Chardonnay and Pinot Noir. Bottle cost ranges from $14-$68.

Bishop's Peak's objective is to produce honest wines of good value that reflect the distinctive character of the county's two winegrowing regions. The grapes for Bishop's Peak wines are purchased from growers who share the Talley family's commitment to quality. Wines usually include Chardonnay, Pinot Noir, Cabernet Sauvignon and Syrah and prices range $12-$22.

A unique feature of Talley is their support for The Fund for Vineyard and Farm Workers. Each year one wine is produced and all of the grapes, materials and services are donated and all proceeds go to the Fund, which provides grants to the organizations that assist these important workers in the community.

The Talley tasting room allows beautiful views of the farming valley, an excellent gift shop and a large, gracious picnic area

From Hwy 101, take the Grande Ave exit in Arroyo Grande. Travel east through the Village and keep right at the three-way stop sign; follow the signs toward Lake Lopez. Winery located 5.5 miles on the left.

Tolosa Winery

4910 Edna Rd/Hwy227

San Luis Obispo

805-782-0500

Tasting Daily 11-5

Two centuries ago, Mission San Luis Obispo de Tolosa established the first vineyard in the Edna Valley and produced the most renowned wines of early California. Today, Tolosa Winery embraces this heritage by not manipulating the grapes to change flavors or characteristics. Their Chardonnay, Pinot Noir, Syrah and other varietals are honest to the grape. The wines come from estate plantings and run $15-$52 per bottle.

Tolosa was created in 1998 and the tasting room opened in 2004. Although the winery has the potential of producing many more cases of wine than they do at present, local owners Bob Schiebelhut and Jim Efird follow a slow, handcrafting process that nurtures the wine through periodic gentle racking and minimal filtration. Not a good way to produce millions of cases of wine, but a sure way to allow nature to determine the character of each vintage.

When you visit Tolosa, you'll visit one of the most dramatic tasting rooms on the Central Coast, with glass walls looking out over the stainless steel tanks, flanked by plaques describing the winery's "Self-Guided Tour of the Winemaking Process." The tasting room is architecturally modern combining elements of the winery in its design, from the cork floor to stainless steel ceilings, glass bar and wood panels.

Every Saturday in the summer you can enjoy a flight of four wines with four gourmet cheeses in their Heritage Room or on the patio. Tickets are limited, reservations are suggested.

Winery located south on Rt 227 (Edna Rd) at the corner of Buckley.

Wild Wood Vineyard & Winery

555 El Camino Real

San Luis Obispo

805-546-1088

Tasting Wed-Sun 11-5

And By Appt

Wild Wood Winery is owned and operated by the Wood Family. The 80-acre Estate is located at the base of the Cuesta Grade in San Luis Obispo and enjoys the cool evening climate of the Edna Valley yet has a warmer daytime temperature similar to Paso Robles. The unique microclimate is ideal for growing wine grapes unique to the Central Coast of California.

Craig Wood produced his first vintage in 2001, but does not call himself a winemaker. He refers to the hands-on training he was given by a number of the top vintners in the area, and the lessons he learned about grapes. His credo is that to make good wine, you have to start with good grapes. To make great wine, you must start with great grapes. So he calls himself a wine grower, and takes pride in his vineyard work.

The family vineyards have grown since 1999, and include Syrah, Cabernet Sauvignon, Sangiovese, Malbec, Cabernet Franc, Pinot Noir, and Alberanio. Thus far, Wildwood has bottled and offers Viognier, Chardonnay, two Syrahs, Pinot Noir, Sangiovese, Rose, a Bordeaux blend and Cabernet Sauvignon. Pricing is from $15-$35 per bottle.

Located directly on Hwy 101, 1 1/2 miles north of the Monterey St exit in San Luis Obispo.

Wolff Vineyards

6238 Orcutt Rd

San Luis Obispo

805-781-0448

Tasting Tues-Sun 11-5

Winter Th-Sun 11-5

The vineyard was planted 30 years ago by one of Edna Valley's winegrowing pioneers, Andy MacGregor. The new owners, Jean-Pierre and Elke Wolff, renamed the vineyard in 1999 when they expanded the vineyard and added their artisan winery.

The vineyard includes 55 acres of Chardonnay and 37 acres of Pinot Noir grapes. Twelve additional acres are planted in Teroldego, Syrah, Petite Sirah and Riesling. The 30 year old Chardonnay blocks (the oldest producing Chardonnay in the Edna Valley appelation) are dry farmed, giving the wine a site-specific "terroir" characteristic. The Petite Sirah is the first planted in the Edna Valley. This unusual cool climate Petite Sirah has quickly gained national review and recognition.

Wolff's very-limited production is hand-crafted using traditional Burgundian wine-making methods. Prices range $20-$25 per bottle.

From the moment you park in the tasting room lot, you'll see the Wolff's commitment to maintaining and improving the ecology of the property. The tasting area is outdoors (except in poor weather) on a lovely patio surrounded by flowering plants. Beyond that, you'll be amazed as Jean-Pierre explains the sustainable winegrowing practices they apply. And you may be rewarded as you sight the quail, kestrel, red-tail hawk and barn owl - even golden eagles that their natural habitat conservation draws to the vineyard.

Located on Rt 227 just south of Price Canyon Rd.

Winery Notes

Winery_____ **Date**_____

City or Area_____

Wine Comments

_____

_____

_____

_____

_____

_____

_____

_____

_____

Winery_____ **Date**_____

City or Area_____

Wine Comments

_____

_____

_____

_____

_____

_____

_____

_____

_____

Winery Notes

Winery_____ **Date**_____

City or Area_____

Wine Comments

_____

_____

_____

_____

_____

_____

_____

_____

_____

Winery_____ **Date**_____

City or Area_____

Wine Comments

_____

_____

_____

_____

_____

_____

_____

_____

_____

Winery Notes

Winery_____ **Date**_____

City or Area_____

Wine Comments

_____

_____

_____

_____

_____

_____

_____

_____

_____

Winery_____ **Date**_____

City or Area_____

Wine Comments

_____

_____

_____

_____

_____

_____

_____

_____

_____

Winery Notes

Winery_____ **Date**_____

City or Area_____

Wine Comments

_____

_____

_____

_____

_____

_____

_____

_____

_____

_____

Winery_____ **Date**_____

City or Area_____

Wine Comments

_____

_____

_____

_____

_____

_____

_____

_____

_____

Santa Barbara County Area

The Santa Barbara County AVA

Approximately half of the annually produced grapes are sold to wineries outside the County at some of the highest prices in California. Chardonnay and Pinot Noir have been the flagship varietals of the county but Rhône and Italian varietals are becoming a large portion of the grapes grown.

The Santa Maria Valley AVA

There are several historic and prestigious vineyards here: Bien Nacido, Nielsen, Sierra Madre and Tepusquet. There are only about a dozen wineries in the Santa Maria Valley. These few wineries, though, are among the best and most reputed producers in California. Traditionally, Chardonnay and Pinot Noir have been the leading varietals in this region.

The Santa Rita Hills AVA

The Sta. Rita Hills are regarded as one of the premier Pinot Noir growing regions. Chardonnay and Syrah also have strong footholds.

The Santa Ynez AVA

The cooler western section of the AVA is planted mostly in Chardonnay and Pinot Noir and a few other Bordeaux varietals while the eastern, warmer, section is dominated by highly regarded Syrah and other Rhône varietals.

Sorry We Missed A Few

We believe the following wineries do offer tasting, but for some reason they chose not to respond to our requests for information. If you visit them, we hope you'll let them know what they missed.

Alexander & Wayne, Arthur Earl, Cambria, J Wilkes, Roblar, Royal Oaks.

Addamo Vineyards

400 E Clark Ave

Orcott

805-937-6400

Tasting Tu-Sun 11-7

The Addamo Family originated in Sicily, where they produced wine for personal consumption for many generations. From his grandparents small-production family estate in Sicily, to his parents acres of Cabernet Sauvignon in Hollister, California, David Addamo, the proprietor has always had a passion and strong interest in growing grapes and making wine. With a background in agriculture and business, it was just a matter of time until David was able to combine his passion with his expertise and produce the highest quality grapes, in the best location for winemaking. In 2000, David and his family moved to the Central Coast, and planted the vineyard on 120 acres in Orcutt. He now proudly grows and produces eight varietals of all estate wines.

With the Vineyard manager, Bill Kesselring and winemaker, Justin Mund, David's vision is to produce the very finest, hand-crafted wines their terroir can achieve. They believe the level of quality is established in the vineyard. Their grapes are balanced at the soil level, and hand-harvested to guarantee unsurpassed quality. They use the finest French Oak barrels for aging to ensure flavor complexity, and balance. This, combined with uncompromising winemaking practices, enables them to create wines of distinctive quality.

Today, they offer Riesling, Chardonnay, Grenache, Syrah, Pinot Noir and an elegant Italian varietal with few plantings in California, Dolcetto. Prices run $19 to $35 per bottle.

Their tasting room and gift shop are located in historic Old Town Orcutt. The western flavor of the village offers a unique blend of antique shops, boutiques and restaurants, so plan to wander for a while.

From Hwy 101, exit Clark in Santa Maria and proceed west on Clark to Old Town Orcott.

Alma Rosa Winery & Vineyards

201-C Industrial Way

Buellton

805-688-9090

Tasting Daily 11-4

Founders of Sanford & Benedict Vineyard (1971) and Sanford Winery (1981), Thekla and Richard Sanford are proud to present wines from their new winery, Alma Rosa Winery & Vineyards. With a commitment to sustainable farming and green business practices, and over 100 acres of certified organic estate vineyards, Alma Rosa offers Pinot Noir, Chardonnay, Pinot Blanc, Pinot Gris, and Pinot Noir-Vin Gris (dry rosé). Retail pricing is $16-$49 per bottle.

Richard Sanford is recognized as the first to plant Pinot Noir in the Santa Ynez Valley and a pioneer and zealot for Pinot Noir in Santa Barbara County. ("Let's go to Sanford Winery," the leading character, Miles, suggests to his buddy in the film, *Sideways*. "They make the best Pinot Noir in California.") If not a winemaking legend, he's the next best thing. He was way ahead of his time when he rounded up investors and started a winery outside of Buellton in 1969.

Now, with over 35 years of winegrowing experience in the region, Thekla and Richard believe this new beginning gives them a greater opportunity to honor the unmistakable relationship between the healthiness of the soil, the energy of the vines, and ultimately the soul of the wine. And with over 100 acres of certified organic estate vineyards they will continue to focus on excellence in Pinot Noir and Chardonnay and on producing wines with extraordinary balance and depth.

Their newest "first"? All wines are sealed with a screw cap – no more corks. Richard says he just got tired of tasting corked wines.

Currently, their tasting room is a temporary location. Hopefully, they'll be able to be in new quarters by the summer of 2007. Call the phone number above for an update.

From Hwy 101 in Buellton, exit at the Hwy 246 exit and proceed 1/2 mile west then turn left on to Industrial Way.

Ampelos Cellars & Vineyard

Solvang and Lompoc

805-736-9957

*Tasting As Below

Or at the Winery By Appt

Ampelos is a Greek word meaning "vine". Peter and Rebecca Work believe that all great wines are made in the vineyard, they also have strong ties to Greece, so "ampelos" truly represents their focus.

They purchased the land in 1999, hoping that one day they might plant a vineyard and maybe make their own wines! Their vineyard consultant advised them that they had a great piece of property and, with a lot of courage and patience, could have a great vineyard.

The next few years were spent learning how to farm, pruning the vines, coaxing them onto the trellis, nurturing the soil and preparing for the first harvest. To get a jump start on learning their new trade, in 2002 they purchased a ton of Pinot Noir and two tons of Syrah and started to make their own wine, under the stewardship of son Don, assistant winemaker at Sea Smoke Cellars. They continued with this direction in 2003, increasing volume a bit and adding a Rosé of Syrah.

2004 brought the inaugural Ampelos Vineyard harvest! They picked 15 tons of Pinot Noir and 6 tons of Syrah, as well as continuing their program of purchasing grapes from warmer regions to "add to the spice cabinet". Since production is small, wines are often sold-out or "not available till next year." But you'll often find Grenache, Syrah, Pinot Noir, Viognier and a blend they call *Syrache*, a Rhone-style blend of Syrah and Grenache. Prices range in the $28-$34 area.

The name ampelos has additional family ties – Rebecca and Peter were married on a small Greek island, and fell so much in love with the island that they created Ampelos Resort there. Ask them about spending vacation time – and drinking wine there.

*Tastings sometimes available at "Cabana" 1539 Mission Dr 'C' in Solvang (Wed-Mon 11-6) and at "Tastes of the Valley" 1672 Mission Dr in Solvang (Daily 11-8) or call the number above for directions and a tasting appointment at the winery.

Andrew Murray Vineyards

2901-A Grand Ave

Los Olivos

805-693-9644

Tasting Daily 11-5:30

Andrew Murray fell in love with the emerging Rhône varieties, Syrah and Viognier, in the late '80s while traveling through the Rhône Valley of France. He took that passion further when he headed out for a short internship in Australia in 1992 to learn more about the famed Australian Shiraz. There he fell so in love with Syrah that he overstayed his planned three months by almost a year.

When he returned home, he earned a degree in viticulture and enology from U.C. Davis and started his vineyard and winery, working with growers who mirrored his passion for excellence. He found vineyard owners who matched his desire for perfection, and who farmed their vines to extremely low yields with the most advanced viticultural methods. Andrew's razor sharp vision can be summed up in the company motto, "Handcrafted wines from steep hillside vineyards, planted exclusively to Rhône Varieties."

All of the focus, passion, and dedication have paid off. Today, Andrew Murray Vineyards is considered, "One of Santa Barbara's finest wineries," by Robert Parker, Jr. and the editors of Food and Wine magazine were in agreement when they named Andrew as the "Tastemaker of the Year" in 2004.

In his tasting room, you'll usually find a number of Syrahs and Viogniers along with Chardonnay and at least two blends – *Enchante*, a white Rhone blend and *Esperance*, which is a blend of Grenache, Syrah, and Mourvedre. Prices vary from $16 to $47 per bottle.

In addition, they craft a number of single vineyard wines each vineyard. As Andrew explains, there's little to no winemaker ego involved in those wines, rather they are very carefully tended from the vineyard to the bottle.

From Hwy 101, take the Hwy 154 exit and turn inland about 2 miles to Los Olivos. Turn right on Grand Ave.

Arcadian Winery

Ballard or Santa Ynez

*Tasting Fri-Sun 12-4

Or at the Winery By Appt

While in college on an athletic scholarship, Joe Davis, the son of a Monterey fishing family, took a job in a wine shop. One Christmas, a good customer brought Joe a gift of a 1978 Clos de la Roche Grand Cru, Domaine Dujac. One sip and he was completely taken with the flavor and sheer deliciousness of the wine, "To have winemaking as a life pursuit and to make wine like this," he thought, "would be the most wonderful thing in the world." And so his quest began.

In 1985, he met and went to work for Dan Lee of Morgan Winery. While primarily making award-winning Chardonnay, Davis never lost site of that fantastic Burgundy and in 1990, he presented a classic Pinot Noir production plan to Morgan Winery.

He employed these procedures for all of his Pinot Noir vintages (1986-1994) at Morgan and then took this knowledge to a General Managers position at Bernardus Winery. Finally in 1996, on his own and ready to fulfill his dream, he released Arcadian Winery's first vintage of Chardonnay to rave reviews.

Following his gut instinct, creating Burgundian style Pinot Noir, Chardonnay, and Syrah allows Joe Davis the complete realization of his dream. His mission remains to make wines that fully express the uniqueness of the vineyard and the region while capturing the voluptuous flavor of the grape and the kiss of cool California breezes and warm sunshine.

Produced as vineyard-designated, his various bottlings of the three grapes run $30-$80 per bottle.

Tasting at "The Ballard Inn" (Fri-Sun 12-4) at 2436 Baseline Ave, Ballard or by appointment by calling the Winery at 805-928-9178 or Davis's cell at 805-452-7413.

Photo by Shelley Strazis

Artiste Impressionist Winery & Tasting Studio

3569 Sagunto St Studio 102

Santa Ynez

805-686-2626

Tasting Daily 11-5

How's that for a company name? Combining a reverence for tradition and a philosophy of winemaking as an artistic expression, Artiste wines are labeled with gorgeous works of impressionist art. Each of their wine blends is named after the title of the painting that graces its bottle.

Each year, Bion Rice artfully canvases a selection of vintages and varietals from exceptional winegrowers and winemakers throughout California. Comparable to an impressionist artist mixing colors on a palette, Bion fuses a balance of wines together to compose neo-classical blends he refers to as impressionist cuvees.

With each blend, Bion captures a sense of old world style with new world personality, handcrafting liquid works of art for your palate. Artiste's highly sought-after wines are limited productions of less than 300 cases each and are exclusively available through Artiste Tasting Studio, Artiste.com, and select restaurants.

The blends, with names such as *Rendezvous, First Dance, Kind of Blue* and *Impromptu,* sell in the $22 to $50 price range.

Also of interest, the tasting room/studio is filled with the impressionist works of the six artists whose works grace the Artiste labels; all for sale. Note especially the paintings by Christina LoCascio using wine, not paint, as the medium.

As you sip and stroll around their comfortable Tasting Studios in Old Historic Santa Ynez, you're encouraged to share your own impressions of the wines, the art and artisan foods. Salut!

From Hwy 101 in Buellton, exit Hwy 246 east towards Solvang. Drive through Solvang and into Santa Ynez. Turn left on Edison, right onto Sagunto St. Artiste is 1/2 block down Sagunto on left.

Photo by Kirk Irwin

Au Bon Climat Winery

Solvang
805-688-7111
*Tasting Daily 11-8

Founded in 1982, Au Bon Climat (which means "a well-exposed vineyard") produces internationally-recognized Pinot Noir, Chardonnay, and Pinot Blanc wine from grapes grown in California's Santa Barbara County.

The winery is located on the world-famous Bien Nacido Vineyard, and is owned by winemaker Jim Clendenen. Au Bon Climat was listed on Robert Parker's Best Wineries of the World in both 1989 and 1990, while Jim Clendenen has been named Winemaker of the Year in 1992 by the Los Angeles Times, and Winemaker of the Year in 2001 by Food and Wine Magazine.

Clendenen graduated from the University of California, Santa Barbara, with High Honors in Pre-Law in 1976. It was during his "junior year abroad" in 1974, while turning 21 in France, that he discovered life beyond tacos. After graduation, a one month stay in both Burgundy and Champagne convinced him to attempt a career in wine rather than continue on to law school.

Beginning with the 1978 harvest, Jim was assistant winemaker at Zaca Mesa Winery for three vintages, a valued training experience. In 1981 his vision broadened with three harvests in one year as Jim worked crush and directed the harvest at wineries in Australia and France. In 1982, Clendenen decided, along with now ex-partner Adam Tolmach, to start his own winery in leased quarters.

In addition to the Pinot Noir, Chardonnay and Pinot Blanc that Au Bon Climat is famous for, they offer a number of other red and white varietals, including Barbera and a number of blends. Prices range from $12 to $150 for a Pinot Noir, *Larmes de Grappe* produced from grapes the likes of which Jim has never seen.

*Tasting in "Tastes of the Valley" 1672 Mission Dr in Downtown Solvang.

Babcock Winery & Vineyards

5175 E Highway 246

Lompoc

805-736-1455

Tasting Daily 10:30-4

One of California's brightest stars in the field of winemaking is Bryan Babcock. Not only was Bryan selected by the Los Angeles Times as one of the "Ten Best Winemakers of the Year", he was also named by this influential daily as "Most Courageous Winemaker of the Year" for his daring style. The prestigious James Beard Foundation chose Bryan as one of the "Top Ten Small Production Winemakers in the World," the only American chosen for this oenological dream team. In choosing Bryan for this award, David Moore wrote, "Bryan Babcock best exemplifies the traits I look for in a great winemaker.

Since 1984 Bryan has been producing wines of exceptional quality from his family owned winery located on the far western edge of the Santa Ynez Valley in northern Santa Barbara County.

Still family-owned and operated, Babcock Winery and Vineyards is an expanding 20,000-case winery with 80 acres currently planted to Chardonnay, Sauvignon Blanc, Pinot Grigio, Pinot Noir, and Syrah. Experimental varieties such as Albarino and Tempranillo from Spain, and Pignolo from Italy, are being evaluated.

Babcock wines feature cool climate, estate-grown fruit as well as grapes from select local vineyards. Highly intellectual and flavorful, each wine possesses distinctive characteristics. These unique qualities are further showcased in a "Terroir" program with multiple annual offerings of Pinot Noir, Chardonnay, Syrah and Cabernet Sauvignon labeled with specific vineyard block designations. Within a vintage, one varietal may have several different designations. Since 1996, they've also offered a popular Bordeaux blend called *Fathom*. Wines are generally priced $15-$50 per bottle.

From Hwy. 101 exit at the Solvang /Lompoc (Hwy. 246) exit and go west on Hwy. 246, toward Lompoc, about 9 miles on your right. Babcock shares a driveway with Melville Winery.

Beckmen Vineyards

2670 Ontiveros Rd

Los Olivos

805-688-8664

Tasting Daily 11-5

Planted in 1996, Tom and Judy Beckmen's 365-acre Purisima Mountain Vineyard was one of the most ambitious hillside vineyard endeavors in the history of Santa Barbara County. With high elevations, a unique microclimate and the same rare limestone subsoil as found in the great Rhone region, this vineyard is perfectly suited for producing outstanding Rhone varietal offerings. In addition to Purisima Mountain Vineyard, their original 40-acre Santa Ynez Valley Vineyard outside Los Olivos contributes to the wines of their respected estate program.

A small, estate winery, Beckmen Vineyards was founded on the belief that the making of superior wines requires hands-on craftsmanship. Conceived as a "palette of small vineyards," each cultivated area on Purisima Mountain is individually tended in accordance with its unique needs, balancing a passion for quality, with a respect for the land. Since 2006, Purisima Mountain Vineyard is 100% biodynamic. Simply put, biodynamic farming is an organic, chemical free and self-sustaining method of working the land, and continues their son Steve's vision of hands-on farming.

Beckmen produces a full line of excellent estate grown Rhone varietals including Syrah, Grenache, Grenache Blanc, Grenache Rose, Marsanne, and *Cuvee Le Bec* (a blend of Grenache, Mourvedre, Syrah and Counoise) that exemplify the capabilities of the region. They also produce small quantities of first-rate Cabernet Sauvignon and Sauvignon Blanc made from smaller vineyard lots that are well suited to these varietals. Wines run $10-$48.

Take Hwy 101 to Buellton and exit on Hwy 246 towards Solvang. Past Solvang, Hwy 246 ends at Hwy 154. Turn left on Hwy 154 and drive north to Roblar. Turn left on Roblar and as it curves to the right, continue straight onto Ontiveros. Follow the signs into the winery.

Bedford Thompson Winery

448 Bell St

Los Alamos

805-344-2107

Tasting Daily 11-5

After receiving a Bachelor of Science degree from UCLA in food science in 1977, Stephan Bedford began his wine career in Santa Cruz working in an agricultural research lab which led to the cellars of Ridge Vineyards. Then came a two year stint as an oenologist for Felton-Empire Vineyards. His first position as winemaker was in 1982 at Mt. Eden Vineyards and then in 1985 Stephan became winemaker at Rancho Sisquoc Winery, serving there for 11 years. Not only did the wines receive high acclaim, he was named Winemaker of the Year by the Central Coast Winegrowers Association.

Stephan began consulting for other wineries including Beckmen Vineyards, Fess Parker Winery and Foxen Vineyard. In 1996, as Winemaker, General Manager and Vice President of Foley Estates and Lincourt Vineyards, Stephan took on the monumental task of guiding the transition of two existing Santa Barbara County wineries, each with a 15,000 case capacity and under the same new ownership, and restructuring them under one umbrella.

Stephan struck out on his own in 1994 forming a partnership with David Thompson to establish Bedford Thompson Winery & Vineyard. David grew the grapes from his exceptional vineyard located in the hills of the Los Alamos Valley, and Stephan made them into wine. The Syrah was an instant hit and has become the signature wine for Bedford Thompson. In July of 2003, Stephan Bedford became sole proprietor.

Now, with his own label, he's offering Chardonnay, a dry Gewürztraminer, Pinot Gris, Mourvedre, Syrah, Grenache, Cabernet Franc and Petite Syrah. All priced from $13 to $45.

Tasting room located in downtown Los Alamos.

Photo Copyright 2002 Diana Healey

Benjamin Silver Wines

Los Olivos

*Tasting Daily 11-5

Who would have guessed that a kid from Amherst, Mass., with a B.S. degree in Animal Sciences (Pre-Veterinary) and a B.A. degree in Italian from the University of Massachusetts, would end up in Santa Barbara as an up-and-coming winemaker? Benjamin Silver did just that after catching the wine bug in 1993 at a summer job at Chicama Vineyards on Martha's Vineyard.

After graduating from college in 1994, Benjamin used his science background to land a harvest-intern Lab Technician position with winemaker Daniel Gehrs at Zaca Mesa Winery. After harvest, the winery offered him a full-time position as Lab Supervisor. "Dan took me under his wing as an apprentice winemaker and nurtured my passion for viticulture and winemaking" explained Benjamin. Upon Gehrs' departure in 1998, Benjamin took over Zaca Mesa's winemaking helm.

Benjamin also began to experiment with small quantities of Zinfandel, Sauvignon Blanc, Cabernet Franc, and Nebbiolo. This experimentation laid the foundation for the eventual formation of his Silver label. He left Zaca Mesa in 2000 to pursue the development of his own label, while also taking over as winemaker for White Hawk Vineyard.

Benjamin Silver Wines currently produces extremely small bottlings of Pinot Noir, Cabernet Franc, Cabernet Sauvignon, Viognier, Mourvedre, Syrah, Nebbiolo and Sangiovese from Santa Barbara County. Prices are $20-$45 per bottle.

Tasting at "Wine Country" 2445 Alamo Pintado in downtown Los Olivos.

Photo by John Fitzpatrick

Bernat Winery

7879 Grand Ave

Los Olivos

888-WINES4U

Tasting Daily 11-5

With a passion for bicycling, the owner, Samuel Marmorstein, had cycled through the Santa Ynez Valley on numerous occasions. "I was always amazed at the beauty, serenity and peace that prevails here," Sam reveals, "I decided that to own land, plant grapes and create wines crafted by hand, made more sense to me than life in the big city."

In 1995, Sam Marmorstein purchased 10 prime acres in Los Olivos, California, and began planting Chardonnay and Syrah grapes. Bernat Vineyard and Winery was born (and named after his father).

The owl on the wine label's logo honors the owls that protect and watch over his namesake vineyard in the Santa Ynez Valley.

In 1999, Bernat Winery, the smallest licensed producer, debuted its first estate-grown Chardonnay wine - 24 cases. The first harvest sold out in two months. After that success, Sam continues to use "old-world" methods of hand pruning, hand harvesting, and minimal processing of Chardonnay and Syrah grapes in making wine. Retail prices are $22.50-$30.

In late 1995, when a former deli in downtown Los Olivos was for sale, Sam seized the opportunity and created The Los Olivos Café. When the retail space adjoining the Café became available in 2001, Sam expanded his successful restaurant by opening the Wine Merchant - a completion of his original vision to have a "one-stop source for great wine and food in Santa Barbara County."

The Wine Merchant now features over 300 local and international vintages and is the exclusive distributor of Bernat Wines. Also included is the tasting bar, presenting a selection of local and international wines by the glass – and always featuring Bernat.

Located in Downtown Los Olivos.

Blackjack Ranch Vineyards & Winery

2205 Alamo Pintado Rd

Solvang

805-686-4492

Tasting Th-Mon 11-5

Proprietor Roger Wisted offers this history to explain his passion; "Blackjack Ranch is the product of 30 years of imagination and preparation. At the age of 14, I began studying the wines and winemaking of France and California. Two years later, I was fermenting small batches of wine in the produce section of my parent's grocery store. By 17, I was collecting the wines of Bordeaux and Burgundy. In 1990, I invented and introduced a casino card game called "California Blackjack" in Los Angeles. The standard game of "21" was outlawed in California in 1873, but my game was different in that two aces was a "Natural" and technically that made the game "22", not "21". The vineyard was planted in 1996 and is named in honor of the game."

It is Wisted's goal to produce wines at Blackjack Ranch that will be both pleasurable and memorable. The Ranch is planted with Syrah, Merlot, Cabernet Franc, and Chardonnay. The topography ranges from level to treacherously steep rolling hillsides with blocks such as Billy Goat Hill, Suicide Hill, and Hamburger's Hill (named after a Black Angus with which that hill is shared). Blackjack Ranch began production in 1997.

Today, Blackjack Ranch takes pride in offering Pinot Noir, Merlot, Syrah, and Cabernet Franc, as well as *Harmonie* (their Bordeaux blend) and Chardonnay. Bottles run $18-$75 each.

The tasting room is California Rustic, having been constructed from materials salvaged from the buildings which previously existed on Blackjack Ranch. The original bar was built from one of the bowling alley lanes salvaged from the old Solvang Bowling Alley.

From the intersection of Hwy 101 and 246 in Buellton, go east toward Solvang. Proceed through Solvang to the stoplight intersection of 246 and Alamo Pintado Rd. Go left (north) proceed four miles and the Winery will be on your left.

Brander Vineyard

2401 Refugio Rd

Los Olivos

805-688-2455

Tasting Daily 11-4

Summer Hours 10-5

C. Frederic "Fred" Brander, owner and winemaker, was born in Buenos Aires. At a young age he moved with his family and settled in Santa Barbara. Fred graduated from Harvey Mudd College with a degree in Chemistry, and then went on to pursue studies in Enology at UC Davis. While attending college, he started his own wine import company, focusing on wines from France and Argentina.

Wishing to make his own wines, Fred and his family established The Brander Vineyard in the Santa Ynez Valley in 1975. The initial planting was mainly Bordeaux grape varietals and in 1977, the first Sauvignon Blanc grapes were taken to a neighboring winery where Brander produced a wine so distinctive it captured Santa Barbara County's first gold medal for a wine at a major wine competition.

Since its inception, the Brander Vineyard has been highly acclaimed as a top Sauvignon Blanc producer, and for many years the only wine was an estate-bottled Sauvignon Blanc. Today, the focus is still Sauvignon Blanc, with one main bottling and three distinctively different reserve wines. Two of these are named for the next Brander generation: *Cuvée Natalie* and *Cuvée Nicolas*; the third Sauvignon Blanc is the multiple award-winning *au Naturel*.

A small quantity of red wine is also produced from estate grapes, featuring the classic Bordeaux varietals (Cabernet Sauvignon, Merlot and Cabernet Franc). As well as single varietal bottlings, extremely small amounts of *Bouchet* (a Bordeaux blend) and Reserve Cabernet Sauvignon are offered. Another label, Domaine Santa Barbara was established in 1995 as a premier producer of Santa Barbara County Burgundian wines, with a focus on Chardonnay. Prices are $14-$50.

Take Hwy 101 to Buellton and exit on Hwy 246 towards Solvang. Past Solvang, Hwy 246 ends at Hwy 154. Turn left on Hwy 154 and drive north to Roblar. Turn right on Roblar and at the split turn left and drive 1/4 mile to the winery gates on the left.

Bridlewood Estate Winery

3555 Roblar Ave

Los Olivos

805-688-9000

Tasting Daily 10-5

Turn in through the gate, up the tree-lined drive, and the first thing you see is Syrah – vines rolling uphill to the broad green yard. Bridlewood's winemaker, David Hopkins, says this is a place uniquely suited to Syrah; south-facing, limestone cobbles the size of baseballs, and the cool wind coming up through the hills.

Paddocks and barns beyond the visitor's center reveal that Bridlewood itself is a working horse farm, as well as a winery. A place once famous for thoroughbred horses, now producing thoroughbred wines.

In the tasting room, you can enjoy a glass of Viognier, or try one of the limited production Syrahs like the rustic *Dusty Trails* or the distinctive red Rhone blend *Arabesque*. Bridlewood Estate Winery creates distinctive wines that are approachable, well balanced, and filled with flavor - principally Syrah and Viognier, because they respond well to the art of winemaking and to conditions in the vineyards of the Central Coast. They also make small quantities of other varietals that can be found exclusively in their tasting room, like Pinot Noir, Roussanne and Estate Zinfandel. Prices vary from $15-$40. But a little known fact – Bridlewood occasionally sells selected wine at a discount in the tasting room.

Their well-informed staff offers special tastings every month – different "flights" of several glasses each that showcase the style and variety of Bridlewood wines. And while there, visitors can tour the estate in a horse-drawn carriage, picnic beside the courtyard fountain or simply sip a glass of wine in the deep shade of the veranda.

From Hwy 101 north of Buellton, exit at Hwy 154, and just past Los Olivos, turn left on Roblar Ave. At the split, turn right, remaining on Roblar and drive 1/2 mile to the gates on the left.

Brophy Clark Cellars

Los Olivos or Nipomo
*Tasting Daily 11-5:30
Or at the Winery By Appt

Brophy Clark Cellars is a unique partnership that combines the talents of wine-maker, John Clark with the viticulture expertise of his wife, Kelley Brophy Clark.

John got his start in the wine industry in 1985 when he was hired as a cellar worker at Corbett Canyon Vineyards in the Edna Valley. Within two years, he was promoted to winemaker and was eventually named vice-president of winemaking. John managed all aspects of production as it grew from 150,000 cases to two million.

Today John's role at the Wine Group, Corbett Canyon's parent company, has shifted to that of Vice President of Premium Wines.

In 1988, after serving as technical advisor and viticulturist for a prominent Santa Maria Valley vineyard management firm, Kelley founded her own business, Coastal Vineyard Consulting, which specializes in pest management and viticultural consulting. She covers more than 2,000 acres and consults for many of the region's preeminent vineyards.

Fulfilling a long-time dream to work together making their own wine, John and Kelley founded Brophy Clark Cellars in 1996.

Kelley's mother also plays a role in the family business. As an accomplished watercolor artist, Mary Campista painted the beautiful landscapes that grace the Brophy Clark bottles. The Sauvignon Blanc label is a scene from Oso Flaco, a pristine area of the Nipomo Dunes known for its rare birds and wildlife. The red wine label for Pinot Noir, Syrah and Zinfandel is a watercolor of Montaña de Oro, a beautiful, yet rugged stretch of the San Luis Obispo County coastline. Wines run $13-$26 per bottle.

*Tasting at "The Los Olivos Tasting Room" 2905 Grand Ave. Los Olivos. Or, you can call 805-929-4830 for an appointment and directions to taste at the winery.

Buttonwood Farm Winery & Vineyard

1500 Alamo Pintado Rd

Solvang

805-688-3032

Tasting Daily 11-5

Buttonwood Farm Winery is a small gem set amidst the splendor of Santa Barbara County's Santa Ynez Valley. Their 39-acre vineyard stretches across a sun-drenched mesa on the eastern portion of a 106-acre property. They started planting in 1983 and now have 33,000 vines, small in the world of wine, but huge to them.

Buttonwood's varietal mix of Sauvignon Blanc, Semillon, Marsanne, Merlot, Cabernet Sauvignon, Cabernet Franc, and Syrah reflects the preferences of owners Betty Williams and her son-in-law, Bret Davenport, for Bordeaux and Rhone style wines. As they expected, those varietals grow perfectly in their warm, eastern Santa Ynez Valley location. Wines sell for $14-$30 per bottle

But it's one thing to grow outstanding fruit and quite another to make excellent wine. That's where winemaker Michael Brown's expertise comes in. Educated in his native Australia as well as at UC Davis, Mike spent six years gaining experience at wineries throughout Santa Barbara County. By the time he arrived at Buttonwood he knew how to translate the quality of their fruit into remarkable wine; wine meant to be consumed with food; wine with aging potential.

The winery was completed in time for the crush of 1989. They now produce 8,000 cases of wine a year and quite frankly, have a great time doing it. How could they not, given spectacular surroundings and the congenial winemaking atmosphere of Santa Barbara County? The satisfaction of what they do spills over to the tasting room where laughter and lively conversation abound.

Take Hwy. 101 to Buellton, go east on Hwy.246 to Alamo Pintado Rd. Go north on Alamo Pintado to Buttonwood Farm.

Byron Vineyard & Winery

5250 Tepusquet Rd

Santa Maria

805-934-4770

Tasting By Appt

Byron Vineyard and Winery was founded in 1984 by Ken Brown. With years of experience as a winemaker in Santa Barbara County, Ken recognized the region's potential for great wines in the Burgundian style, and was the first winemaker to introduce Rhone-style grape varieties to the area. The first crush at Byron produced 7,600 cases, and they soon gained national recognition for high quality Pinot Noir and Chardonnay.

In 1990, the Robert Mondavi family purchased Byron, and Brown became Winemaker and General Manager. Today, Byron is owned by the Legacy Estate Group, who also own Freemark Abbey Winery in St. Helena and Arrowood in Sonoma Valley

In March 2001, Jonathan Nagy joined Byron Vineyards as assistant wine-maker, where he trained with winery founder Ken Brown and was promoted by Ken to winemaker in the spring of 2003. According to Ken, "Jonathan has a great wine knowledge and savvy instincts. At only 31 years of age, he has one of the best palates I've ever tasted with and I am confident that he will continue to produce world-class wines."

Byron produces three wines under their label. In addition to the Chardonnay and Pinot Noir, they've become known for their Pinot Blanc. *Io* was introduced as a separate label in 1999 with the release of the 1996 vintage. The result of more than a decade of experimentation, *Io* is a Rhone-inspired blend of Syrah, Grenache and Mourvedre from Santa Barbara County. Byron has now added a number of vineyard-designated Syrahs to their portfolio. Prices range from $24 to $55.

From Hwy 101 in Santa Maria, take the Betteravia Rd exit and head east for about 6 miles. There will be a left fork onto Santa Maria Mesa Rd – take it for about 5 miles and bear left onto Tepusquet Rd. Byron is 1/2 mile up the road on the right.

Calzada Ridge

Ballard

*Tasting Fri-Sun 12-4

Calzada Ridge is a pristine gem situated on a ridge in the southeastern section of the Santa Ynez Valley AVA. It is dedicated soley to the Rhone varietal, Viognier, and produces less than 100 cases of this hand crafted wine from this single, exceptional vineyard.

Richard & Pamela Harris moved to Santa Ynez in 1996 to escape a lifetime in the motion picture industry. Richard has garnered numerous accolades and awards for his many and varied projects from an Emmy award for the critically acclaimed "Indictment, The McMartin Trial" to an Academy Award for Film Editing the blockbuster film "Titanic." Pamela was the Associate Producer on "Titanic" and was nominated for an Oscar herself for producing the visual effects in the movie "Cliffhanger."

The same painstaking, loving detail they brought to their craft has been transferred to the winemaking venture on Calzada Ridge. Upon seeing the perfectly situated, slightly hilly, rocky soiled site, it was Richard's dream to create a wine he and Pamela would love to drink themselves. With these high standards always in mind, he personally tends the vineyard and oversees all aspects of its operation. Everything is done by hand, from the pruning to the leafing to the harvest. No pesticides or other chemicals are used on the vines.

Richard sometimes refers to this venture as a "hobby gone awry" but clearly the pride he takes in the recognition Calzada Ridge Viognier has received is every bit as fulfilling as hearing his name called at the Academy Awards. His single bottling sells for $30.

Tasting at "Ballard Inn Tasting Room" 2436 Baseline Ave, Ballard.

Carhartt Vineyard

2990A Grand Ave

Los Olivos

805-688-0685

Tasting Th-Sun 11-5

The Carhartt Vineyard and Winery is located on the historic Rancho Santa Ynez, where Mike Carhartt's family has raised cattle, horses and feed since the early 1900's. Wanting to continue the tradition of working the land, the Carhartts planted a vineyard in 1995. The ten acre plot sits high on a mesa overlooking the barns and ranch house, and is well suited for warmer climate grapes such as Syrah and Merlot.

Although they originally intended to only sell the grapes to local wineries, Brooke and Mike decided to vinify small amounts of their grapes for their own label and produced two barrels of wine in 1998. Production has grown since then, although quantities are still extremely limited. Each bottle of the Carhartt Syrah and Merlot is adorned with a version of the family's heart-shaped cattle brand.

The Carhartt winemaking philosophy echoes that of their farming practices – hands-on, handmade and an acute attention to detail. All of the wines are crafted in a converted barn on the ranch. This close proximity of the winery to the vineyard ensures that the fruit is in its ultimate condition for processing. The wines are not filtered or fined.

Two red wines are produced from the estate Carhartt Vineyard: a Merlot and a Syrah; in addition, a very small amount of *Chase the Blues Away Rosé* is produced. From neighboring vineyards they've added a Sauvignon Blanc and a Pinot Noir. Their wines sell from $19 to $30 per bottle.

And so, Rancho Santa Ynez and the Carhartt traditions continue and evolve – still a family business and still devoted to the land.

Tasting room in downtown Los Olivos, one block north of the flagpole in the smallest building in town.

Carina Cellars

2900 Grand Ave "A"

Los Olivos

805-688-2459

Tasting Daily 11-5

Carina Cellars is the result of an avid wine collector with a dream who meets an accomplished winemaker with a vision. When attorney and businessman David Hardee and winemaker Joey Tensley met in 2002, they were quick to recognize the benefits of combining their passion. With Hardee's talent for business, Tensley's talent for wine making, and a shared belief in only the best, Carina Cellars was born.

Not having vineyards of their own makes it imperative to source grapes from growers who are as dedicated to their vines as David and Joey are to their wines. Carina looks for vineyards that represent the terroir of the Santa Ynez and Santa Maria growing regions and which will produce wines on which they are proud to place the Carina Cellars label. Each bottle proudly bears the name of the vineyard as a show of respect to the growers.

Santa Barbara County vineyards produce some of the most intriguing and intense Rhône grapes possible, from which Carina is able to produce spicy Syrah, earthy Mourvedre and fruit-laden Grenache. They are also very fortunate to be able to obtain Cabernet Sauvignon grapes from a premier Napa Valley vineyard. These grapes become an integral part of the *Iconoclast* blend as well as a black-curranty Cabernet Sauvignon. They also offer a Viognier or two each vintage. In general, wines sell at $22-$70 per bottle.

The winery is located a few miles from the tasting room - in Buellton, and tours and tastings at the winery itself are available by appointment. And between their tasting room and the winery are many other wineries, restaurants, historical points of interest, recreational opportunities and just plain beautiful scenery.

Located in downtown Los Olivos.

Carr Vineyards and Winery

414 N Salsipuedes St

Santa Barbara

805-965-7985

Tasting Daily 11-5

After graduating from the University of Arizona as a graphics design major, Ryan Carr moved to Santa Ynez to pursue a career in winemaking. In 1998, Ryan had the opportunity to work in the Central Coast Winery making wine for Stolpman Vineyards. After learning the trade, he produced his own first vintage in 1999. The vintage, made in his garage, was a whopping 10 cases and was given to friends and family. After making such a great wine from grapes he had grown, Ryan felt this was the only way winemaking should be done. Working as assistant winemaker at Kahn Winery, he was able to produce his first commercial bottling under his own label. That vintage sold out before he was able to produce the next.

Carr Vineyards & Winery is a small hand-crafted winery located in downtown Santa Barbara. The winery and tasting room are housed in a 1940's World War II Quonset hut with a faux cave interior reminiscent of the underground caves in Burgundy.

The winery currently produces 2000 cases with plans to expand to 4500 cases. All of the wines produced at Carr Winery are sourced from Santa Barbara County vineyards directly managed by Ryan Carr. The focus of the winery lies with Pinot Noir grown in the Santa Rita Hills Appellation. This region has been recognized for producing some of the finest Pinot Noirs in the world. Although the focus is on Pinot Noir, the vast microclimates of Santa Barbara County allow the winery to produce several other great wines.

Today Carr Winery offers Pinot Gris, Pinot Noir, Syrah and Cabernet Franc, all in the $18-$40 price range.

From Hwy 101, exit at Milpas Rd and go north (away from the beach). Turn left on E Gutierrez St and right on N Salsipuedes St. Winery on the right.

Casa Cassara Winery & Vineyard

Hwy 246 West & 291 Valley Station Rd

Buellton

805-688-8691

Tasting Wed-Mon 10-5:30

When Bennie Cassara first set foot on his mountain top retreat he knew this was the place where he and his family could get away from the daily grind. That was April of 1981; in the following years the family utilized the property located just three hours north of their home in Long Beach as a weekend retreat.

Over the next few years Bennie brought up horses for his grandchildren, raised cattle, chickens and even a few goats. In 1990 the first vines were planted on the tiny hilltop estate. Bennie was told that his property would be the perfect growing environment for Pinot Noir grapes. It took several years and a great deal of work before the first grapes were ready for market. The first wine produced from the vineyard was actually made in 1995; John Krska made the equivalent of about one gallon of wine. Bennie, John and Dan Cassara tasted the fruits of the harvest. Brian knew then that a world class Pinot Noir could be produced from the grapes in this vineyard.

In 1998 John Krska came to work for Casa Cassara Winery and made a commitment to produce the very best grapes this small hilltop vineyard was capable of producing. Now, John serves as General Manager and shares winemaking with Brian Freeborn, whose experience includes stints at Fess Parker, Bridlewood, Lucas & Lewellen and Kahn. At Bridlewood and Lucas & Lewellen, Brian had the opportunity to work with consulting winemaker Dan Gehrs.

The 2000 Pinot Noir production run was their first. Over the past few years, Syrah, Merlot, Riesling, Chardonnay and Sauvignon Blanc have been added. Prices are in the $14-$34 range.

From Hwy 101 in Buellton, take the Hwy 246 exit west towards Lompoc to the Valley Station Rd intersection (just past the Fire Station). Winery on the left.

Cold Heaven Cellars

448-B Bell St

Los Alamos

805-344-3640

Tasting Fri-Sun 11-5

"My mission as a winemaker is to illuminate and define Viognier, to elevate its profile and explore its potential through keen observation and copious tasting. I seek to sound the depths of this enigmatic grape, to reveal its secrets and shine a bright light on the extraordinary fruit grown in the cool vineyards of the Santa Maria and Santa Ynez Valleys of California's Central Coast," says Morgan Clendenen, owner and winemaker at Cold Heaven Cellars.

After traveling yearly to the Condrieu region of France, numerous tastings of California Viogniers, and experimentation with different vineyards and micro-climates, Clendenen believes that Viognier which maintains a natural acidity is the best expression of the grape.

Cold Heaven's definitive style is fresh, bright, and delicious, alone or with food. Cold Heaven wines develop nicely in bottle, some drinking fresh up to 5 years, atypical of most California Viogniers.

In 2006, she released *Deux C*, an international blend made up of Sanford & Benedict vineyard fruit from Santa Barbara County, combined in equal parts with legendary winemaker Yves Cuilleron's French grapes from the Northern Rhône appellation of Condrieu.

Finally, for those rare times when a Viognier just won't do, Cold Heaven offers a Pinot Noir from the Clendenen family's own Le Bon Climat Vineyard in the Santa Maria Valley and a Syrah she calls *Second Sin*. Cold Heaven wines sell in the $20-$50 range. Along with Cold Heaven, she offers wines from the Clendenen Family Vineyards at Heaven & Earth in Los Alamos.

Tasting room located in Los Alamos at the "Heaven and Earth Gift Shop," just off Hwy 101.

Consilience Wine

2933 Grand Ave

Los Olivos

805-691-1020

Tasting Daily 11-5

Consilience was founded in 1999 when after years of planning the aspirations of two couples became a small reality. There of course is a long story, but the short of it began when winemaker Brett Escalera, his wife Monica, and Tom and Jodie Daughters all met back in 1990 with many common values and interests. Wine and the lifestyle surrounding it were of particular interest, and after years of planning, education and good old fashioned perseverance, Consilience started with a small production of 1997 Syrah from Santa Barbara County.

Production has grown, but Consilience remains a small producer of premium wines loosely focused around the typical Rhone varietals. It all starts with the grapes, and they've been fortunate to establish relationships with some of the best vineyards and growers around Santa Barbara County, from whom they purchase most of their fruit. This has been pivotal in their quest to reliably produce the big, intense wines that have defined their style.

The wines are all crafted in small enough production to allow careful hand-crafting with attention to capturing the grape's identity and maintaining a very high quality from wine to wine. While loosely focused on Syrah and other Rhone varietals, they also produce other wines such as Viognier, Roussanne, Genache Blanc, Pinot Noir and Petite Sirah out of genuine interest, and will add others as the very best fruit becomes available. Prices are in the $16-$36 range.

With all the wines, they work to capture a sense of elegance and finesse, but you won't find a weak-kneed wine in the list.

With an eye towards producing carefully nurtured, bold, and exciting wines that the common man can actually afford, they don't have a chateau for people to visit, or pay for. They do however, have a humble tasting room in the quaint little town of Los Olivos.

Located in downtown Los Olivos.

CORE Wine

Los Olivos

805-714-5057

*Tasting Daily 11-5

Or By Appt

Dave Corey is the owner of Vital Vines, a viticultural company that provides technical support for vineyard property owners, vineyard managers and winemaking personnel in the promotion of sustainable agriculture.

With a major commitment and a second mortgage, Dave cut down on some of his vineyard consulting work to focus on winemaking for CORE, the hands-on management of Alta Mesa Vineyard and facilitating the wine sales.

Becky Corey began her interest in the wine industry while still attending high school in Temecula, California. She worked in the Culinary Department at Callaway Winery in addition to regular events for a local caterer specializing in winery functions.

She was one of the first students to participate in the Cal Poly Wine Marketing Certificate program. Currently, she operates a consulting business that specializes in winery hospitality and visitor programs and also works with Dave to promote CORE wines.

CORE is known for Rose, Saroyan Grenache, a number of blends including a red *Blend 163, Hard Core, Elevation Sensation - Alta Mesa Vineyard, Mister Moreved, and Candy Core*. Prices range from $14 to $38 per bottle

Tasting occasionally in "Wine Country" at 2445 Alamo Pintado in Los Olivos or by appointment by calling the winery at the phone above.

Costa de Oro Winery

Hwy 101 @ Stowell Rd

Santa Maria

805-928-2727

Tasting Daily 11-6

Gold Coast Farms was founded by Ron Burk and Robert Espinola. They struck up a friendship and began growing greenhouse tomatoes, and kiwis on the weekend. Their weekend hobby soon turned to a thriving business when they founded Gold Coast Farms in 1978.

Out of a passion for farming, Ron and Bob have "grown" their business to include a variety of crops. Their decision to grow grapes appeared to be fate. On a bluff at Fuglar's Point, where the soil proved to be poor for vegetable growth, they decided to try wine grapes. The well drained, sandy loam soil, although difficult for vegetables, was perfect for Chardonnay and Pinot Noir grapes.

Today, 19 acres of Pinot Noir and 11 acres of Chardonnay cover this beautiful and unique landscape of the Santa Maria Valley.

Enter Ron's son Gary, who was living in LA and pursuing a career in music. In 1993 on a visit home to Santa Maria, Gary was fortunate enough to share a dinner with Au Bon Climat's Jim Clendenen and Dominique Lafon of Domaine des Comtes Lafon. After that evening, Gary was hooked ... funny what a great glass of Meursault will do! In 1994 he was invited to work harvest at the Au Bon Climat/Qupe facility and was hired full time in 1995. He worked in production and marketing for ABC/Qupe until August of 2002 when he left to devote all of his time and energy to Costa De Oro.

Costa de Oro offers Sauvignon Blanc, Estate Chardonnay, Reserve Chardonnay, Estate Pinot Noir, Reserve Pinot Noir, Cabernet Sauvignon, Syrah and a Tempranillo dessert wine, all in the $14 to $50 price range.

The tasting room is unique in that they sell their "estate-grown" produce (strawberries, sweet corn, etc) so there's a virtual farmer's market every day.

Located at the Stowell Rd exit off Hwy 101 in Santa Maria.

Cottonwood Canyon Vineyard & Winery

3940 Dominion Rd

Santa Maria

805-937-8463

Tasting Daily 10-5:30

Cottonwood Canyon Vineyard & Winery is a small ultra-premium winery specializing in Estate Chardonnay and Pinot Noir. Founded in 1988 by the Beko family, Cottonwood Canyon joins traditional Burgundian wine-making practices with American ingenuity to produce age-worthy and memorable wines.

Their season usually begins with bud-break in mid-February and ends with the mid-October harvest. This long, very cool growing season results in a high skin to liquid ratio, creating very high acid levels in the fruit. This, in combination with their "hands off" wine-making philosophy, results in a very age worthy wine program unique to Cottonwood and most French Burgundies. However, Cottonwood has climatic advantage over Burgundy. With moderate temperatures throughout the growing season, they're able to achieve higher sugar levels while maintaining the naturally high acidity so critical to long-lived wine.

The estate is currently planted to 18 acres of Pinot Noir and fewer than 18 acres of Chardonnay. They planted 5 acres of Syrah a few years ago and have added that to their offerings. Wines sell for $20-$48.

A unique feature of Cottonwood is their cave. The 2000 square foot cave was dug in 1995-96 and maintains a constant 62° temperature with 95% humidity; perfect for storing wine. Cottonwood offers tours of the cave on Sat. and Sun. at 11am, 1pm and 3pm – except when it's raining. Midweek tours can sometimes be arrange by advance appointment.

From Hwy 101 take Betteravia Rd exit. Turn east and drive approximately 3 miles. Turn right onto Dominion (look for their sign). Drive approximately 1.5 miles. Winery entrance is on the left.

Curran Wines

1557 Mission Dr

Solvang

805-688-2100

Tasting Wed-Mon 11-5

Shortly after graduating from Fresno State with a degree in winemaking, Kris Curran became the assistant winemaker at Cambria Winery in Santa Maria. This experience led to an offer to be the winemaker and general manager for Koehler Winery, located in Los Olivos. In addition to crafting Koehler's first vintage of both red and white wines, Kris was responsible for overseeing the winery's development from its inception.

In 2000, Kris was tapped by Sea Smoke Cellars to set up their winery and head the winemaking team. At Sea Smoke she focuses solely on Pinot Noir produced from their estate grown vineyards in the Santa Rita Hills appelation. Sea Smoke's first vintage was in 2001 and, although a fledgling winery, they have already received much acclaim.

Kris' own label, Curran, was started in 1997. In 1999 she rejected the Pinot Noir fruit she received, from a new vineyard, due to lack of ripeness and had to reexamine her philosophy for the label 'Curran'. Deciding that great Pinot Noir was difficult to come by, unless you owned and managed the vineyards (a luxury she experiences with the Sea Smoke team), Kris decided to seek out small producers of other varietals who were willing to work closely with her to ensure the optimum ripeness and integrity of the grapes. Currently, Kris is producing Syrah, Sangiovese and Grenache Blanc; all of which are locally sourced from premium, selected vineyards in the eastern end of the Santa Ynez Valley. Prices range from $22 to $45 per bottle.

Kris feels she has the best of both worlds; "I work with some great Pinot from the Santa Rita Hills AVA (Sea Smoke) and am able to round out my portfolio with some very interesting varietals that prefer the warmer environment found on the east end of the Santa Ynez Valley."

Located in Downtown Solvang.

Curtis Winery

5249 Foxen Canyon Rd

Los Olivos

805-686-8999

Tasting Daily 10-5

Under the guidance of Winemaker Chuck Carlson, Curtis Winery is exclusively committed to the crafting of Rhône-style wines. They are inspired by the extraordinary terrain of Santa Barbara County's Santa Ynez Valley, which is today recognized as one of the world's leading appellations for Rhône varietals. Since 1995, Curtis Winery has built a reputation for wines of quality and distinction, with an emphasis on the authentic expression of vineyard and vintage.

Their wines hail primarily from their estate vineyards with contributions from select local vineyards. The Ambassador's Vineyard was planted in 1990 as the cornerstone of the estate. Crossroads Vineyard followed in 1997, and is today recognized for producing one of the region's most acclaimed Syrahs. Small blocks of Grenache and Roussanne are also integral to their estate program.

Carlson's focus on Rhône-style wines is expressed in the following three tiers: vineyard-specific Syrahs, then Viognier, Roussanne, Grenache and Mourvedre from estate and select local vineyards and finally their *Heritage Cuvée, Heritage Blanc* and *Heritage Rosé* offering unique, flavorful cuvées for everyday enjoyment. Wines are in the $14-$32 range.

Part of the Firestone family, there are savings in tasting and purchase offered between Curtis and Firestone Wineries. If you enjoy the wines, ask for details.

From Hwy 101 take the Zaca Station Road/Highway 154 exit located seven miles north of Buellton. Head east at the stop sign. The road dips and curves southward. Take an immediate left onto Zaca Station Road and continue for 2.5 miles: Curtis Winery is located on your left, 1/4 mile past Firestone Vineyard.

Photo by Bob Dickey

Daniel Gehrs Wines

2939 Grand Ave

Los Olivos

800-275-8138

Tasting Daily 11-5

Daniel Gehrs became a "wine enthusiast" during his college years in the Northwest during the early '70's. He made small lots of wine for himself and his friends, not all of it grape, not all of it good. But for parties it was something besides beer and some of it wasn't even too bad!

He also started appreciating traditional wine and after going through the Boone's Farm-Rhine Castle-Mateus-Lancer's stage got to liking things like Almaden Mountain Claret or Burgundy. On a "starving student's" budget, you can't be much more choosy than that.

In 1974, he joined Paul Masson. While at Masson he and his wife Robin discovered an overgrown, mostly abandoned old mountain vineyard that was to become their first big venture - Congress Springs. They were at Congress Springs Vineyards in the Santa Cruz Mountains from 1974 to 1990. When they left CSV in the spring of 1990 they founded Daniel Gehrs Wines.

In January of 1993 they made a momentous change when he accepted the position of winemaker at Zaca Mesa Winery with the understanding that he could bring the Daniel Gehrs brand with him and continue producing it on a limited scale at Zaca Mesa. While there, Gehrs really established his reputation as a wine-maker, producing, among other fine wines, a Syrah that went all the way to Wine Spectator's #6 in the top 100 wines of the year for 1995.

Completely on his own now, he's producing Chenin Blanc, Chardonnay, Pinot Noir and Syrah. He also offers extremely limited quantities of Viognier, Merlot, Zinfandel and Cabernet Sauvignon. Under the Gehrs label and two other labels for his family of wines – Vixen and Oasis – retail pricing is in the $12-$45 range.

Tasting room located in Downtown Los Olivos.

Dierberg Family of Wines

2445 Alamo Pintado

Los Olivos

805-693-0744

*Tasting Daily 11-5

Jim and Mary Dierberg restored an old winery building in Hermann, Missouri some thirty years ago and founded Hermannhof Winery. Hermannhof has become one of the best known wineries in the Hermann, Missouri appellation and produces a variety of American and French hybrid varietal still and sparkling wines.

Jim and Mary's love of Cabernet Sauvignon ultimately led them to California. The ten year search for a world class vineyard site took them to all corners of the state. The breathtaking visual aspects of Star Lane Ranch and the potential for growing Bordeaux varietals convinced Jim and Mary that the eastern end of Santa Ynez Valley was the right place to grow premium grapes. They acquired two additional properties with near perfect microclimates for growing Burgundian grapes. The Santa Maria Valley property is currently producing exceptional Chardonnay and Pinot Noir and the Santa Rita Hills Vineyard is being developed.

Dierberg Estate Wines are dedicated to offering premium, distinctive Pinot Noir and Chardonnay that reflects the unique personality of the vineyard. Wines run in the $40-$48 range.

Star Lane Estate Wines originate in the warmer, most eastern corner of the Santa Ynez Valley. They have dedicated production to premium wines made from classic Bordeaux varietals: Cabernet Sauvignon, Cabernet Franc, Merlot, Malbec and Petit Verdot. Prices run $20-$35 per bottle.

Three Saints Wines are a vivid expression of carefully selected grapes from all three of the Dierberg Family's vineyards, offered at compelling value. Prices range $20-$26 per bottle.

*Located in Downtown Los Olivos at "Wine Country". Dierberg plans to open their own tasting room on Hwy 246 just west of Buellton in the summer of 2007. Call the number above for details.

East Valley Vineyard

Solvang or Santa Ynez

805-455-1412

*Tasting Wed-Mon 11-6

Or at the Winery By Appt

The Dascomb family purchased property in Santa Ynez Valley in 1974. Don Dascomb and his sons went to work planting the vineyard, primarily Cabernet Sauvignon, resulting in the birth of East Valley Vineyard. Over the years, the vineyard produced quality fruit which has been purchased by Babcock, Beckman, and Longoria.

In the late 1980s an unfavorable reputation developed regarding Cabernet Sauvignon wine produced out of the Central Coast—it was regarded as too "veggie." By the year 2000, due to market trends, most vineyards made the decision to change to other varietals. Not the Dascomb family. Don and his son, Dave, knew the climate and soil were right for this varietal. And Dave realized the key to making a premium Cabernet is to allow the fruit to fully mature – reach peak ripeness. As a result, East Valley owns and operates one of the oldest Cabernet vineyards in Santa Barbara County.

They are offering six varieties of red wines. The estate Cabernet Sauvignon is considered to be one of the best 'Cabs' in Santa Barbara County. Their Syrah, grown in Edna Valley near San Luis Obispo, comes from a perfect growing climate. In addition, they offer Pinot Noir, Sangiovese and two blends and well as a Vintage Port. Prices are $24-$37 per bottle.

East Valley Vineyard and Winery is well on their way to becoming Dave's vision. That is, a boutique winery producing premium wines - never too large to invite you out to their small vineyard, sit back and share their history, vision, and wine.

Tasting occasionally at "Cabana" 1539 Mission Dr 'C' in Solvang or by previous appointment at the winery by calling the number above and obtaining directions.

Epiphany Cellars

2963 Grand Ave

Los Olivos

805-686-2424

Tasting Th-Mon 11:30-5:30

Some people are fortunate enough to experience an event that serves to add direction and clarity in their life.

For Eli Parker, this event was his family's foray into the wine business in 1987, a move that would prove to be an important turning point in his professional life. Eli embarked on a journey which began with apprenticeships and associations with several critically acclaimed winemakers and, in the process, revealed his innate winemaking talent.

Winemaking has truly been an epiphany for Eli.

Epiphany is a winemaker's wine, one which satisfies Eli's passion for and fascination with winemaking. Crafting interesting wines of exquisite quality is the sole reason for the conception of Epiphany.

Epiphany's foundation is built upon the outstanding grapes harvested from the best vineyards throughout Santa Barbara County and beyond. In most cases the Epiphany wines are made with grapes from a single vineyard source in order to accentuate the unique characteristics and terroir of that vineyard. Other Epiphany wines blend grapes from multiple vineyards in order to marry different flavor nuances thereby adding depth and complexity to the final wine.

Eli produces Syrah, Petite Sirah, Grenache, Grenache Blanc, Rosé and two red blends – *Revelation* and *Gypsy*, along with Roussanne and Pinot Gris. Prices are in the $14-$35 range.

In 2006, Eli Parker was named Andre Tchelistcheff Winemaker of the Year by the San Francisco International Wine Competition. This competition is the largest and most prestigious wine competition in America. The 34 judges are made up of wine retailers, sommeliers, wine writers, beverage managers and other respected members of the wine business from all over the country.

Located in Downtown Los Olivos.

Falcone Family Vineyards

Solvang

*Tasting Daily 11-6

During the week, John and Helen Falcone are the husband and wife winemaking team at Rusack Vineyards. Along with their great day jobs, they have a passionate project – Falcone Family Vineyards.

Dating back to the mid-seventies, their dedication to the wine industry has culminated in planting their own small vineyard and producing their own brand.

Born into an Italian winemaking family, John started his wine odyssey at age 19, working for his uncle at The Monterey Vineyard. Prior to joining Rusack, John worked for many years in the Napa Valley, including a position as head wine-maker at Atlas Peak Vineyards. Helen Falcone also worked in the Napa wine industry holding the positions of assistant winemaker at Chimney Rock Winery and Codorniu Napa wineries.

During visits to John's family, they discovered the wonderful growing areas surrounding Paso Robles.

They've chosen to focus on two varietals at their family vineyard. They chose Cabernet Sauvignon because it is such a noble varietal that to not attempt to create a stellar Cab on the Central Coast would seem a missed opportunity that they didn't want to regret later in their careers. With Syrah, a varietal with a potential they simply love, they have tried to create a wine that is elegant, layered and mysterious enough to satisfy any drinker with some degree of patience and adventure. Both wines sell for $28 per bottle.

Tasting by request at "Cabana" 1539 Mission Ave 'C' in Solvang.

Fess Parker Winery & Vineyard

6200 Foxen Canyon Rd

Los Olivos

805-688-1545

Tasting Daily 10-5

When Fess Parker was cast in the roll of Davy Crockett in the mid-1950's, it caused an international sensation and changed his life forever. So too did the purchase of 714 acres in the Santa Ynez Valley change the course of the Parker family's history.

Realizing the potential of Santa Barbara County as a premium grape-growing region, Fess and his son, Eli, originally set out in 1989 to plant a small vineyard and sell fruit to local producers. The Fess Parker Winery and Vineyard now farms almost 700 acres on four vineyards throughout Santa Barbara County.

Working as a family has always been a great source of pride and pleasure for the Parker family. Eli Parker began in the family business as assistant winemaker in 1989. After several years of learning the craft at the side of renowned and accomplished winemakers, Eli took the reigns as winemaker himself with the 1995 vintage. In 1996 Eli formally assumed the title and responsibilities of President. In the early 1990's, Ashley ran the first tastings out of the barrel room and represented the winery at trade shows. In 1998, Ashley became Eli's partner, working on the public relations and sales and marketing teams. The presence of Fess and his wife Marcy as the founding visionaries of the winery is a vital and enduring one.

Priced from $14 to $40, the wines include Viognier, White Riesling, Chardonnay, Pinot Noir, Syrah and red and white blends. An additional label is Parker Station – everyday wines at $14 each.

The tasting room is a visual treat, offering wines and gifts and lots of coonskin caps. Visit at the right time and yours could be autographed.

From Hwy 101 north of Buellton, take the Hwy 154 off-ramp. Proceed 100 yards to Zaca Station Rd. and turn left. Follow Zaca Station for 5 miles and the winery entrance is on the right.

Fiddlehead Cellars

1597 E Chestnut Ave

Lompoc

800-251-1225

Tasting Th-Sat 11-4

And By Appt

Kathy Joseph established Fiddlehead Cellars to capture the pure essence of the two grape varietals that she loves best – Sauvignon Blanc and Pinot Noir.

Her early Pinot Noir grape source was the famed Sierra Madre Vineyard in the Santa Maria Valley, but the sale of the vineyard left a hole in Kathy's Pinot Noir program. And there were no replacement sites that could meet Kathy's high expectations.

Forced into action, and with a typical "Kathy attitude", she set about to develop her own vineyard and spent countless months looking for the perfect place. She ultimately approached the owner of a flower farm (that was not even for sale) who was amenable to her offer. Kathy predicted its success based on some of the extraordinary wines of its "across the street" neighbor, the historic Sanford & Benedict Vineyard, which shared the same soil series and exposure to ocean breezes. Fiddlestix Vineyard was carefully planned and developed over a two year period and has fulfilled her every expectation of that ideal place.

Now in her eighteenth vintage as "Head Fiddle", Kathy continues to passionately pursue her goal of creating stylistic Sauvignon Blancs and silky, intense Pinot Noirs. Terroir-driven, Fiddlehead's Sauvignon Blanc wines hail from the stellar eastern-end of the Santa Ynez Valley, while her estate Pinot Noirs show-case the cooler Santa Rita Hills in the western-most part of that transverse valley. And loving the nuances of place, Kathy continues to craft intriguing Pinot Noir from Oregon's Willamette Valley. Her wines vary in price from $24-$50.

From Hwy 101 in Buellton, take the Hwy 246 exit west towards Lompoc. In Lompoc, turn right on N 7th St, then right on E Chestnut Ave.

Firestone Vineyard

5000 Zaca Station Rd

Los Olivos

805-688-3940

Tasting Daily 10-5

Firestone Vineyard wines hail from eight estate vineyards near California's celebrated Santa Barbara coast, where an unparalleled marine climate and expressive soils yield wines of extraordinary complexity and elegance.

Here, atop three breathtaking mesas in the heart of the Santa Ynez Valley, third-generation winegrower Adam Firestone advances a family tradition of estate vineyards that represent a singular commitment to quality, consistency and character.

Founded as Santa Barbara County's first estate winery in 1972, Firestone Vineyard today remains a cornerstone of coastal estate winemaking, producing highly acclaimed wines that capture the distinctive flavors of their vineyards and region.

With the vineyards planted in numerous varietals, Firestone has the opportunity to produce any number of wines and blends, and they do. Top of the line is their Ambassador - a limited-production, Bordeaux-style wine crafted with passion and precision from their most prized vineyard blocks. The Ambassador represents the finest expression of the estate and is structured for extended cellaring.

Next is their reserve line - Firestone Reserve wines are crafted from only the finest vintages, when select blocks of estate fruit mature to the highest caliber. Next, the Firestone Estate wines hail from estate vineyards with contributions from select neighboring vineyards. Finally, for their Vineyard Select wines, Firestone ventures beyond their own estate, working with local growers to source grapes from premier appellations across the Central Coast. All the wines are priced from $10 to $35 per bottle.

From Hwy 101, take the Zaca Station/Highway 154 exit. At the stop sign, turn right, then take immediate left onto Zaca Station Road. After two miles, you will see Firestone Vineyard on the left.

Flying Goat Cellars

Solvang & Los Olivos
*Tasting Daily 11-5

Norm Yost has been making wine for over twenty years, and has a particular passion for Pinot Noir. He first came to Santa Barbara County as the winemaker at Foley Estate's new facility in Santa Rita Hills, but he and his wife Pam ventured out on their own in 2004 to concentrate on Flying Goat Cellars.

Once the Yosts decided to create their own label, they pondered and agonized over a name. "Yost Wines" just didn't do it - they wanted the winery to reflect a sense of fun in conjunction with making and selling a premium wine.

With this mission of merriment in mind and musing over a name for the winery, they decided to take the path of many vintners and name the winery after our "kids". The kids, in their case, were two pygmy goat pets, who inspired all with their unrestrained spiral loops, flipper turns and straight-legged leaps. The Yosts launched the winery with this same spirit of enthusiasm, and Flying Goat Cellars was born. Their energy and passion for Pinot Noir echoes the kid's antics, so with this kind of zeal they offer limited lots of handcrafted wine made from fruit of the finest vineyards in Santa Barbara County. They've added a little bit of Pinot Gris and even a sparkling, bubbly Rosé de Noir to the list, and all sell in the $18-$44 range.

A good friend of Norms used to say, "Wine is food to be consumed with food". It's all about enjoyment with food, friends and family. So, Norm has what he call his "Mission of Merriment", which is to produce great wine that is reasonably priced and ready to drink upon release. He wants to have fun making and selling the wine. And hopes you join his crusade!

Tasting occasionally at "Wine Country," 2445 Alamo Pintado , Los Olivos (Daily 11-5) and "Cabana", 1539 Mission Dr 'C' in Solvang (Wed-Mon 11-6).

Foley Estates

6121 E Highway 246

Lompoc

805-737-6222

Tasting Daily 10-5

William (Bill) Foley II is the founder and Chief Executive Officer of Fidelity National Financial Corporation, a publicly traded, Fortune 500 Company. As a resident of Santa Barbara with his wife Carol and their four children, Bill was well aware of the potential to produce world-class Pinot Noir and Chardonnay in the cool coastal north of the county. His passion for wine led him to buy the historic J. Carey Cellars located near the hamlet of Ballard in the Santa Ynez Valley in 1997. He renamed the winery Lincourt after his two daughters, Lindsay and Courtney.

Believing that the finest Pinot Noir and Chardonnay in California could be produced in the cool western valleys of Santa Barbara County, Bill located and purchased Rancho Santa Rosa in 1998. Situated in the Santa Rita Hills AVA, Bill planted Rancho Santa Rosa to two hundred thirty acres of Pinot Noir, Chardonnay and Syrah and built his second state of the art winery, Foley Estates.

A historic parcel located in the Santa Rita Hills region of the Santa Ynez Valley, Rancho Santa Rosa had formerly been a thoroughbred horse ranch. The property had the steep, south facing hillsides and the limestone soils that are the "holy grail" to Pinot Noir and Chardonnay vintners.

Foley whites include Chardonnay and Pinot Gris, while the reds include Pinot Noir and Syrah. A Rosé rounds out the offering. Wine prices fall in the $18-$50 price range.

From Hwy 101, exit at Buellton onto Hwy 246, heading west toward Lompoc. Drive approximately 7 miles to the winery.

Foxen Vineyard

7200 Foxen Canyon Rd

Santa Maria

805-937-4251

Tasting Daily 11-4

Bill Wathen and Dick Doré have been making wine together since 1985, when they founded Foxen Winery at the historic Rancho Tinaquaic in northern Santa Barbara County.

Since that time, their dedication has remained the same—the creation of very small-production, vineyard-designated wines using a "minimalist" approach to winemaking. The winery is named in memory of William Benjamin Foxen, an English sea captain and Dick's great-great grandfather, who came to Santa Barbara in the early 1800's. In 1837, this Santa Barbara County pioneer purchased the Rancho Tinaquaic, a Mexican Land Grant that originally totaled nearly 9000 acres and comprised most of what is now known as Foxen Canyon. Captain Foxen adopted the distinctive "anchor" as his ranch cattle brand, which has become a trademark of the winery. It is very fitting that Foxen Winery makes its home on the 2000-acre Rancho Tinaquaic, which remains in family hands.

Foxen's estate ten-acre vineyard was planted by Dick and Bill in 1989 on the Doré family's historic Rancho Tinaquaic. In their frugal "shoestring budget" style, the "Foxen Boys" gathered the canes for their little vineyard from already-pruned cuttings from historic Santa Maria Valley vineyards during evening hours in Dick's old orange pickup truck. For this reason, they affectionately refer to their special cane collection method as the "Volar de Noche" or "fly by night".

Today, Foxen offers Chardonnay and Chenin Blanc along with Pinot Noir, Syrah, *Cuvee Jeanne Marie* (a Rhone blend of Syrah, Grenache, Mourvedre and a small amount of Viognier), a Bordeaux blend called *Foothills Reserve*, a Sangiovese and a late-harvest Viognier. Current releases run $18-$46.

From Hwy 101 north of Buellton, exit at Hwy 154 and turn left onto Zaca Station Rd which will turn into Foxen Canyon Rd. Winery on the right after a drive through the Canyon.

Gainey Vineyards

3950 E Highway 246

Santa Ynez

805-688-0558

Tasting Daily 10-5

In 1962, Dan C. and his son Dan J. Gainey purchased an 1800 acre ranch on the eastern end of the Santa Ynez Valley. With over 1000 acres of rangeland devoted to cattle, 600 acres of farmland, 100 acres of Arabian horses facilities and 100 acres of vineyards, the Gainey Ranch was and still is the largest diversified farming operation in the valley.

In the early 1980's, the Gaineys became convinced that the unique geographical and climatical conditions of the area gave it the potential to produce world class wines. They planted 50 acres in 1983 and opened their Spanish style winery in 1984. The winery quickly became one of the most popular wineries to visit in the area and was named as "one of the best wineries to visit on California's Central Coast" by Wine Spectator magazine.

In the 1990's, the family purchased and planted a 120 acre parcel along Santa Rosa Road in what would later become the Santa Rita Hills AVA. The Gainey Vineyard thus became the first winery to own properties in both the warm, eastern end of the valley, where the family concentrates on Bordeaux varieties, and the cool, western end of the valley, where they have planted Pinot Noir, Chardonnay and Syrah.

Thus, they offer Sauvignon Blanc, Chardonnay and Riesling along with Merlot, Cabernet Franc, Syrah and Pinot Noir. The wines run $14-$36.

Gainey is unique in offering regular winery tours. Tours, presenting an unusually close look at the winemaking process, are conducted daily at 11am, 1pm, 2pm, and 3pm. Reservations are required only for groups of 10 or more. And be sure to check their Summer Concerts schedule – a series they've offered for many years.

From Hwy 101 in Buellton, take the Hwy 246 exit towards Solvang and continue on through Santa Ynez to Gainey's entry gate on the right.

Great Oaks Ranch & Vineyard

Los Olivos
*Tasting Daily 11-5

Go West, young couple! After Michael Lippman earned his Law degree and Nancy a History degree from Skidmore College, they left their native Rochester, NY in the early 70's to seek out the sun and lifestyle of California. The very night that they arrived in Los Angeles, Nancy and Michael were invited to a movie screening and were unknowingly on their way to a career in the entertainment industry.

Lippman Entertainment was formed to represent producers, songwriters and artists. One of Lippman Entertainment's early clients shared their love of the West, horses and the cowboy culture. When Bernie Taupin purchased land in the Santa Ynez Valley, the Lippman's and their two sons would often stay in the guest house on the property. A year later, a ranch not far from Taupin's came up for sale, and the Lippman's jumped at the opportunity. The 66-acre Great Oaks Ranch & Vineyard was theirs.

Nancy had always wanted a vineyard and decided to convert some of the pastures and hay fields of the ranch to vineyards. She dove right into learning everything about vines and wines, taking classes through the local Alan Hancock Community College's Viticulture and Enology program and finding the best people to help her plant what has become one of the premier vineyards in the Santa Ynez Valley. While many of the grapes are sold to a select group of local winemakers, the quality of the grapes and Nancy's passion for the project convinced Andrew Murray to become winemaker for Great Oaks Ranch & Vineyards estate wines.

They offer Sauvignon Blanc, Syrah and *Windmill Hill*, a Cabernet Sauvignon/Cabernet Franc cuvee. Retail prices range from $20 to $36 per bottle. The wines are in extremely limited supply.

Tasting, when wine is available, at "Wine Country" 2445 Alamo Pintado in Los Olivos.

Photo by Lisa Thompson Photography

Hartley Ostini Hitching Post Winery

406 E Hwy 246

Buellton

805-688-0676

Tasting Daily 4-6

On the Central Coast of California, BBQ has always meant grilling over an open fire of red oak, a style of cooking that is native to the area and goes back to the days of the Spanish Rancheros. The Buellton Hitching Post II was established in 1986, but their roots started at the Casmalia Hitching Post in 1952. It was there that Frank & Natalie Ostini brought "Santa Maria Style BBQ" to its peak of perfection.

They are also one of a very few restaurants creating their own wines for sale in the restaurant and to the public.

Hartley-Ostini Hitching Post wines are made by Buellton Hitching Post owner/chef Frank Ostini and his good friend, former fisherman Gray Hartley. Frank and Gray first made wine at home in 1979. They bottled their first Pinot Noir in 1981. The project moved to a winery in 1984 to make the first wines under the Hitching Post label.

Their passioned focus has been to work with the Central Coast's best vineyards to produce many Pinot Noirs, a couple of Syrahs and a Cabernet Franc blend. A great example of these wines is the Hartley-Ostini Hitching Post *Highliner*. "Highliner" is one of the best fishermen in the fleet, and this name honors the great men of the Alaskan Salmon Fishery alongside whom Gray worked for 28 years. A special wine, it is meant to be the "best of their fleet" of Pinot Noirs. Their wines are priced in the $18-$44 range.

Tasting is done in the restaurant's lounge. As you enter, the place may look familiar, especially if you saw the movie "Sideways." Yes, this is the bar, and *Highliner* was the wine, and only the waitress Maya (Virginia Madsen) is missing.

From Hwy 101 in Buellton, exit at Hwy 246 - the Lompoc/Solvang exit. Travel east towards Solvang for 1 1/2 miles. Restaurant on the right side of Highway 246.

Huber Cellars

Solvang

*Tasting Daily 9:30-5:30

The Huber Estate was established in 1986, and the first vines were planted in 1987, making it one of the oldest vineyards in Santa Rita Hills. The premier grapes of the appellation, Pinot Noir and Chardonnay, are grown on the estate, as is a German red grape varietal called Dornfelder.

Dornfelder? Norman and Traudl Huber originally hail from Germany, with family backgrounds in carpentry and farming. A few years ago, friends were visiting from Munich, and upon their return decided that a bit of the "old country" was needed in the vineyard, and sent a gift of certified nursery stock of Dornfelder vines. The vines flourished, and a little bit of the Chardonnay has been grafted over to Dornfelder each year. Huge, bold wines that are almost ink black and loaded with flavor – not your typical German wine. A bit of heritage, with a California attitude, perhaps!

Norman Yost is the consultant winemaker for Huber Cellars. In addition to over twenty years of winemaking experience, Norm brings a wealth of knowledge and passion for Pinot Noir and Chardonnay to the team. True, this is his first experience with Dornfelder! "I find it very exciting to work with the fruit from the Huber Vineyard", states Yost. "It is one of the few vineyards in Santa Rita Hills with mature vines, and definitely shows the nuances of "terroir" in the wines. And working with Dornfelder? Well, that's just a trip! What an amazing varietal!"

Huber offers the three wines in a price range of $21 to $38 per bottle.

Tasting occasionally at "Olde Mission Wine" 1539 Mission Dr. 'B' in Solvang.

Jaffurs Wine Cellars

819 E Montcito St

Santa Barbara

805-962-7003

Tasting Fri-Sun 12-4

And By Appt

Jaffurs Wine Cellars is dedicated to producing great Rhone varietal wines with a new-world independence. Owner/winemaker Craig Jaffurs, produced his first professional wines during the 1994 harvest. All his wines are carefully made in small lots. Only about 3000 cases are produced each year. They work closely with growers in the Santa Ynez, Santa Rita, Los Alamos, and the Santa Maria growing regions. They limit vineyard yields and require that optimal farming practices are observed. All their wines are crushed, pressed, cellared and bottled in their Santa Barbara facility. 2007 is their 14th harvest!

Craig has been making wines since 1989. He is a refugee from the aerospace industry where he spent 17 years as a cost analyst. He worked as a "cellar rat" at Santa Barbara Winery for five harvests where Bruce McGuire, their winemaker, began prodding Craig toward a career in wine. Several home winemaking vintages and a few classes at U.C. Davis later, the winery was born. When his first wine, the 1994 Santa Barbara County Syrah got rave reviews, the future was set.

Jaffurs owns no vineyards. They purchase premium wine grapes from six Santa Barbara County vineyards including Thompson, Bien Nacido, Melville, Westerly, Paradise, and Stolpman Family.

In addition to those wines, which sell in the $23-$75 price range, Jaffurs sometimes offers special bottlings in the artist Hank Pitcher's art label series – Craig and Hank's toast to surfing and the Central Coast life. Those offerings do sell out quickly.

From Hwy 101 in Santa Barbara, exit at Milpas St. and turn north (away from the ocean) and go four blocks to Montecito St. Turn left. Go 100 feet and turn right into their parking lot.

J. Kerr Wines

Los Olivos
*Tasting Daily 11:30-5:30

Photo by Kirk Irwin

John Kerr began his winemaking career at Brookside Winery in Ventura in 1972 shortly after returning from Vietnam as a decorated veteran. There, he planted vines and worked in their tasting room.

In 1980 John moved to Monterey County and began seriously pursuing a winemaking career. He worked at Chalone and Jekel wineries before spending four years at Ventana Vineyards and Winery where he was in charge of production. In 1984 he returned to Santa Barbara County where he became an independent consulting winemaker, assisting Babcock Winery, Brander and Houtz wineries, John began working for Byron Winery in 1986. In 1995 he went to work for the Firestone family as winemaker at Carey Cellars (now Curtis). John continued on as the Curtis winemaker until the spring of 1998 when he decided to focus on his own singular wine production.

1986 was the year of the first J. Kerr crush. Concentrating on Chardonnay, which is the mainstay of J. Kerr Wines, John began making reds in 1988 with a Syrah. Today, in various bottlings, the wines sell for $15-$30.

John ages his wine differently than most wineries. "In any given year the vineyard can throw you the biggest curve for fruit flavors development, which I call maturity. Accounting for all of the variables, I've found that to make the best, richest fruit flavor complexities along with ageability, the wine needs to mature in the barrel for about two years. So, when most wineries are bottling the current vintage just prior to the next harvest, I don't feel my wines have had the chance to develop fully in this short a time frame. I think once you taste my wines, you'll agree the wait is worth it!"

Tasting usually available at "Los Olivos Tasting Room" 2905 Grand Ave, Los Olivos.

Jorian Hill Vineyard

Solvang

805-686-8490

Occasional Tasting By Appt

There are some vintners who acquire grapes, and some have grapes thrust upon them.

Gary and Jeanne Newman, devoted cultivators of the small-lot, estate-grown wines of Jorian Hill, did not set out to own a winery. Their goal was to find a family home in the Santa Barbara County foothills that they had loved and explored for many years. They found that home in 2005: an idyllic 20-acre estate nestled in the rolling hills of Ballard Canyon. And to their surprise, on a southwesterly-facing hill, they found something else: seven and a half lush acres of top-quality Syrah and Viognier vines.

As veterans of the entertainment business - Gary is President of 20th Century Fox Television, and Jeanne is a partner in a top entertainment law practice - they had a distinct set of skills to apply to the task of creating a premium winery. In their Los Angeles-based careers, Gary and Jeanne have both earned respect by building winning teams, by valuing the inspiration and inclusion of their family, and by displaying an uncompromised passion for excellence. The winery's winning team includes renowned winemaker Bruno D'Alfonso, formerly of Sanford Winery, as well as top vineyard assessor Jeff Frey (whose clients include Sea Smoke, Au Bon Climat and Qupé). Also part of the team are the Newman children - Jordan, Reed and Hillary - who have helped to pick and taste grapes, endured the harvest-time bee stings that inspired the vineyard's bumblebee logo, and lent their names to be blended into the name Jorian Hill.

Jorian Hill Viognier sells for $22.50, the Syrah for $30.

Tasting by appt only – call at least two weeks in advance.

Kalyra Winery

343 N Refugio Rd

Santa Ynez

805-693-8864

Tasting Daily 11-5

Mike Brown is a worldly kind of guy. He's come all around the world - or at least halfway, from Australia to California - to make wine in Santa Barbara County. Why?

Because the surf is great in this part of the world and the Santa Barbara County is one of the most progressive and fast moving winemaking regions in the country. He wanted a piece of all that.

After years of study and work at wineries in Australia and the Central Coast, in 1989 Mike decided to create his own label. The name is a translation from the Australian Aboriginal meaning "a wild and pleasant place". The philosophy behind these wines is that good wine should be a direct reflection of the fruit used and that it should highlight the distinct varietal characteristics of the regions it came from. At the same time, he continues as the winemaker for Buttonwood Farms Winery.

The white wine list includes Sauvignon Blanc, Chardonnay (stainless steel fermented), off dry Gewürztraminer, Semillon and a bright new Pinot Grigio. The red portfolio adds Nebbiolo and Sangiovese as well as Cabernet Franc, Merlot and Cabernet Sauvignon as well as a dry style Cabernet Franc Rosé. The dessert wines from Kalyra include fortified Muscats, Vintage and Ruby Ports and the now famous Tawny Port as well as a number of limited release late harvest and Eiswein styles. Prices run $14.50 to $32.

In 1997 Mike decided to make some wines from his native Australia under the M. BROWN label. He travels down under each year to source fruit for a classic Shiraz, a dry Riesling and, for something really unique, a Shiraz/Cabernet blend featuring wines from Australia and California blended together!

From Hwy 101, exit on Hwy 246 in Buellton and travel east through Solvang. In Santa Ynez, turn right on Refugio Rd. Winery on the right.

Ken Brown Wines

Ballard or Lompoc

*Tasting Fri-Sun 12-4

Or at the Winery By Appt

Ken Brown is recognized as one of Santa Barbara County's pioneering winemakers and innovators. He was among the first vintners to realize the tremendous promise for Pinot Noir and Chardonnay in this cool-climate appellation in the mid-1970's. He was also the first winemaker to introduce the Syrah grape, as well as Pinot Gris and Pinot Blanc, to Santa Barbara County.

As founding winemaker at Zaca Mesa, Ken had the opportunity to help design the winery, select the winemaking equipment and set the standards. His wines were highly acclaimed, and he was one of a handful of winemakers to catapult Santa Barbara County into an established appellation.

Lured by the appeal of making great Pinot Noir and Chardonnay, Ken, with his wife, Deborah and several partners founded Byron Vineyard & Winery in 1984 in the little-known Santa Maria Valley. Byron Winery enjoyed early success and gained national recognition for Pinot Noir and Chardonnay.

With the benefit of nearly 30 years experience in this region, Ken's goal in founding Ken Brown Wines is to focus on exceptional Pinot Noir from leading vineyards in the Santa Rita Hills and several other select locations in the county. With the introduction of Ken Brown Wines in 2005, Ken feels that he has reached a place where he can optimize the best sources of Pinot Noir with uncompromised winemaking. His first wines feature Pinot Noir in addition to limited bottlings of Syrah, Vin Gris and Chardonnay. Prices are $18-$50.

*Tasting at "Ballard Inn Tasting Room" 2436 Baseline Ave, Ballard or at the Winery by calling 805-448-3791 or 688-4482 for an appointment and directions.

Kenneth Volk Vineyards

5230 Tepusquet Rd

Santa Maria

805-938-7896

Tasting Fri-Sun 10:30-4:30

And By Appt

Proprietor Ken Volk has been making Santa Barbara and Central Coast wines for more than a quarter century. Perhaps best known as the founder of Wild Horse Winery, Ken has earned a reputation for crafting world-class wines, particularly Pinot Noir and Chardonnay from the Santa Maria Valley.

In many ways, Ken's landing in Santa Maria is sort of a full circle journey. He made home wines from the nearby Rancho Sisquoc Vineyard in the 1970's, and his first professional wine under the Wild Horse label was a 1983 Pinot Noir from the nearby Sierra Madre Vineyard. Rodolfo Callado, of Mesa Vineyard Management, who oversees the management of Kenneth Volk's small estate vineyard, was Ken's first employee at Wild Horse.

A combination of outstanding vineyards and innovative winemaking techniques help Kenneth Volk Vineyards craft uniquely-styled luxury wines.

The primary focus is Chardonnay and Pinot Noir from Santa Maria Valley, a region long renowned for Burgundian varietals. The unique soil, paired with the cooling influence of the ocean, provides the ideal growing conditions for these wines. Ken also has a longstanding interest in and affinity for Bordeaux varieties from Paso Robles. The winery currently produces Cabernet Sauvignon and Merlot from the westernmost locations of the region, an area that Volk thinks is among the best California has to offer for these wines. They also produce small amounts of heirloom wines from unique vineyard sites from throughout California's Central Coast. Prices vary from $14-$48.

From Hwy 101 in Santa Maria, exit at Betteravia and head east. Betteravia becomes Foxen Canyon Rd (176). Veer left at the fork onto Santa Maria Mesa Rd. Drive past the Cambria winery and go straight at the stop sign where Santa Maria Mesa Rd becomes Tepusquet Rd Winery is located 1/2 mile ahead on the right.

Koehler Winery

5360 Foxen Canyon Rd

Los Olivos

805-693-8384

Tasting Daily 10-5

When Kory Koehler acquired the 100 acre property in 1997, all of the estate grapes were being sold to local wineries. Koehler soon recognized that some of the best wines in the valley were being produced with grapes harvested from her vineyards, and she resolved to launch her own winery and tasting room. From the start, Kory's vision was to create a world-class winery committed to making premium wines at affordable prices. Koehler began by turning the property over to one of the most skilled and knowledgeable vineyard managers in central California, Felipe Hernandez. Felipe painstakingly tends the sixty-seven acres planted to Cabernet Sauvignon, Chardonnay, Sauvignon Blanc, Riesling, Syrah, Sangiovese, Grenache and Viognier.

As the vineyard aged, Koehler recognized the need to bring on a wine-maker of impeccable credentials to match the quality of the grapes. Chris Stanton, one of the Sonoma Valley's most respected winemakers, was appointed to head the winemaking operations at Koehler beginning with the 2005 vintage. Stanton, soft-spoken and utterly in love with making wine, was the winemaker at Mayo Winery in Sonoma, where he created dozens of high-scoring wines. Born and raised in Napa and Sonoma, 2007 was his 26th year of winemaking.

Now, Koehler is aiming for some outstanding vintages. Their wines sell in the $12-$40 range. So now would be a good time to visit.

Weather permitting, guests may also partake of a sip of wine on the spectacularly beautiful grounds, surrounded by the Koehler family's remarkable menagerie of unusual animals and exotic birds.

From Hwy 101, exit at Hwy 154 and turn left onto Zaca Station Rd which will turn into Foxen Canyon Rd. Winery on the right.

Lafond Winery & Vineyards

6855 Santa Rosa Rd

Buellton

805-688-7921

Tasting Daily 10-5

In 1962 Pierre Lafond opened the first winery in Santa Barbara County – Santa Barbara Winery - since prohibition. It would be more than ten years before a second winery opened. Today, there are over 100.

Initially Lafond used grapes from outside the county, notably Zinfandel from Bill York's vineyards in Templeton, York Winery, later York Mountain Winery. By the late 1960s Lafond was using some Santa Barbara County grapes. Unfortunately, his source was also supplying grapes to a large Napa Valley winery, which because of increased public interest and consumption began taking every grape. When Lafond's supply was cut off, he decided to plant his own vineyard, purchasing 105 acres west of Buellton. In 1971 the Lafonds planted grape vines covering 65 of those acres in the Santa Rita Hills at the western tip of the Santa Ynez Valley. The main plantings are Pinot Noir, Chardonnay and Syrah in that order with smaller blocks of Riesling and Grenache. Current releases normally sell in the $18 to $45 range.

Lafond's hiring of winemaker Bruce McGuire in November 1981 set the course for the stellar reputation his wines have achieved today. "We were a very amateur operation until Bruce came," Lafond admits.

In 1996 Lafond Vineyards purchased additional property across the river and planted 30 acres of Pinot Noir and Syrah. And in 1998, Pierre and his son David began construction on the new Lafond Winery. And in the spring of 2001, Lafond Winery opened to visitors.

From Hwy 101, take the Santa Rosa Rd Exit in Buellton and drive west 5.6 miles.

Lane Tanner Winery

Los Olivos

805-929-1826

*Tasting – Hours Below

In 1980, Lane Tanner picked up a temporary job at Konocti Winery labeling bottles. They found out she was a chemist and asked her to do some lab work for them. Lane tells: "The first day I was in the lab, I was introduced to their consultant, Andre Tchelistcheff, as the new enologist (I had no clue what that was). All day long, Andre kept telling the winemaker "Have Lane test this, have Lane check that". At the end of the day, Konocti asked me to stay on because Mr. Tchelistchef definitely liked me and they didn't want to tell him that they had lied to him. My new career was born."

After a stint at Firestone Winery, Lane began her own company in 1984 with one client. She began making wines for the Hitching Post restaurant. In 1989 she started the Lane Tanner label. She started out making Pinot Noir and her methods for Pinot production have not changed much in the last 25 years. She uses the best Pinot grapes available in Santa Barbara County. She harvests the grapes when they taste right, not when the sugar hits a certain number.

Pinor Noir is her main wine but now she makes a few cases of Syrah each year. Her production is small because she can't stand the idea of someone else touching those babies. As with any parent, she feels that no one can understand their needs as she does. Prices run $21.50 to $33 per bottle. Production runs about 1800 cases a year.

Lane adds: "To sum it up, I am making a product for people who are searching for the more subtle, elegant nuances of the Pinot Noir (and Syrah) grape."

*Tasting often in "Tastes of the Valley" at 1672 Mission Dr in Solvang (Daily 11-8) and "Ballard Inn Tasting Room" at 2436 Baseline Ave in Ballard (Fri-Sun 12-4) and sometimes at "Los Olivos Tasting Room" at 2905 Grand Ave in Los Olivos (Daily 11:30-5:30).

La Vie Vineyards

308 N 9th St - D

Lompoc

805-291-2111

Tasting Fri-Sun 11-5

Or By Appt

La Vie Vineyards is a handcrafted winery dedicated to the production of fine and elegant wines of exceptional character and quality. During the sweet years of college, Ariel Lavie and Angela Hobbs fell in love with wine and each other, and the story unfolds into a passion for Pinot Noir. Studying Biology/Botany and Environmental Studies/Economics at UC Santa Cruz until 1997, they found themselves destined at graduation to find the ideal piece of land for premium wine production on the west coast. In 1998, they obtained a 40 acre ranch in the heights of the Santa Rita Hills and surrounded themselves with the greatest Pinot Noir Vineyards of the region.

For two vintages they worked with Clos Pepe Vineyard and applied their sustainable agricultural backgrounds to the newly planted vineyard. Since then they have worked with a number of the best producers in the area and have acquired a diverse style incorporating traditional and nouveau wine making techniques. They intend to keep a small annual production and focus on growing their young vineyard.

They produce several bottlings of Pinot Noir and Chardonnay, but limit quantities to a few hundred cases a year. Along with using estate fruit, La Vie also buys grapes from several premium vineyards including Clos Pepe, Sweeney Canyon, Fiddlestix, Sanford and Benedict, and Vigna Monte Nero.

Currently, their efforts have resulted in a number of Pinot Noirs bottled under vineyard designation as well as a couple of Chardonnays. Occasionally they'll offer other varietals, like Viognier or Riesling. Prices range from $30 to $48 per bottle.

From Hwy 101 in Buellton, take Hwy 246 west to Lompoc. In Lompoc, turn right on N 7th St, go one block and turn right and follow the street to N 9th.

Lincourt Wines

1711 Alamo Pintado

Solvang

805-688-8554

Tasting Daily 10-5

Founded in 1996 by Bill Foley, Lincourt is a producer of ultra premium wines from the Santa Maria and Santa Ynez Valleys. A long time wine enthusiast, Bill has been particularly enchanted with the wines of Burgundy. In 1994, when he and his wife Carol relocated their family to Santa Barbara, he discovered that the potential to produce some of America's most distinguished versions of Pinot Noir and Chardonnay lay just miles north of his home. In 1997, Bill acquired a 30-acre estate and winery in the Santa Ynez Valley, named the winery in homage of his two daughters, Lindsay and Courtney, and hired renowned winemaker Alan Phillips. Together Alan and Bill have contracted fruit from the regions finest vineyards and in concert with the estate fruit have established Lincourt as one of Santa Barbara's most compelling wine portfolios.

Originally a dairy farm, the property retains the rural charm and simplicity of an earlier era. The quaint tasting room is located in the former farmhouse, a 1926 Sears Craftsman kit home. The barns have been converted to a winery and barrel rooms, and equipped to allow for handcrafted, premium winemaking.

Lincourt is blessed to source fruit from many prestigious Santa Ynez Valley vineyards including two estate vineyards: the Alamo Pintado and La Cuesta Vineyards. Planted in 1973, the estate has under vine Cabernet Sauvignon, Merlot, Syrah and Sauvignon Blanc. Additionally, they offer Chardonnay and Pinot Noir. Wines sell for $16-$35 per bottle.

From Hwy 101, exit in Buellton onto Hwy 246, toward Solvang. Go through Solvang and turn left onto Alamo Pintado Rd. Winery about 2 miles up the road, on the left hand side.

Lions Peak Vineyards

1659 Copenhagen Dr
Solvang
805-693-5466
Tasting Fri-Mon 11-5
Or By Appt

Lions Peak, one of the oldest vineyards in the Central Coast, is set in the very heart of the historic San Miguel Region. The Estate has been the Soni family home since 1992 and consists of 120 acres. The rustic Victorian Manor House overlooks the vineyard, and evenings are often spent on the veranda viewing the beautiful valleys and surrounding vineyards.

Lion's Peak produces premium quality wines that are artistic and singularly unique. That artistry is also manifested in the magnificent wine labels that grace the bottles. Ken boasts at his website that "each label tells a story with an expression of artistic design that epitomizes the philosophy of the marriage of fine wine and art."

The vines at Lions Peak Vineyards were first planted in 1971. The mature old vines on their own varietal rootstock produce wines with remarkable depth of character and complexity.

Lions Peak produces Cabernet Sauvignon, Petite Sirah, Mouvedre, Cabernet Franc, Viognier, Marsanne and a Cabernet Port. Blends include *Lionnesse, Bon Courage and Lulu.*

They decided to make several sweeter wines in response to customers who asked for them in the tasting room. A new wine they call *Sisters*, a blend of Marsanne, Viognier and Rousanne with a little Orange Muscat and a late-harvest Viognier are currently available. Wines are priced $16-$45.

The Sonis take their hands-on approach to winemaking seriously, from the vineyards to the winery to introducing Lions Peak to the public. "We are always here at the tasting room," Jennifer said. "We feel it's very important to teach and talk about wines. It becomes like a family. We are the face of the winery."

Located in downtown Solvang.

Longoria Wines

2935 Grand Ave

Los Olivos

805-688-0305

Tasting Fri-Sun 11-4:30

Mon, Wed, Th 12-4:30

Richard Longoria Wines, established in 1982, is a family operated wine business owned by Rick and Diana Longoria. Rick Longoria, who arrived on the local wine scene in 1976, became the first cellar foreman for The Firestone Vineyard. By 1982 he felt confident in his skills and in the quality of some of the county's best vineyards to venture into the wine business for himself, and with financial help from his father he produced 500 cases of Chardonnay and Pinot Noir from Santa Maria valley vineyards.

In 1985, The Gainey Vineyard lured Rick away from J.Carey Cellars to produce wines for their ambitious and exciting new winery project. During his twelve years as winemaker, Rick's winemaking skills established Gainey as one of the top quality wineries in the area. He also continued to produce very small quantities of Longoria wines, just enough to keep the label active.

In 1997 Rick gave up steady employment to devote his full energies to his winery business. And in 1998 Rick and Diana opened the doors to their own tasting room in one of the oldest buildings in downtown Los Olivos. The metal sided building dates back to the early 1900's and was originally the machine shop for the valley.

When visiting, you'll usually be offered Chardonnay, Pinot Noir, Cabernet Franc (normally his *Blues Cuvee* wine), Syrah, Merlot, a red table wine and an occasional small release that Richard is testing. Recently, he's been proud of two Spanish varietals, allowing him to acknowledge the Spanish origins of the Longoria name. Prices are in the $16-$85 (for a very special Pinot Noir) price range.

Tasting room in downtown Los Olivos.

Lucas & Lewellen Vineyards

1645/1665 Copenhagen Dr

Solvang

805-686-9336

Tasting Daily 11-5:30

Royce Lewellen first met Louis Lucas shortly after moving from Solvang to Santa Maria in 1975. Both were members of the Santa Maria Wine & Food Society and the Rotary Club of Santa Maria. Louis was growing wine grapes in the Santa Maria Valley and selling them primarily to wineries in Napa and Sonoma Counties, where wines made from his grapes won high honors. They became friends, especially enjoying the Wine and Food Society events together.

In 1996, the friendship led to a partnership, and L&L as they refer to the company, was born. Together, they acquired several premium wine producing properties to add to the two vineyards Lucas had owned. Their vineyards are located in the three principal wine grape growing regions of Santa Barbara County: the Santa Maria Valley, the Los Alamos Valley, and the Santa Ynez Valley, allowing them to utilize the 3 different climate zones that are unique to Santa Barbara's County's coastal climate.

Shortly, winemaker Dan Gehrs was contacted by the two partners and asked to join them in creating Lucas & Lewellen wines. Since producing their first vintage together in 1999, they have continued to win numerous significant awards for the wines of Lucas and Lewellen.

The L&L wines include Cabernet Franc, Cabernet Sauvignon, Merlot, Pinor Noir and Syrah along with Chardonnay, Sauvignon Blanc, Viognier and Muscat Canelli. Prices run $14-$32. Their Mandolina label offers estate-grown Italian varietals including Pinot Grigio, Barbera, Nebbiolo, Moscato, Sangiovese, and "Super-Tuscan" blends (of Bordeaux and Italian varietals), selling for $12-$32.

Tasting in downtown Solvang – L&L wines at 1645 Copenhagen Dr and Mandolina at 1665 Copenhagen Dr.

Margerum Wine Company

813 Anacapa St

Santa Barbara

805-966-9463

Tasting Sat-Sun 11-3

Doug Margerum began his wine and food career at a young age. After graduating from UCSB with a degree in business economics Doug, with backing from his family, started the Santa Barbara *Wine Cask* in 1981. What began as retail wine store expanded to include a simple bistro. The restaurant and adjacent Intermezzo café now serve over 50 wines by the glass and a wine list that offers over 3,500 bottles of wine. Since 2002, Intermezzo also serves as the Margerum Wine Company tasting room.

In 2005 Doug opened Wine Cask Los Olivos with an adjacent Intermezzo café and a lovely al fresco patio with outdoor fireplace.

Doug explains his gradual move to winemaker: "After twenty years in the wine business it had always been a dream of mine to have a small production winery where I did most of the work myself. I currently operate out of a leased building between Curtis and Andrew Murray. The term being bantered around in France for what I am doing is a production called 'garagiste.' The 'garagiste' philosophy, for me, is that I am part of a growing group of vintners looking to return wine making to its previous form of production – hand-crafted and personal. I strive to make wines that I personally enjoy and my hope is others will enjoy them as well. The approach to this is the antithesis of mass production. I choose to make wines that are distinctive, have a place and personality to them, and are made to my own standards."

Margerum produces a wide selection of premium wines – from Sauvignon Blanc and Pinot Gris to single vineyard Syrahs and a Pinot Noir. Not to be missed is *M5*, Doug's Rhone-style red blend. Prices run from $18-$60 per bottle.

Located in Downtown Santa Barbara.

MCKEON - PHILLIPS
2005
Reserve Chardonnay
Lot GC
Santa Maria Valley • Santa Barbara County
PRODUCED & BOTTLED BY MCKEON-PHILLIPS • SANTA MARIA, CALIFORNIA • ALC. 14.3% BY VOL

McKeon-Phillips Winery

2115 S Blosser Rd Unit 114

Santa Maria

805-928-3025

Tasting Daily 11-6

McKeon-Phillips Winery is the best kept secret in Santa Barbara County. Nestled quietly away in the Vintner's Plaza in Santa Maria, they have been producing increasingly outstanding, award-winning, handcrafted and unique wines since 1982.

Ardison Phillips, the proprietor and winemaker, has a eclectic background that makes him a living icon on the central coast. He is an internationally collected and recognized artist. He has designed virtually all of the labels that adorn the bottles of the McKeon-Phillips wines, with the exception of two labels that have been designed by his son Bailey.

Ardison began producing wine in 1976 under the Studio Grill Private Selection label in Hollywood. In addition to winemaking, Ardison has a passion for pairing food with wine. He teaches Pairing Food and Wine classes at Alan Hancock College in Santa Maria throughout the year.

Bailey McKeon-Phillips is currently serving as cellar master and overseeing the production of wine at McKeon-Phillips. Bailey has learned in the best of possible ways. The wine trade has been taught to him by his father, in the method of apprenticeship that has virtually disappeared from this country. Bailey has a formal education in winemaking, but his real experience has come from the act of doing, the act of making, from creating alongside his father the wines that come from McKeon-Phillips Winery.

Currently, they offer a number of Cabernet Sauvignons along with Pinot Noir, Merlot, Syrah, a Bordeaux blend as well as a Super Tuscan blend and Chardonnay and Sauvignon Blanc. Prices range from $15 to $65 for one of their premium Cabs.

From Hwy 101 in Santa Maria, exit at Betteravia Rd into the city and turn right on S. Blosser Rd. Tasting room on the left.

Melville Vineyards & Winery

5185 E Highway 246

Lompoc

805-735-7030

Tasting Daily 11-4

In 1989, Melville Vineyards, a family owned and operated enterprise was founded in Sonoma County's Knights Valley, where Ron Melville grew high quality, much sought after Chardonnay, Merlot, and Cabernet Sauvignon. In 1996, Ron's desire to grow Pinot Noir and Chardonnay brought Melville Vineyards to Lompoc's Santa Rita Hills.

The shared enthusiasm of Ron's sons, Brent and Chad Melville, and winemaker, Greg Brewer has sparked a family project. Brent is vineyard manager of Verna's Vineyard, Chad fills the same position at Santa Rita Hill Vineyard. Brewer, who was assistant winemaker to Bruce McGuire at Santa Barbara Winery, also served as winemaker and general manager at Sunstone before joining Melville.

Today, they have 139 acres planted in the Santa Rita Hill Vineyard with 255,000 vines of Pinot Noir and Chardonnay, and two Rhone varietals, Syrah and Viognier. They also have 100 acres on Verna's Vineyard in Cat Canyon, two miles north of Los Alamos in the Santa Barbara County Appellation, which is primarily dedicated to Syrah and Viognier.

Currently, they offer estate bottlings of Syrah, Chardonnay and Pinot Noir, selling in the $20-$36 range.

Their beautiful two-story winery resembles a romantic Mediterranean Villa. Set within a landscape of lavender bushes and poplar, oak, and sycamore trees, the winery is the nucleus of estate grown Pinot Noir, Chardonnay, and Syrah vines. While enjoying your glass of fine Pinot Noir, you will be seated in an exquisite tasting room, encased by a rotunda of French doors, overlooking a picturesque garden setting and courtyard.

From Hwy. 101 exit at the Solvang /Lompoc (Hwy. 246) exit and go west on Hwy. 246, toward Lompoc, about 9 miles on your right. Melville shares a driveway with Babcock Winery.

Michael Grace Wine

Solvang or Santa Maria
*Tasting Daily 9:30-5:30
Or at the Winery By Appt

Michael and Grace McIntosh set out to create wines that are thoroughly enjoyable, flavorful but not overpowering, light on alcohol content, handmade and modestly priced. By doing most of the work themselves, they believe they can remain true to producing a handcrafted, limitedly supplied wine that can be enjoyed during a casual meal or a special occasion. They specialize in the unique wines of the Southern Rhone area of France.

Michael has been making wine since 1998. What began as a hobby grew into a passion for sourcing good fruit from good vineyards to make great wine! They believe in the European tradition where wine is enjoyed as a regular part of the meal - They therefore believe it is important to make an affordable, quality wine.

Although the label is new, their winemaking is steeped in traditional techniques that have produced premium quality wines across the centuries. They ferment in small 1/2 to 1 ton bins; remove seeds, and separate grape skins from free run juice. The skins are pressed and barreled separately then blended back in to attain the desired balance of tannins, color, and flavor. After 24 - 30 months of aging in French oak barrels, the wines are bottled unfined and unfiltered.

Their wines include Syrah, Grenache and a blend of Grenache/ Mourvedre/ Syrah. Prices are in the $22 area.

Tasting at "Olde Mission Wine Co." 1539 Mission Dr 'B' in Solvang. For an appointment and directions to taste at the Winery, call Grace at 805-291-1008.

Morovino Wine

433 Alisal Rd "B"

Solvang

805-693-8466

Tasting Wed-Sun 12-5

Morovino is a small winery located in the heart of the Santa Barbara wine country. It was started in September 1994 by Guerrino "Gerry" Moro. Gerry Moro grew up watching his family make wine in Italy. So when they immigrated to the U.S., Moro had winemaking in his veins. (An interesting side note about Gerry—he represented Canada in the 1964 and the 1972 Olympics in the pole vault and decathlon, and is still active today teaching kids to pole vault.)

Morovino started by making and bottling 500 cases of wine in 1994, and is now producing 4,000 cases of a variety of wines. The wines are fermented and aged in American and French oak barrels. The grapes are purchased from some the best, matured vineyards in the county.

Moro, the Italian-born owner and winemaker, produces limited amounts of premium quality wines including Zinfandel, Merlot, Barbera, Sangiovese, Dolcetto and Chardonnay from the best mature vineyards in Santa Barbara County. The Morovino tasting room is relaxed and casual, with a no-fuss presentation from Gerry of the wines that he loves. Though he concentrates on Italian styled wines, Morovino's *Tango,* a 50/50 blend of Zinfandel and Merlot, is their most famous and sought-after wine. Prices fall in the $16-$25 range

More wines may follow as Gerry finds the vineyards that produce the premium grapes he requires.

For now he's content to "play golf, make a little wine, and be happy." That's the Italian way.

Located in downtown Solvang on the main street, across from the Post Office.

Mosby Winery

9496 Santa Rosa Rd

Buellton

805-688-2415

Tasting Mon-Fri 10-4

Sat-Sun 10-5

The Mosby Winery is one of the earliest wineries in Santa Barbara County. The land is part of the old *Rancho de la Vega*, which derives its name from the Spanish "river bottom or meadow."

The old de la Cuesta Adobe at Mosby's Winery and Vineyards was built in 1853 by Dr. Roman de la Cuesta for his bride, Micaela Cota. All of the lumber used in the construction of the house was carried by oxen and mule pack over the rough trails of Gaviota Pass.

The house was built with 13 rooms around an open court. The old adobe remained with the de la Cuesta family until the 1950s when the two remaining de la Cuesta sisters sold the property. Bill and Jeri Mosby purchased the property in 1976 to become one of the early wine pioneers in Santa Barbara County. The first thing Bill did was plant vines. "Noah did that," he says quietly. "First thing he did. Plant a vineyard."

The Mosby Winery Tasting Room is located in the restored de la Cuesta Carriage House near the old Adobe, which is home to the Mosby Winemaker Dinners.

While Mosby's specialty is the growing and vinification of fine Italian varietal wines, he also makes award-winning grappa, wild plum and raspberry distillatos. His experienced palate and careful, ongoing search for interesting new varietals has resulted in vintage after vintage of Sangiovese, Nebbiolo, Pinot Grigio and more. And then there's his latest addition, Dolcetto — the everyday wine of Piemonte. Prices run $12-$44 per bottle.

The Mosbys like to remind their visitors: "Remember: Wine is not only for special times. Wine makes the times special."

Located at Highway 101 and Santa Rosa Road 1/4 mile south of Buellton.

Ojai Vineyards

Ballard

*Tasting Fri-Sun 12-4

The Ojai Vineyard, owned by Adam & Helen Tolmach, works closely with a dozen different vineyards on the Central Coast of California and produces wines from Syrah, Grenache, Mourvedre, Pinot Noir, Chardonnay, Sauvignon Blanc and Viognier. About 6000 cases are produced each year, divided between 15 bottlings, most of which are vineyard designated wines. Retail prices are in the $16-$56 price range.

The key to producing special wine is in the care taken growing the grapes. There is an inverse relationship between quantity and quality when it comes to grapes, so rather than purchasing theirs by the ton, they have long term agreements with growers to buy the fruit by the acre. This lets Ojai culture the vines and thin the crop to their strict specifications, yet allows the grower to receive a fair return.

In the winery they like to watch the development of the wine carefully, yet prefer to do as little as possible. Twenty-five years of experience has shown them that the least amount of moving, pumping, fining and filtering is always best. The ultimate objective is to show off the distinctive character of a vineyard site.

Adam relates an experience that pretty much explains his winemaking thoughts. "In 1981, after working the harvest in Burgundy, Sarah Charmberlain, Jim Clendenen and I visited quite a number of wineries there. It struck me that it didn't seem to matter whether a proprietor had a cellar with lots of fancy equipment or not, the quality of the wine produced had a lot more to do with how thoughtful the winemaker was. I ran with that spirit when I started The Ojai Vineyard."

*Tasting at "Ballard Inn Tasting Room" 2436 Baseline Ave, Ballard.

Oreana Winery

205 Anacapa St

Santa Barbara

805-962-5857

Tasting Daily 11-5

Surrounded by the soothing blare of Steely Dan music and the clank of glass bottles, Oreana Winery produces micro-batches of Pinot Noir, Syrah, Chardonnay, Sparkling Wine and Verdelho, once Portugal's most common white wine, at the cooperative winery, Cellar 205, located in downtown Santa Barbara. Using a name borrowed from the grand days of California Rancheros, owner/winemaker Christian Garvin truly embraces the renegade style of the Central Coast.

Finding little demand for his Communications degree from UC Santa Barbara in 1996 and having worked in restaurants since his early days in New York, Christian jumped at the chance to join a college friend who was working at the Fess Parker Winery. After a raucous harvest season spent living in a trailer with two other cellar rats and a vineyard dog, the future was set. He teamed with the assistant winemaker and together they launched Kahn Winery, known for mind-blowing Syrah. After seven years he was looking for a new challenge that presented itself in the form of an abandoned building near Santa Barbara Winery and Jaffurs Cellars in Santa Barbara. Another winery – or three - in the neighborhood made sense, and Oreana was born.

So today, Oreana Wines are tasted in Cellar 205, the winemaking cooperative housed on Anacapa Street in what was once a tire shop that now plays host to two expert, grape-loving prodigies: Christian Garvin and John Bargiel, guys who know what they're doing and how to have a good time doing it (check out the Ms. Pac-Man machine).

Oreana very-limited production wines sell for $16-$40.

Located in Downtown Santa Barbara, south of Hwy 101.

Ovene Winery

Solvang

*Tasting Daily 9:30-5:30

Ovene Winery, Inc. was founded by Jeff & Genni White in March 2004. The winery is a culmination of 18 years of home winemaking preceded by 5 years of sales management in the wine business.

Jeff and Genni started making wine in their garage in 1986. The early years included great memories of having 5 gallon glass carboys exploding in the Jacuzzi and finished bottles of wine blowing corks off in the garage after hot summer days. For 18 years they dragged all of their friends, the neighbor kids and whoever would go with them to pick grapes early in the morning. They would fill trash cans, pickup trucks and garbage bags full and take the grapes back to their home in Yorba Linda where they would crush the grapes with a hand cranked Italian crusher/destemmer. They always saved a few hundred pounds of grapes to be crushed "Lucy style". All the kids and any newbie's would be obliged to wash off their feet and squish grapes until their feet turned purple. What fond memories!

Ovene Winery produces Central Coast Pinot Noir, Chardonnay, Viognier, Pinot Blanc, Sauvignon Blanc, Cabernet Sauvignon and Muscat Canelli. Their first release was a Rose of Syrah. Wines are priced at $15-$30 per bottle.

Ovene Winery is the culmination of a lifetime of their family's passion for food and wine. Ovene is dedicated to Jeff's Grandmother Merthel Ovene McConnel. Granny was an inspiration to several generations who taught them the love of God, family values, traditions and a passion for food and wine. She was known as Groovy Granny and always said to save the best for last.

*Tasting usually available at "Olde Mission Wine Co" 1539 Mission Dr 'B' Solvang.

Palmina Wines

1520 E Chestnut Ct

Lompoc

805-735-2030

Tasting Th-Sun 11-4

And By Appt.

Palmina is a Californian celebration of the rich, wonderful lifestyle and attitude toward food, wine, friends and family that exists in Italy.

Steve Clifton, winemaker and owner, produced the first Palmina wines in the basement of his home in 1995. His career in the wine industry had begun in 1992 when he begged his way into a tasting room position at Rancho Sisquoc winery. Little by little he forced his way into the cellar and in time Steve worked his way up to Assistant Winemaker under Stephan Bedford. Over the next few years Steve's on the job schooling would include production and winemaking positions at Beckmen, Brander and Domaine Santa Barbara wineries.

A trip to Italy inspired him to find work in an Italian restaurant in Laguna Beach where under the mentorship of his good friend Michael Whipple he learned all that he could about Italian wines.

Chrystal Clifton completes the Palmina picture. Educated at the University of Bologna and fluent in Italian, Chrystal is invaluable in forging the relationships with wine producers in Italy which have supplied phenomenal insight in forming Palmina's philosophy and style. Steve and Chrystal were married in Friuli, Italy (where else) in the Spring of 2004.

Palmina white wines include Traminer and Malvasio Bianca. Reds include Barbera and Dolcetto and four blends – *Savoia. Sisquoc, Alisos and Mattia*. Prices are from $20 to $50.

Often sold out, ask if there's any *Botasea*. "Botasea" is a word in the Venetian dialect which means "little barrel". This is Chrystal's "little project" which she first conceived when she was a student in Italy and dreaming of making a beautiful and delicious Rosato.

From Hwy 101 in Buellton, take Hwy 246 West to Lompoc. Turn right on N 7th St. then right on E Chestnut Ct.

Presidio Winery

1603 Copenhagen Dr #1

Solvang

805-693-8585

Tasting Daily 11-6

Presidio Vineyard & Winery was founded in 1991 from winemaker Douglas Braun's concept of bringing European viticultural philosophy to Santa Barbara County . His idea was of a high-density, low-yield per vine vineyard, planted low to the ground to maximize the refraction of heat from the soil, at the winery's estate Presidio Vineyard located west of the Santa Rita Hills near Lompoc . This certified organic and biodynamically farmed vineyard's cool climate and southern-facing exposure is particularly well-suited for Pinot Noir, Syrah, and Chardonnay.

Presidio's vineyard management blends modern viticultural techniques with traditional farming methods. Douglas' involvement in the vineyard is year-round from pruning to harvest. Controlling pruning to limit crop levels, meticulous canopy management, and precisely monitored minimum drip irrigation with organic compost fertilization to maximize concentration result in the highest quality fruit; the essential start to a superior wine.

As the Santa Ynez Valley has been under the ocean several times in the past 150,000 years, the vineyards are deeply rooted in vertical Monterey shale - a result of thousands of year of marine depository and geological uplift. Closer to the surface, the sand and loam are excellent for drainage. For these reasons, the cooler western part of the Santa Ynez Valley in Santa Barbara County has the ideal climate and soil conditions to produce fine Pinot Noir, Syrah, and Chardonnay.

Their wines, in the $20 to $43 price range, include estate and non-estate selections of those three wines as well as an unfiltered Port.

Located in Solvang at the corner of Mission Dr and Atterdag St.

Qupé Wine Cellars

Los Olivos and Solvang
*Tasting Daily – Hours Below

In 1975, after working harvest at his first winery job, Bob Lindquist discovered the potential of Santa Barbara's winegrowing region when he opened and managed a tasting room in Ventura County. While managing a retail shop in Los Olivos, he got fired for attending a Kinks concert against the wishes of the shop owner, but he was immediately hired as Zaca Mesa Winery's first tour guide – a job that included cellar work. There he met winemakers Ken Brown and Jim Clendenen who taught Bob the basics and inspired him to become a winemaker which he did by founding Qupé in 1982.

Qupé employs traditional winemaking techniques to make wines that are true to type and speak of their vineyard sources. Their goal is to make wines with impeccable balance that can be enjoyed in their youth, yet because of the good acidity from cool vineyard sites can also benefit from ageing. They are committed to sourcing grapes from some of the best and most prestigious vineyards in Santa Barbara and San Luis Obispo counties.

For his first vintage Bob produced Syrah, Chardonnay, and a Rosé of Pinot Noir. Soon, Bob's love of the assertive and complex wines of the Rhône Valley led him to focus Qupé on the production of Rhône varietals, particularly Syrah. Chardonnay continues in the portfolio because of Bob's connection to the wonderful fruit sources in the Bien Nacido Vineyard. Other whites include Viognier, Marsanne and Roussanne along with a *Bien Nacido Cuvée*. Besides a number of Syrah bottlings, Qupé produces a Grenache and a *Los Olivos Cuvée*. The wines range in price from $18-$40.

Tasting often in "Wine Country" at 2445 Alamo Pintado in Los Olivos (Daily 11-5) and usually at "Tastes of the Valley" at 1672 Mission Dr in Solvang (Daily 11-8).

Photo by Kirk Irwin

Rancho Sisquoc Winery

6600 Foxen Canyon Rd

Santa Maria

805-944-4332

Tasting Daily 10-4

Located in northern Santa Barbara County on the Sisquoc River 18 miles east of Santa Maria, Rancho Sisquoc is part of an 1852 Spanish land grant. To the Chumash Indians of the area, "Siaquoc" meant "gathering place" - and today Rancho Sisquoc is again a gathering place, this time for wine lovers.

The 37,000 acre ranch was purchased in 1952 by James Flood. The cattle business is the same as it has always been, but beans and barley have been replaced with vegetables and grapevines. The initial planting in 1968 consisted of nine acres of Johannisberg Riesling and four acres of Cabernet Sauvignon. Current acreage is 320 and growing.

Today, as you drive the road that snakes along the edge of the valley floor to the ranch headquarters and tasting room, you leave the rush of the twentieth-first century behind. The farmhouse and barn date from the early 1900s, and artifacts of an earlier age lend the ranch a feeling of when the pace was slower and unhurried.

You'll find Riesling, Sylvaner (the only producers of this varietal in California), Sauvignon Blanc, Chardonnay, Merlot, Cabernet Sauvignon, Syrah, Malbec, Pinot Noir and some exciting red blends, all priced at $12-$30 each.

A unique landmark at Rancho Sisquoc is San Ramon Chapel, standing at the entrance to the ranch and shown on the wine labels. It was built in 1875 by Frederick Wickenden at the request of his wife, Ramona Foxen Wickenden. Officially dedicated in 1879, the Chapel was built on stilts, often resulting in cancelled services due to cold winds. However, in 1976, the Chapel was brought back to life, and Mass is now celebrated each Sunday at 10:30 AM.

From Hwy 101 in Santa Maria, exit at Betteravia Rd and drive east. Betteravia becomes Foxen Canyon Rd and make a series of left and right turns. Continue till you reach San Ramon Chapel and follow the signs to the winery.

Rideau Vineyard

1562 Alamo Pintado

Solvang

805-688-0717

Tasting Daily 11-5

Rideau Vineyard was founded in 1997 by New Orleans native, Iris Rideau. Early on in the winery's inception, Iris decided to dedicate her estate vineyard entirely to Rhône varietals. She felt that Rhône wines were not only ideally suited to the Santa Ynez Valley AVA, but also instinctively felt that they were best suited to the Creole cuisine of her childhood. Indeed, as the vines matured, and the first estate wines were produced, Iris soon began hosting a series of Creole-inspired dinners, with each dish paired with a Rhône varietal. The dinners were wildly successful, and soon became full-fledged winery events.

Within their 16 acres of planted vineyard, one can find Syrah, Viognier, Mourvedre, Roussanne and Grenache. They also honor long-standing contracts with some of Santa Barbara County's most esteemed vineyards. From Bien Nacido they receive Chardonnay and Pinot Noir grapes from a winery designated block year after year. From Sanford and Benedict, they purchase Pinot Noir grapes. From Paradise, they are contracted for over 15 tons of Syrah and from La Presa's pristine vineyard managed by their winemaker, Andrés Ibarra, they obtain Petite Sirah grapes. They have also been fortunate to work with some of the best Tempranillo growers in California. Rideau sells their wine in the $28-$65 price range.

The Rideau Vineyard is rich with history dating back to 1769 when it was owned by the King of Spain and supervised by Mission Santa Barbara. It includes one of few two-story adobes in California. Over the years it served as a stagecoach stop, a famous inn, a guest ranch and a working ranch, as well as being designated Santa Barbara County Historical Monument No. 12.

From Hwy 101, exit onto Hwy 246 in Buellton towards Solvang. Past Solvang, turn left onto Alamo Pintado. Winery about 1 1/2 miles on the right across from the miniature horses.

Rusack Vineyards

1819 Ballard Canyon Rd

Solvang

805-688-1278

Tasting Daily 11-5

Rusack was established in 1995 by Geoff and Alison Rusack with a commitment to creating world-class wines. The owners' vision was to offer a limited production of ultra-premium wines. According to Geoff, "With us quality must be our first priority." In the years since 1995, this dedication to quality has meant some dramatic changes.

The most visible change is in the vineyard. Following the 2001 harvest, many of the original vines were pulled out and replanted. Utilizing cutting edge technology and taking advantage of Ballard Canyon's unique terroir, varieties to be grown were carefully chosen and limited to those clones best suited to the microclimate. Syrah, Sangiovese, and Sauvignon Blanc have been planted, along with smaller lots of Cabernet Franc, Merlot and Petit Verdot to be blended into their renowned Bordeaux-style red wine *Anacapa*.

John and Helen Falcone occupy a unique niche as one of the few husband and wife winemaking teams in California's wine industry. Born into an Italian winemaking family, John started his wine odyssey at age 19, working for his uncle at The Monterey Vineyard. Prior to joining Rusack, John worked for many years in the Napa Valley, including a position as head winemaker at Atlas Peak Vineyards. Helen held positions of assistant winemaker at Chimney Rock Winery and Codorniu Napa wineries. Their decision to join Rusack was prompted by their desire to "get back to hand-crafting wines" and their belief that Santa Barbara County is now one of the best places for a small production winery to live up to its potential for producing great wines.

So today, along with *Anacapa*, Rusack offers Sangiovese, Pinot Noir, Syrah, Sauvignon Blanc and Chardonnay, in the $17-$36 area.

From Hwy 101, take the Hwy 246 (Solvang/Lompoc) exit in Buellton towards Solvang. Drive 3/4 mile and turn left onto Ballard Canyon Rd. Continue along, taking a left at the 'T' intersection. Rusack is 2 miles from the "T" on the left.

Sanford Winery & Vineyards

5010 Santa Rosa Rd

Lompoc

800-426-9463

Tasting Daily 11-4

In 1971 Sanford Winery and Vineyards discovered an overlooked, grape-growing treasure in the Santa Rita Hills. Recognizing a magical combination of climate and soil conditions much like those in France's famed Burgundy province, Sanford planted the area's first Pinot Noir in its Sanford & Benedict vineyard.

Pinot Noir has thrived in the Santa Rita Hills ever since, and so has Sanford Winery. The pioneering winery's Pinot Noir ranks among the best and most distinctive in the world. And Sanford's leadership helped put Santa Barbara and the Santa Rita Hills on the map of the world's great wine regions. Certified as an American Viticultural Area (AVA) in 2001, today the area is renowned for its Chardonnay as well as Pinot Noir. And Sanford has long been a leading producer of both. Each year they produce a number of Pinots and Chardonnays from each of their famous vineyards. Wine prices are in the $14 to $45 range.

The summer of 2007 will bring a major, new addition to Sanford: the opening of a brand new tasting room July 1, 2007, next to their beautiful stone and adobe winery and estate vineyards at La Rinconada. This new tasting room will be located at 5010 Santa Rosa Road, approximately 10 miles west of U.S. Highway 101. With the addition of the tasting room, Sanford will be able to provide visitors with a complete winery experience, all in one location, including tours of the winery and surrounding vineyards.

From Hwy 101 just sorth of Buellton, take the Santa Rosa Rd off ramp. Drive west onto Santa Rosa Rd. Proceed 10 miles to Winery and Tasting Room.

Santa Barbara Winery

202 Anacapa St
Santa Barbara
805-963-3633
Tasting Daily 10-5

Santa Barbara Winery was started in 1962 by Pierre Lafond. It was the first winery in Santa Barbara County since the end of Prohibition in the early 1930's. At that time no vineyards existed in the area and grapes were trucked in from San Luis Obispo County some distance away.

Santa Barbara Winery planted its first vineyard, the Lafond Vineyard, in 1972. It is now just under 100 acres. It was not, however, until the arrival of winemaker Bruce McGuire in 1981 that the winery achieved its present status and recognition.

Over the years Bruce has crafted many exceptional wines and today embracing the latest and finest technology the wines are even better. An example is the new 'Triage' technology they are using to process red grapes where leaves, stems and any other debris is removed from the must prior to fermentation.

The vineyard, of course, is the key. Everything starts there and today the Lafonds have a program replacing, gradually, the old vines with clones that have preformed well in their vineyard or in a neighbor's vineyard.

In 2001 they opened the Lafond Winery at the vineyards to process and produce only red wines while continuing to make white wines at Santa Barbara Winery.

Santa Barbara offers a wide range of wines. Sauvignon Blanc, Chardonnay, Riesling, Syrah, Pinot Noir, Cabernet Sauvignon, Zinfandel and an occasional dessert wine. Prices are $13-$45.

From Hwy 101 in Santa Barbara, exit at the Garden St off-ramp, turn south towards the beach and then left on E. Yanonoli St three blocks to the winery.

Shoestring Winery

800 E Highway 246

Solvang

800-693-8612

Tasting Daily 11-5

How many horse trainers do you know that want to make wine? And of course, they all head for Napa, right? That's what Bill and Roswitha Craig did. Then one stormy night, sitting in their rented home near St. Helena, they watched a James Garner-narrated documentary called *Santa Ynez Carriage Classic*. Roswitha asked "Where's that?" and a few days later, they were driving south.

After a couple of visits, they found a stud farm turned polo ranch of 65 acres, with room, eventually for about 35 acres of vineyards. It became theirs in 1997.

They'll readily tell you that they drove to the West coast with not much more than a dream... hence the name "Shoestring". Ten years later with steadfast determination and dedication of countless hours of hard work, Shoestring Winery is a reality.

About half their wine comes from juice from their own vines, about half is sourced from vineyards they work with to meet their needs.

They invite you to stop by and taste their wonderful wines. Roswitha recalls that they were told early on to "make wines that you like, because if they don't sell, you'll be drinking them for a long time."

So when you visit, you'll be sharing their Pinot Grigio, Rosé, Sangiovese, Cabernet Sauvignon, Merlot and Syrah. Prices fall in the $22-$28 price range.

And while you're there, you can meet a couple of beautiful horses – a reminder to the Craig's of an earlier life.

From Hwy 101 in Buellton, take the Buellton/Solvang exit onto Hwy 246 heading towards Solvang. Winery located on the right, approx. 1 mile from the Hwy. 101 exit.

Stolpman Vineyards

1659 Copenhagen Dr "C"

Solvang

805-688-0400

Tasting Daily From 11

Tom and Marilyn Stolpman planted their first grapes in 1992 and today have 120 planted acres. The vineyard continues to be a dynamic location for the planting of Syrah, Sangiovese and Rousanne. In addition, the estate contains an assortment of other varietals which include Nebbiolo, Sauvignon Blanc, Grenache, Cinsault, and Merlot.

The vineyards at Stolpman were originally planted with the sole intention of selling the fruit to other Central Coast wineries. Now, with their own estate wine program, they continue to provide fruit to other wineries but on a smaller, more selective scale. In many cases, producers choose to bottle wine from Stolpman fruit separately under a vineyard-designated label.

Under estate-bottling, they produce "vineyard crafted wines" that include Angeli, Estate Syrah, Hilltops Syrah, *L'Avion*, *La Croce* (a Syrah/Sangiovese blend), *Limestone Hill Cuvee*, Nebbiolo, *Poetry in Red, Poetry in White*, Rosato (a perfect aperitif) and Sangiovese. Pricing is generally in the $18-$60 range.

In 2003, Stolpman Vineyards instituted the La Cuadrilla Project - each year, the 13-member full-time vineyard crew (in Spanish, "La Cuadrilla") is given a small section in the vineyard to manage as they please. Pruning, watering, and fruit yield decisions on these rows are all made by the vineyard crew. During harvest, La Cuadrilla decides when to pick the fruit, and the winemaking team helps them vinify the grapes. At the end, La Cuadrilla divides the wine among its members – about two cases per member – and the members have a better understanding of how their work in the vineyard has a direct influence on what ends up in the bottle.

Tasting in Downtown Solvang.

Summerland Winery

2330 Lillie Ave

Summerland

805-565-9463

Tasting Daily 11-5

Nebil "Bilo" Zarif, the owner of Summerland, is best known for his development of premium Central Coast vineyards. After founding Barnwood Vineyards, he incorporated it with the Laetitia Winery. Under his guidance, the reputation of the two properties was raised to world recognition. After selling Laetitia and Barnwood, Bilo is devoting his energies to raising Summerland to even higher standards.

Throughout the growing season you will find Zarif and his winemaker, Etienne Terlinden making frequent trips to their vineyard sources to insure that the contracted fruit for their program is farmed to the specified yields and quality.

For the past 15 years, Zarif has had a secret collaborator in Michele Pignarre Le Danois, a world-class oenologist from Bordeaux. Oenology, a scientific approach to winemaking and tasting, requires up to five years of schooling to earn a master's degree in the 18th century specialty. Ms. Le Danois has been at it for 35 years.

Zarif flies in the wine-blending expert with the experienced palate to help each vintage be the best it can be. Over five days, Mr. Terlinden and Ms. Le Danois taste 400 different barrel samples, placing them together like pieces of a puzzle.

Summerland offers two tiers of wine – their Central Coast Collection, exhibiting excellent varietal character with a Central Coast flavor. And their Single Vineyard Collection, dedicated to single-vineyard bottlings from top vineyards in the region. Between the two, Summerland offers a wide selection of Viognier, Sauvignon Blanc, Chardonnay, Syrah, Pinot Blanc, Merlot, Cabernet Sauvignon and a Rhone blend, *Trio*. Prices run $14-$20 and $22-$55 in the two tiers.

From Hwy 101 in Summerland (just south of Santa Barbara) take Exit 91. Tasting room on the north side of the Freeway, between Hollister and Colville.

Sunstone Winery

125 Refugio Rd
Santa Ynez
805-688-9463
Tasting Daily 10-4:30

When Fred and Linda Rice and their three children moved in 1989 from Santa Barbara to a peaceful 55-acre Santa Ynez ranch to grow wine grapes, little did they know that they would end up happily presiding over one of the largest organic vineyard estates in the County. Today, the Rices' 77 acre, sun-dappled land, planted to Rhone and Bordeaux varietals, meets all California Certified Organic Farmer (C.C.O.F.) standards.

The site of the winery was originally a horse barn, which was seriously damaged when an oak tree fell on it after heavy rains and winds. Thanks to that storm, Sunstone now has one of the most attractive wineries and tasting rooms in the Valley. Aromas of French lavender and rosemary greet visitors as they approach the winery's inviting courtyard and tasting room.

The architecture recalls wineries in the Provencal countryside, and the relaxed ambiance in the tasting room includes a kitchen complete with wood-burning oven. Over 5,000 square feet of stone barrel-aging caves are built into the hillside.

Bion Rice, the winery president, recommends experiencing Sunstone wines at the winery. "Tasting our wines is tasting the terroir of this special place," he says. "As you walk in, you are surrounded by the soils and the vines that create our wines. You can feel the temperate winds that sweep between the rows, creating the perfect climate for Bordeaux and Rhone varietal grapes."

So they offer a wide selection of Cabernet Sauvignon, a Bordeaux blend called *Eros*, Syrah, Chardonnay, Pinot Grigio, Sauvignon Blanc, Viognier and Rosé. Prices vary from $13 to $50.

From Hwy 101 in Buellton, exit Hwy 246 towards Solvang. Go through Solvang and into Santa Ynez. Turn right on Refugio Rd. Winery on the right.

Tantara Winery

4747 Ontiveros Ln

Santa Maria

805-938-5051

Tasting By Appt

Tantara was the name of a horse owned by winery co-owner Bill Cates some years ago. After Tantara was retired to pasture, she defied predictions of an imminent demise and lived to a ripe old age. Horses symbolize elegance, grace and power and in Tantara's case, long life, all of which are qualities they embrace for their wine.

California's Central Coast, from Santa Barbara to Monterey is blessed with ideal growing conditions for Pinot Noir and Chardonnay. Since 1997, Cates and his partner and co-winemaker, Jeff Fink, have been dedicated to producing the very finest Pinot Noir and Chardonnay. Located on the beautiful Bien Nacido Vineyard in Santa Barbara County, their wines are vineyard designated from Central Coast growers such as Bien Nacido, Talley, Pisoni, Gary's, Laetitia and Dierberg.

In addition to two acres of Bien Nacido G Block Pinot Noir, in 1999 they planted ten acres of Pinot Noir and two acres of Syrah which will bring their own vineyard holding to about fourteen acres. This fruit will make up their estate bottling.

Because of their commitment to detail and the finite amount of fruit that meets their standards, total production will be 5,000 cases. Wines consist of Chardonnay, Pinot Noir (a number of vineyard-designated bottlings), Syrah and Pinot Blanc. Prices are in the $24 to $80 range.

From Hwy 101 in Santa Maria, exit at Betteravia Rd, go east for 7 miles to the fork, bear left, go 0.9 (nine tenths) mile to Bien Nacido Vineyard. Look for the sign and street number - 4705 on the left. Turn left at the sign and go 1.25 miles on the paved road through the vineyard to the winery.

Tensley Wines

2900 Grand Ave "B"

Los Olivos

805-688-6761

Tasting Fri-Sun 11-5

And By Appt

Joey Tensley's first experience with wine took place when he was just twelve years old. While taking part in a soccer tournament in Bordeaux, his team toured a winery. Joey vividly recalls the chill of the old caves and the aromas of wines fermenting in barrel. From that moment on he knew what he wanted to do with his life – make wine. "Which pretty much made me the only kid growing up in Bakersfield, California, with that particular dream," Joey says.

In 2002 Joey met freelance television and film writer Jennifer Beck whose interest in wine also went back to a time she spent in France when she was twelve. She lived in Paris for a year with her mother who was a wine importer at the time. Jennifer and Joey were married less than a year after meeting, and son, Oliver Gunnar Tensley, came along in 2003. "Talk about being raised in the wine business. This kid is in the vineyard with Jennifer and me taking sugar samples, tasting grapes, riding around the winery on his tricycle while we're washing barrels. He even teethed on corks."

Today, Tensley Wines is a family owned and operated winery focusing on vineyard designated Syrah within Santa Barbara County. Established in 1998, the first release of Tensley totaled just 100 cases. In 2006, production reached 3,300 cases and included seven single-vineyard Syrahs, the most in the County. Their wines are priced at $28-$38 per bottle.

Jennifer has even launched her own brand, Lea Wines, which produces small quantities of hand-crafted Syrah Rose and Pinot Noir from Santa Barbara County. Tensley has introduced a white Rhone blend, *Tensley Blanc*, and a Grenache-Syrah blend named for Joey's niece, *BMT.*

Located in downtown Los Olivos.

Photo by Kirk Irwin

Verdad Wines

Solvang and Los Olivos
*Tasting Daily – Hours Below

Verdad's mission is to make small amounts of delicious wines using Spanish grape varietals. Their goal is to make wines which express the true flavors of the varietal and the unique terroir in which they're grown.

Louisa Sawyer Lindquist is the inspiration behind Verdad. In the late 80's, while working at a retail store on Long Island, Louisa became enamored with the beauty and finesse of Spanish Albariño. When she began working for a fine wine importer and distributor in New York, she had the opportunity to work with the Classical Wines of Spain portfolio and expand her knowledge.

After moving to California, Louisa began dating Bob Lindquist, the owner/winemaker of Qupé Wine Cellars, and introduced him to Spanish wines. In time they began planting small blocks of Albariño and Tempranillo at the Ibarra-Young Vineyard in the Santa Ynez Valley, experimenting with clones and organic growing techniques.

As the plantings at Ibarra-Young matured and began to produce fruit, Louisa went to Spain to work harvest. As she talked with the people across the country, she noticed that one of the favorite expressions, repeated on a regular basis was "es la verdad" (that's the truth). That became her inspiration to naming the fledgling brand "Verdad".

Verdad offers Albariño and Tempranillo as well as a Rosé; pricing runs $14 to $20. The wines are produced at Qupé under Bob's direction.

*Tasting often available in "Wine Country" at 2445 Alamo Pintado in Los Olivos (Daily 11-5) and "Tastes of the Valley" at 1672 Mission Dr in Solvang (Daily 11-8).

Waltzing Bear Wines

Los Olivos

805-686-9699

*Tasting Daily 11-5

Waltzing Bear Wines was started in 2002 by Brad Lowman with much encouragement from the late, great Bob Senn, who introduced him to many of the winemakers and winegrowers in Santa Barbara County, including Brian Loring of Loring Wine Company and the folks from Tantara Winery, Jeff Fink and Bill Cates.

In 2002, Brad made his first vintage with the assistance of Brian, who also generously hosted and mentored Brad on his style and philosophy of wine making.

Also in 2002, Brad volunteered time almost daily during harvest at Tantara Winery as they expanded their operations into a new building. Jeff Fink serves as Brad's other mentor.

Since 2003, his wines have been made at Tantara Winery, located in the middle of the beautiful Bien Nacido Vineyard east of Santa Maria. Brad spends September and October each year working full time at the winery to produce his wines before returning home to the Los Angeles area to resume work at his "day job".

And each year Brad bottles a number of vineyard-designated Pinot Noirs. Pricing is generally in the $36 to $45 range.

Why name it Waltzing Bear Wines? Because the waltz is the most elegant dance, and Pinot is the most elegant wine, and Brad is as clumsy as a bear on the dance floor, but still enjoys the elegant things in life!

Tasting usually available at "Wine Country" 2445 Alamo Pintado Ave, Los Olivos.

Whitcraft Winery

36A S Calle Cesar Chavez

Santa Barbara

805-730-1680

Tasting Sat-Sun 12-4

And By Appt

A long-standing member of the Santa Barbara winemaking community, Chris Whitcraft is obsessed with producing the highest quality wines. His signature varietals are Pinot Noir, Chardonnay and Lagrein. Prices run $30-$50, and you'll find a selection of bottlings, especially among his Pinot Noirs.

Chris entered the wine profession over 30 years ago, first as a retailer then as a journalist, wholesaler and ultimately a producer of wines. Through this evolution, he built robust relationships with major industry players such as Burt Williams (Williams & Selyem); Dick & John Graff (Chalone); Ken Burnap (Santa Cruz Mountain Vineyards); and Michael Benedict (Sanford & Benedict). These individuals were major influences in Chris' passion for Pinot Noir - a varietal with amazing potential which is notoriously difficult to master. Working with them, he came to appreciate the importancc of selecting the finest grapes and, in the wine-making process, enabling the natural qualities of that fruit to come through.

Chris' early success in producing high-quality wines enabled him to secure grape contracts from leading producers throughout California (e.g. Bien Nacido; French Camp; Hirsch Vineyards; Melville), providing the platform for producing consistently outstanding wines. While maintaining that tradition, he also continues to seek out new sources of the highest-quality grapes so that he can deliver ever-improving products to his loyal clientele, those who have discovered through him that "Pinot Noir — it's not just for breakfast anymore!"

Located in Santa Barbara south of Hwy 101 between Garden St and N Milpas.

Wild Heart Winery

2933-C Grand Ave

Los Olivos

805-688-7386

Tasting Daily 11-5

Suzanne and Jim Burens founded Wild Heart in 2005 with the goal of creating a wine tasting experience that visitors would remember long after leaving the tasting room. And the friendly, homey atmosphere that resulted almost guarantees you'll have fond memories of Wild Heart.

Jim has always considered himself an entrepreneur, having started five businesses before the wine bug found its mark. Both Jim and Suzanne enjoy wine, and being an artist at heart, Suzanne recognized the connection between fine wine and fine art. In fact, the heart in the winery label will remind you of some of the hand-made jewelry pieces that Suzanne offers in the tasting room.

Carefully choosing the vineyards they work with, Wild Heart offers Viognier, Sauvignon Blanc, Chardonnay, Zinfandel, Syrah, Cabernet Sauvignon and a Syrah/Mourvedre blend named *Capricieux*.

Pricing is generally $24 to $34 per bottle.

Jim and Suzanne are proud that many visitors have returned to taste again and again. That just proves to them that the dream they had for their tasting experience has become a reality. They hope you'll stop by, as well.

Located in Downtown Los Olivos.

William James Cellars

*113 S College Ave

Santa Maria

805-349-1122

*Tasting Tues-Sun 11-5

Or at the Winery By Appt

William James Cellars is the 'Dream Come True,' that began back in college in the early 90's. While attending CSU-Fresno, Jim and Robin Porter gathered with friends at the campus CATI building for wine tastings and social gatherings. After graduation, Jim began making wine in the basement of their house in Northern California. Starting from scratch with kitchen utensils, strainers and trash cans they began smashing grapes away!

Jim won every home-wine making award possible; bronze, silver, gold and best of show. That's why he decided to turn professional!

In 2003, Jim applied for an alternating proprietorship at Fess Parker's Wine Center in Santa Maria. The partnership allows him to use space in Parker's Winery while using his own equipment to produce wine. He made a Syrah and Chardonnay from premiere coastal vineyards, a total of 450 cases. In 2004, Jim added a Central Coast Syrah blending syrah grapes from San Luis Obispo County and Santa Barbara County, for a total of 1200 cases. In 2005, Jim added a Syrah from the Hampton Family Vineyards for a total of 2500 cases. Jim will continue making fine wine from these vineyards in the future topping off at 4000 cases per year. Wine prices run $22-$38 per bottle.

Tastings done as part of a Food and Wine pairing at "Testa's Bistro" at the address above. Call for information or stop in during hours shown. Or to taste at the winery, call Robin at 805-478-9412 for an appointment and directions. Also, sometimes tasted at "Olde Mission Wine Co." 1539 Mission Dr "B" Solvang (Daily 9:30-5:30).

Zaca Mesa Winery & Vineyards

6905 Foxen Canyon Rd

Los Olivos

805-688-9339

Tasting Daily 10-4

The original property was purchased in 1972 by a group of young investors with big dreams. With few other vineyards in the area to learn from, the vineyard was originally planted in 1973 with numerous varieties such as Cabernet Sauvignon, Merlot, Zinfandel, Riesling, Pinot Noir, Grenache, Chardonnay, and Syrah.

Since 2002, Zaca Mesa has ripped out over 100 acres of the original plantings and replanted half using new clones of Syrah, Grenache, Mourvèdre and Viognier. Their vineyard is the sole source for their wines. Nor does Zaca mesa sell any fruit to other winemakers. Thus, Zaca Mesa "Estate Grown and Bottle" wines ensures you a unique, terroir-based wine experience to share with your friends and family. Wines price in the $15 to $52 range.

The winery has long been referred to as "the University of Zaca Mesa." As one of the pioneers in the Santa Barbara County, Zaca Mesa was a training ground for many. Ken Brown was the first winemaker and later started Byron in Santa Maria Valley. Jim Clendenen and Bob Lindquist worked at Zaca Mesa before venturing out on their own to start Au Bon Climat and Qupé, respectively. Other alumni include Lane Tanner, Daniel Gehrs, Chuck Carlson of Curtis, and Adam Tolmach of Ojai. Today the winemaker is Clay Brock. He's worked at a variety of wineries in Napa Valley and the South Coast, eventually working his way up to Assistant Winemaker at Byron Winery in Santa Maria. In 1997, he was appointed Winemaker for Edna Valley Vineyards. Clay oversaw four vintages before coming to Zaca Mesa in 2001.

From Hwy 101 north of Buellton, exit onto Hwy 154/Lake Cachuma and take the First left on Zaca Station Road which becomes Foxen Canyon Rd. Proceed to winery on your left.

Winery Notes

Winery_____ **Date**_____

City or Area_____

Wine Comments

_____

_____

_____

_____

_____

_____

_____

_____

_____

_____

Winery_____ **Date**_____

City or Area_____

Wine Comments

_____

_____

_____

_____

_____

_____

_____

_____

_____

Winery Notes

Winery_____ **Date**_____

City or Area_____

Wine Comments

_____

_____

_____

_____

_____

_____

_____

_____

Winery_____ **Date**_____

City or Area_____

Wine Comments

_____

_____

_____

_____

_____

_____

_____

_____

Winery Notes

Winery_____ **Date**_____

City or Area_____

Wine Comments

_____

_____

_____

_____

_____

_____

_____

_____

_____

_____

Winery_____ **Date**_____

City or Area_____

Wine Comments

_____

_____

_____

_____

_____

_____

_____

_____

_____

Ventura – Malibu Area

The Saddlerock-Malibu-Newton Canyon AVA

This tiny 850-acre AVA is located in Los Angeles County's Malibu area. Producing Cabernet Sauvignon, Chardonnay and a small amount of Merlot.

Giessinger Winery

365 Santa Clara St

Fillmore

805-524-5000

Tasting Mon-Th 11-5

Fri-Sun 11-6:30

The Giessingers were wine producers in their home country of Algeria, but left in 1962 for the United States. A son, Edouard became a Professor at UCLA in laser physics. But the life of a winemaker still held a place in his soul.

In 1997, owner/winemaker Edouard Giessinger opened his namesake winery in a converted welding shop near the Fillmore train depot. He fell in love with the town as he took an unplanned shortcut through the Heritage Valley on Route 126 one lovely day. It was, he decided, just the place to produce his "French-styled" wines.

Sleeping barrels are visible through glass windows in the tasting room, where visitors may sample wines ranging from a Viognier made with grapes grown in Sutter Creek to a Port made with Zinfandel grapes grown in Cucamonga Valley. Also available are specialty wines (including a red called *Forgiveness*) and any number of dessert wines. Prices fall in a wide range – many in the $10 to $19.95 category, with a few up to $39.95.

While you're tasting, you can enjoy one of the five or six "French Gourmet Sandwiches" that the winery offers, and relax in their garden, perhaps keeping track of the trains loaded with tourists as they chug in and out of the adjoining station.

Tasting in Downtown Fillmore as well as at a second tasting room at 210 State St in Downtown Santa Barbara (Mon-Th 12-5, Fri 12-6, Sat-Sun 11-7:00) and by appointment at their Thousand Oaks tasting room at 2219 E Thousand Oaks Blvd #5.

For a weekday appointment in Thousand Oaks, call 805-405-5557.

Herzog Wine Cellars

3201 Camino del Sol

Oxnard

805-983-1560

Tasting Sun-Th 11-9

And Fri 11-4

The Jewish people have a special relationship to wine that predates even the Romans and Greeks. For the ancient Jews, wine played an important role in religious ritual. Today, thousands of years later, it continues to do so. Kiddush, the prayer over the wine, traditionally announces the beginning of the Sabbath on Friday night as well as other holidays.

And so it should come as no surprise that the Herzog family has been making wine for a long time. They trace their winemaking origins back to Philip Herzog, who made wine in Slovakia for the Austro-Hungarian court more than a century ago. Philip's wines were so appreciated by Emperor Franz-Josef, that the emperor made Philip a baron. The Baron Herzog wines - a line of premium yet moderately priced California varietals - are named to commemorate the honor.

In 1985, the Herzog family decided to expand their winemaking operations to California, where they make wine under two separate labels: Baron Herzog and Herzog Wine Cellars. Under the supervision of head winemaker Joe Hurliman, Herzog Wine Cellars has created a center for high-end contemporary winemaking in a tradition that dates back nearly six millennia.

Hurliman sources grapes from across the state from vineyards that meet Herzog's demanding standards. The Winery proudly encourages and supports the efforts of California winegrowers to adopt sustainable winegrowing practices.

Red wines include Cabernet Sauvignon, Zinfandel, Merlot, Syrah and Pinot Noir. Whites include Chenin Blanc, Chardonnay and Sauvignon Blanc. In addition to a White Zinfandel, they offer a number of late harvest and dessert wines. Prices fall between $7-$34.

From Hwy 101 south of Oxnard, exit Del Norte South toward the ocean and turn right at the first street, Camino Del Sol. Winery about 100 yards on the right side.

Malibu Family Wines

31800 Mulholland Hwy

Malibu

888-433-9463

Tasting Wed-Sun 11-5

The rich, fascinating history of Saddlerock Ranch began more than three centuries ago when the vast expanse of land surrounding the Santa Monica Mountains was part of the original Spanish Land Grant. Local caves are filled with ancient pictographs painted by the Chumash Indians, dating back to the Portola Expedition of 1769. The beautiful pictographs of this culture have become very rare due to erosion and weathering, but some of the most well preserved examples remain on the ranch and have been studied by archeologists and photographed for books on the subject.

The rocky terrain and steep south facing slopes provide the perfect environment for growing premium wine grapes. Planting started in 1997 with 14 acres of Cabernet and Merlot. Today the hillside vineyards consist of approximately 60,000 vines on 65 acres and their goal is to have vineyards on 100 acres. Eight varietals are planted, including Cabernet Sauvignon, Merlot, Sauvignon Blanc, Syrah, Malbec, Grenache, Mouvedre and Viognier. The last four are used for blending purposes.

Wines are available in two collections. The Semler label includes Cabernet Sauvignon, Merlot and Syrah, priced $24 to $30 each. The Saddlerock label covers Chardonnay, Cabernet Sauvignon and Merlot, for $14-$18 each.

Set in a wooded and beautifully lawned arena, the tasting room is actually a ranch-style structure that holds an open bar. Umbrella-covered tables with wooden chairs are scattered around, making for an inviting, relaxing tasting area. But note – you will be tasting in the open air. Rainy days may tempt you elsewhere.

From Hwy 101 in Agoura Hills, take Kanan Dume Rd towards the ocean and turn right on Mulholland Dr. Tasting on the left, past the ranch entrance.

Old Creek Ranch Winery

10024 E Old Creek Rd

Ventura

805-649-4132

Tasting Sat-Sun 11-5

Talk about history! The Old Creek Ranch Winery is owned and managed by John and Carmel Whitman. Carmel is the daughter of Mike and Carmel Maitland, the original founders of the winery in 1981. Chuck Branham, also one of the original founders, remains in charge of winemaking.

But even before, there was wine. The Winery is located on the Old Creek Ranch, part of a Spanish 22,000 acre land grant awarded to Don Fernando Tico, dating back to the early history of California. In the late 1800's the ranch was purchased by Antonio Riva from the island of Corsica. He was a chef in Paris, London and later in San Francisco. He built a winery on the ranch at that time. Today the original winery still stands and is depicted as the logo on the label of the current wines.

Riva produced wine until about 1942, including the prohibition years. Wine purchasers would leave an order and money on the clothesline and would return later to pickup a jug of red wine left at the base of an oak tree. On one occasion he was warned that the FBI was coming to raid the winery. All wine beyond what was legal for one family to produce was dumped prior to their arrival.

In 1976 the Maitlands purchased the property with the intention of revitalizing the old ranch. They have planted a cherry orchard, which they are expanding to include plums. The vision is a subsistence ranch just as it was when the Riva family lived there.

In 1981 the first vintage was introduced. Today. Old Creek Ranch Winery produces a wide range of wines – Petite Sirah, Viognier, Syrah, Cabernet Sauvignon, Merlot, Chardonnay and Sangiovese. The wines sell for $17.50 to $29 a bottle.

From Hwy 101 in Ventura, travel north 10 miles on Hwy 33. Winery located between Casitas Springs and Oakview in route to Ojai.

Rosenthal – The Malibu Estate

26023 Pacific Coast Hwy

Malibu

310-456-1392

Tasting Wed-Sun 11-6

Fine wine from Malibu? Southern California's Malibu, home to movie stars and Bay Watch?

Yes, these wines are from grapes grown in Malibu, not on the famous beach, but in a scenic valley four miles from the coast, 1,400-feet up, above the coastal fog, in the AVA Malibu Newton Canyon.

George Rosenthal, owner of movie studios, hotels, and other enterprises, first planted vineyards at his 250 acre estate in 1987, after spending two years checking soil and weather to make sure he planted the correct varietals in the correct locations.

Well, it was a bit more complicated than that. Malibu isn't the home of a large agricultural labor force, so workers had to be found and trained on vineyard development. Then came equipment – easy to get in Northern California, but Los Angeles people don't normally order much in the way of grape stakes, wire, grapevine cuttings and the like. Water had to be found, boulders removed and paths built to support tractors. The work was difficult and very expensive, but today Rosenthal Estate produces a Cabernet Sauvignon selling out at $30 to $50 a bottle, an outstanding Merlot at $25 and a small amount of a splendid Chardonnay that also sells for $25.

A new viticultural area, named Malibu-Newton Canyon, has been established consisting of approximately 850 acres within Newton Canyon, and encompassing all of the Rosenthal-The Malibu Estate vineyards. Grape varietals grown comprise Cabernet Sauvignon, and small amounts of Cabernet Franc, Merlot, and Petit Verdot. Three acres of Chardonnay were planted in 1991. Case production is extremely limited from this boutique winery.

Tasting room located on the south side of PCH, just east of Malibu Rd.

Sagebrush Annie's

4211 Highway 33

Ventucopa

661-766-2319

Tasting Sat-Sun 11:30-5

And By Appt

In 1985, Larry Hogan bottled the first wine under his Barnwood Vineyards label. Larry recognized that the warm days, cool nights and well drained soils of the Cuyama Valley were conducive to wine grape production. And in a few short years, he was proven right as his wines, especially the Cabernet Sauvignon, were judged outstanding by wine experts as well as the public.

The facility that was to become Sagebrush Annie's started out as a simple grocery store. After numerous changes of ownership, it was purchased by the Hogan family in 1989 and became a restaurant serving dinners Friday through Sunday.

In 1990, Larry sold Barnwood Vineyards and devoted more time to Sagebrush Annie's and to his old love - rodeo. But the wine bug was still there, and in 2001, Sagebrush Annie's and Stone Pine Estate wines were born. And again, Larry stayed with his specialty - Cabernet Sauvignon. Prices run $22 - $26 per bottle.

Today, Sagebrush Annie's restaurant becomes the tasting room on Saturday and Sunday. A special menu to accompany the wine tasting is available. Whether you eat or not, you'll enjoy your day in the back country.

Your hosts are Larry and Karina Hogan, the epitome of 'mom and pop'. Your chef is Karina and the BBQ chef is Larry. When wine tasting, your corks are pulled by Larry who will also pour your tastes.

You can't get much more 'mom and pop' or hands-on than that. The Hogans even built their own facilities. Come visit them and taste the wines they have available.

Located just an hour north of Ojai on Highway 33. It is also a 90 minute drive from San Luis Obispo or a short 60 minute skip from Bakersfield.

Winery Notes

Winery_____ **Date**_____

City or Area_____

Wine Comments

_____

_____

_____

_____

_____

_____

_____

_____

_____

_____

Winery_____ **Date**_____

City or Area_____

Wine Comments

_____

_____

_____

_____

_____

_____

_____

_____

_____

_____

Winery Notes

Winery_____ **Date**_____

City or Area_____

Wine Comments

_____

_____

_____

_____

_____

_____

_____

_____

_____

_____

Winery_____ **Date**_____

City or Area_____

Wine Comments

_____

_____

_____

_____

_____

_____

_____

_____

_____

_____

Winery Notes

Winery_____ **Date**_____

City or Area_____

Wine Comments

_____

_____

_____

_____

_____

_____

_____

_____

_____

_____

Winery_____ **Date**_____

City or Area_____

Wine Comments

_____

_____

_____

_____

_____

_____

_____

_____

_____

EASY ORDER FORM

Phone orders: Call **toll-free** 1-877-591-1757 - Have credit card ready

E-mail orders: orders@cawinetastingguide.com – Include information on this form

Postal orders: Old Vine Publishing Company, PO Box 6774, Pine Mountain Club, CA 93222-6774 - Use this form

Fax orders: Dial **toll-free** 1-877-591-1758 - Use this form

Please send _____ copies of *THE Wine Tasting Guide to California's Central Coast* at $19.95 each   _____

Add $1.45 sales tax for each book shipped to CA addresses   _____

Add $4.00 shipping for first book, $2.00 for each additional   _____

shipped to U.S. Call for International Shipping information

Total Payment   _____

Name_____

Address _____

City_____State_____Zip_____

Telephone_____

E-mail address_____

(we require either a phone number or email address in order to reach you should a problem arise)

Check enclosed for $_____ (Make out to Old Vine Publishing Co.)

Charge my   (   ) Visa or (   ) Mastercard

Name on Card_____

Card Number_____Exp. Date_____

Signature _____

EASY ORDER FORM

Phone orders: Call **toll-free** 1-877-591-1757 - Have credit card ready

E-mail orders: orders@cawinetastingguide.com – Include information on this form

Postal orders: Old Vine Publishing Company, PO Box 6774, Pine Mountain Club, CA 93222-6774 - Use this form

Fax orders: Dial **toll-free** 1-877-591-1758 - Use this form

Please send _____ copies of **THE *Wine Tasting Guide to California's Central Coast*** at $19.95 each   _____

Add $1.45 sales tax for each book shipped to CA addresses   _____

Add $4.00 shipping for first book, $2.00 for each additional   _____

shipped to U.S. Call for International Shipping information

Total Payment   _____

Name_____

Address _____

City_____State_____Zip_____

Telephone_____

E-mail address_____

(we require either a phone number or email address in order to reach you should a problem arise)

Check enclosed for $_____ (Make out to Old Vine Publishing Co.)

Charge my (   ) Visa or (   ) Mastercard

Name on Card_____

Card Number_____Exp. Date_____

Signature _____

About Mike O'Beirne

Mike was born far from wine country in Tolono, IL. After graduating with a degree in Business Management from the University of Illinois, he entered the pharmaceutical industry where he served as Trade Promotion Manager for a major brand of mouthwash.

His next career move was as an account executive for a major advertising agency, working on their Proctor & Gamble account. Since then he has occupied ownership positions in the sales promotion, construction and corporate recognition industries.

In 1991/92 Mike served as President of the Awards and Recognition Association, the worldwide trade association of the awards industry.

Mike was first exposed to good wine in Cincinnati, where he and his wife Jo-Ann were members of the local Chapter of the American Wine Society. In following years, he served as broker in the State of Ohio for a large California winery, and believe it or not, a winery operating out of St. Louis using grapes they grew in Arkansas.

After moving to California in 1977, the O'Beirnes began touring the nearby Central Coast and discovered the great wines being produced. In ensuing years, they toured the wineries of Napa, Sonoma, the Russian River, the Monterey-San Jose area, Livermore, the 49er Trail and Temecula. In 1995, he lead his first wine tasting tour into the Central Coast – nine couples touring the Santa Maria area. In 1997, he lead another group on a larger tour covering the Westside of Paso Robles and continues to organize tours today.

In 2002, along with four friends from the Rotary Club of Thousand Oaks, CA, O'Beirne founded the Midsummer Evening of Wine and Arts which over six years has raised more than $280,000 for charity.

Mike currently resides in Pine Mountain Club, CA. He and Jo-Ann have three daughters and four grandchildren.

He can be reached through his website at www.cawinetastingguide.com.